SPEAKING THE LANGUAGE OF DESIRE

The films of Carl Dreyer

Carl Dreyer and Birgitte Federspiel (Inger) during the filming of
Ordet. Courtesy of The Museum of Modern Art Film Stills Archive.

Speaking the language
of desire
The films of Carl Dreyer

RAYMOND CARNEY
Boston University

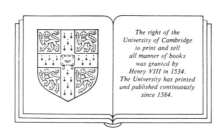

The right of the
University of Cambridge
to print and sell
all manner of books
was granted by
Henry VIII in 1534.
The University has printed
and published continuously
since 1584.

CAMBRIDGE UNIVERSITY PRESS

Cambridge

New York   New Rochelle   Melbourne   Sydney

Published by the Press Syndicate of the University of Cambridge
The Pitt Building, Trumpington Street, Cambridge CB2 1RP
32 East 57th Street, New York, NY 10022, USA
10 Stamford Road, Oakleigh, Melbourne 3166, Australia

© Cambridge University Press 1989

First published 1989

Printed in the United States of America

Library of Congress Cataloging-in-Publication Data

Carney, Raymond.
Speaking the language of desire : the films of Carl Dreyer / Raymond Carney.
p.   cm.
ISBN 0-521-37163-5.   ISBN 0-521-37807-9 (pbk.)
1. Dreyer, Carl Theodor, 1889–1968 – Criticism and interpretation.
I. Title.
PN1998.3.D74C36   1989
791.43'0233'0924 – dc19   88–30236
                                                                          CIP

|00| 276 805

British Library Cataloguing in Publication Data

Carney, Raymond
Speaking the language of desire: the films of Carl Dreyer.
1. Danish cinema films. Directing. Dreyer, Carl Theodor—Critical studies
I. Title
791.43'0233'0924

ISBN 0-521-37163-5 hard covers
ISBN 0-521-37807-9 paperback

TO MY MUSE, MY INGER.

She knows who she is.

Contents

vii

FIGURES OF IMAGINATION AND DESIRE

Introduction

Critical difficulty

What interests me – and this comes before technique – is reproducing
the feelings of the characters in my films. That is, to reproduce as
sincerely as possible the most sincere feelings possible. The important
thing for me is not only to catch hold of the words they say, but also
the thoughts behind the words. What I seek in my films, what I want
to obtain, is a penetration to my actors' profound thoughts by means of
their most subtle expressions. For these are the expressions that reveal
the character of the person, his unconscious feelings, the secrets that
live in the depths of his soul. That is what interests me above all, not
the technique of the cinema.

Carl Dreyer, Interview with Michael Delahaye

THE pages that follow are an attempt to bring the
work of one of the world's greatest filmmakers
back to life for a new generation of viewers.
There is, at present, a real need for the rehabilitation of
the work of Carl Dreyer. The problem is that, as things
now stand, his films are almost unknown to the average
(or even the considerably above-average) filmgoer. Although he is one of the acknowledged masters of world
cinema, Dreyer's films are surprisingly rarely screened
or discussed. With the possible exception of his silent
Passion of Joan of Arc, most of them are not regularly
shown even in our major university film programs.

Even within the small circle of "art film" devotees,
Dreyer seems to lack the following of other "classic"

1

directors. When was the last time the local art house ran a Dreyer festival? When was the last time you heard someone say he or she was rushing down to the Bijou to catch *Day of Wrath, Ordet,* or *Gertrud* for the nth time, the way one commonly hears film buffs talk about favorites like *The Rules of the Game, City Lights, Citizen Kane,* or *North by Northwest?*

Not that Dreyer's life and work are not revered in the abstract. One of his films can almost always be counted on to appear on top-ten lists of "the greatest films ever made." His name is invariably included on lists of the canonical directors. But the homage stays peculiarly abstract and dispassionate. Even as everyone agrees that Dreyer is (in the standard formulas) "one of the greatest filmmakers who ever lived" or "the filmmaker's filmmaker," his work is not thought to be really "fun" to watch.

This sort of critical bad faith is not an uncommon phenomenon in artistic appreciation, and is not entirely attributable to the way most people (film critics included) implicitly patronize film as a form of "entertainment." Many another challenging twentieth-century artist is "respected" in the same strangely dutiful and distant way. We pay our respects to them by avoiding their work.

Dreyer is, in short, one of those "cinematic artists" (in the most chilling sense of the phrase) whose films are publicly promoted as being "good for us," while they are privately conceded to be ponderous, difficult, or downright dull. Renoir is ebullient. Hitchcock is gripping. Welles is dazzling. Chaplin is touching. Dreyer, the dour Dane, is "monumental" and "impressive." I wonder if any filmmaker has ever had the word "masterpiece" applied more dauntingly to his work to warn potential viewers *away* from it.

In the end, the one situation obviously feeds the other. Because Dreyer's work is regarded as being so demanding and esoteric, it is seldom screened or written about. Because it is seldom seen and discussed, it continues to remain alien and incomprehensible. It is only reasonable to wonder how this unfortunate situation arose in the first place. One might make a few conjectures.

There is, to start off, what might be called the Kierkegaard syndrome. Dreyer's fellow countryman, Sören Kierkegaard was not "discovered" by Western theologians and philosophers until almost a century after his death simply because his writing was in Danish and outside of the main traditions of academic discourse. Similarly, some of Dreyer's obscurity and unfamiliarity to European and American audiences is undoubtedly at least in part a consequence of the cultural origin of his work. Living much of his life in Copenhagen, making his sound films in Danish, and featuring Danish actors in most of them, Dreyer simply cuts himself off from the natural cultural constituency possessed by filmmakers from nations with a larger influence in Western Europe and America.

Dreyer's fate seems all the more sealed in America

where the foreign language programs of our universities are the major avenue for the introduction of the works of foreign filmmakers to mass audiences. The works of Buñuel, Renoir, and Fellini are thrust upon thousands of viewers every year in our schools, simply because the languages and cultures they represent are taught in a major way in our language programs. It goes without saying that Danish language, literature, and culture are decidedly outside the main traditions of language school teaching.

As an additional reason for Dreyer's neglect, one might cite the small number of sound films upon which his career must base its claim to our attention. Because of the difficulty he had raising funds for his productions, Dreyer produced only four feature films in the period of sound.[1]

Purists and film scholars may argue that a filmmaker's silent work is of absolutely equal importance to his sound work, but in the real world of ordinary film-going that is obviously not the case. During his lifetime and afterward, Dreyer effectively doomed himself to be ignored by the sort of mass audience for whom one's silent work doesn't even exist as an object of attention. Being

---

1 The four sound films are: *Vampyr* in 1932, *Day of Wrath* in 1943, *Ordet* in 1955, and *Gertrud* in 1964. I am only counting the films that Dreyer himself considered to be his "good" work. In addition to these four, he worked on a feature film (*Two People*) in 1944, which he later repudiated, and directed eight commercial shorts for various purposes during the period 1942–1954.

known principally as a silent film director, at least if one is not making silent comedies, is not exactly the way to make one's career matter to the film-going public at this point in the twentieth century.[2]

One must also consider the less than ideal conditions involving the release and distribution of Dreyer's films – even the sound ones. In his major work, Dreyer functioned as what has come to be called an "independent" director. This gave him relatively complete and unfettered artistic control, even as by the same virtue it usually doomed his productions to relative obscurity. Made on small budgets and lacking the bureaucratic backing of larger corporate entities, his films received extremely limited and financially pinched releases. The consequence was that Dreyer's greatest work was (at best) distributed in poor or mutilated condition, and was (at worst) not distributed at all. (As two examples: to my knowledge, there is still – at this late date in film history – no completely satisfactory print of Dreyer's *Joan of Arc* available; and, at least in this country, his *Vampyr* exists only in copies so far removed from the original print that in certain scenes it is almost unwatchable.)

But surely, one replies, the understanding of major artistic careers is not affected in the long run by such

2 It is interesting to notice that even within our universities and film programs, Dreyer is best known not for his sound work, but for his 1928 silent film – *The Passion of Joan of Arc.* Insofar as that is the case, he is removed from contemporary relevance, even though his work is still "taught" in school.

cultural or linguistic or bureaucratic accidents. One assumes that the final judgments of film criticism are not affected by the fact that Dreyer's work lacks a large cultural or linguistic constituency in Europe or America, or by the poor distribution of his work during his lifetime or the discouraging physical condition of some of it now.

It is in precisely such a situation that one counts on the sophisticated critic to rise to the occasion. When a work or a filmmaker is temporarily in eclipse, the critic's job is to direct our attention beyond the passing artistic fads and fashions of the day to remind us of enduring values and nobler traditions. If there is a chasm of historical incomprehension or cultural misunderstanding that makes a text temporarily inaccessible or incomprehensible, the critic's task is to help to reestablish adequate standards of appreciation. If an important body of work is lost sight of, the critic's function is to remind us of its existence, to bring it back to our awareness. The critic can, in short, mediate between the work and its viewers – to help bring works to the attention of the audiences they deserve. The good critic makes difficult or forgotten films a little (but only a little) easier to see and understand. The critic opens doors to appreciation, clears as many roadblocks from the path as possible.

Yet in this respect, Dreyer's work has been ill served even by his self-elected critical champions. One can't help feeling that Dreyer has, in effect, become the victim of the smallness of his own audience. It has all too often become a coterie audience in the worst sense – an audience of aficionados, connoisseurs, and specialists that, in its apparent devotion to protecting Dreyer from "vulgar" appreciation and "debasing" popularity, has inadvertently worked *against* his films' being more widely seen and enjoyed.

Within the realm of academic criticism, the kinds of writing Dreyer's films have attracted in the past two or three decades have made them seem, if anything, not less, but even more formidable and forbidding than they did upon their release. Since Dreyer seems by default to be a figure known principally by academics, his career has become the intellectual property of highly specialized academic writers, and his work has become captive to highly technical academic criticism. In recent decades, even when Dreyer's films have been critically defended and promoted (as by David Bordwell, Noel Burch, and Paul Schrader, among others), it has invariably been with the terminology and methods of severely abstract, stylistic analysis. The result is that, even when Dreyer's films have been praised, it is in terms so austere or repellent to the normal range of human interests and sympathies that it makes them seem even less accessible and more forbidding than ever. Rather than dispelling it, such criticism has unconsciously only contributed to the stereotype of the dreary, daunting Dane.

Yet, having said all of the above, I have to conclude that, in the final analysis, none of these reasons for Dreyer's neglect is very persuasive. Consider the counter examples. Eisenstein made even fewer sound films than Dreyer and is an absolute staple of undergraduate film courses and "art film" festivals. Bergman, Kurosawa, and Wajda represent cultural and linguistic situations equally removed from the curricula and the cultural constituencies of our universities, and equally distant from the social experiences of most European and American viewers; yet they have not had any difficulty at all finding appreciative and devoted (if necessarily less than blockbuster-sized) audiences for their work in American and European theaters. Finally, the careers of Buñuel, Godard, and Fassbinder all prove that the low-budget work of "independents" can successfully be brought to the attention of fairly mainstream audiences, even without large advertising campaigns or corporate distribution deals.

Nor can one really attribute the neglect of Dreyer's work to his critics. The problem has not been created by critics. It would only exaggerate the importance of critics and teachers of film to assume that they have such an enormous influence over the average audience's understanding of, or attendance at, a film. Dreyer indeed does need to be rescued from his putative defenders and explainers, but one can't blame the defenders for the neglect or misunderstanding in the first place. If Dreyer's critics have made an unintentionally inhumane or narrow case for his work, or have failed to mount a persuasive argument on behalf of its importance to contemporary viewers, Dreyer's films themselves must, at the very least, have lent themselves to the sorts of misunderstandings that have risen up around them, pervasive as they are.

The inevitable conclusion is that the neglect of Dreyer's work is not attributable to linguistic, cultural, or critical forces outside of the films, but is traceable to the films themselves. In short, when all is said and done, there is no blinking the fact that it is not cultural politics or critical careerism that has sealed Dreyer's fate, but the kind of films he makes.

For whatever historical reasons, Renoir, Hitchcock, Chaplin, Buñuel, Welles, Kurosawa, Eisenstein, even Fassbinder – as different as they are from one another – apparently express themselves in terms of a cinematic vernacular that can be understood by even fairly unsophisticated film-goers. The evidence of their almost universal acclaim suggests that they speak a common cinematic *lingua franca* that virtually every film-goer has unconsciously mastered by the age of eighteen. Dreyer apparently does not speak that language, which is why it is hard even for quite sophisticated viewers to appreciate what is going on in his work.

Dreyer's work is somehow harder for a viewer to appreciate than this other work. His films apparently make demands on an audience's attention that the work of these other filmmakers does not. Any film programmer can testify to this from firsthand experience. Audiences, even very intelligent and aware audiences of university faculty and students, almost invariably leave Dreyer's

9

works puzzled or frustrated (if they stay to the end of the films at all) in a way they are not by the work of these other directors. Dreyer makes a kind of movie unlike almost anything else in film.

It seems clear that the cinematic fluency acquired through extensive acquaintance with most popular European and American films can be a positive handicap in appreciating Dreyer's movies. When we approach his films the way we approach most other films, we are almost certain to misunderstand them. Viewers and critics who come to Dreyer's work with eyes trained to follow the sorts of actions and events in the other kind of movie – the movies of Renoir, Hitchcock, or Hawks contemporaneous with Dreyer's films, the movies of Altman or Kubrick or Allen in our own day – will be doomed to overlook or misappreciate virtually everything that *is* going on in Dreyer.

One must actually unlearn certain viewing habits to appreciate Dreyer's work. One must learn to readjust one's view from the way one watches a Chaplin, a Renoir, or a Kurosawa film. One must adjust to a different pace and range of interests; one must master a different way of understanding from that used with most other films.

The different kind of film that Dreyer makes is what the following pages seek to define and appreciate. Needless to say, my assumption is that if Dreyer deserves our attention at all, it is not because he makes frigid Nordic "masterpieces" (in the worst sense of the word), but because he presents passionate human dramas. Dreyer is a thrilling, even breathtaking dramatist, once we adequately appreciate what he is doing in his films.

My goal in the following chapters is, in the largest sense, to rescue Dreyer and his films both from his coterie appreciators and from the unthinking resistance of the viewer who comes to Dreyer with cinematic reflexes and judgments trained since childhood by the experience of very different kinds of films.

Thus at several points, it will be necessary to contrast Dreyer's interests and methods with those of filmmakers with which the reader may be more familiar. (In particular, I will be using the work of Jean Renoir, Dreyer's greatest cinematic contemporary, as a contrast with that of Dreyer.) I would emphasize that my goal is not to make invidious comparisons or rankings, but only to try to clear a space for an appreciation of Dreyer's distinctive difference.

The following pages are written neither for the cult follower of Dreyer's work, nor for the viewer who is already thoroughly comfortable and conversant with it (as few of these as there seem to be). It is written to attempt to open Dreyer's work to the common, intelligent, curious reader and viewer, especially the viewer who may have been bewildered or repelled by a past viewing of Dreyer's work.

Since that is my goal, I deliberately concentrate my argument on the three most accessible of Dreyer's films: his final three sound films, released ten years apart in

11

the final three decades of his life: *Day of Wrath* (1943), *Ordet* (1955), and *Gertrud* (1964). These are the films that provide the best possible introduction to the greatness of Dreyer's work. They are the films that are most likely to be screened at a local theater, or to be available for viewing on video.

The text is sprinkled with references to some of Dreyer's other works, but I assume that if the value of these three crowning masterpieces can be made clear, the curious filmgoer can take care of the rest. Enlarging the argument for the sake of comprehensiveness to include extended discussions of Dreyer's other most important works[3] – as desirable as it might be for other reasons, would have placed both the size and the scope of this book beyond the ordinary viewer I most want to reach.

Above all else, I want to demonstrate that the artist who was apparently (but only apparently) the most esoteric and intimidating of "art film" directors is a man who speaks intimately and passionately to our situations here and now. Dreyer's work needs to be rescued equally from neglect and from the sterile academicism of so-called advanced critical appreciation. He needs to be returned to the common viewer, to the extent that it is possible for any supreme artistic genius to be made democratically available. But to do that will necessarily

3 Which I take to be *The Passion of Joan of Arc, Master of the House, Michael, The Parson's Widow,* and *Vampyr.* All but the last are silent.

require a degree of reeducation, an unlearning of some of the ways of viewing that Hollywood and the most popular foreign films have trained us in.

Like any great artist, Dreyer teaches us how to understand him; but in order to be able to learn from his films we must be willing to humble ourselves enough before the works in order to open ourselves to what they distinctively have to offer. It will be crucial that we not ask his work to be something other than it is. Dreyer's style is his way of teaching a viewer to look and feel differently than he or she does in other films.

As a note to the reader on the organization of the pages that follow, I should mention that I have divided my presentation into two contrasting sections. The first section, "Ways of Knowing," consisting of the first two chapters, is more theoretical in approach, and deals with general questions of how Dreyer's style teaches us to understand him. The second, "Figures of Imagination and Desire," is focused on *Day of Wrath, Ordet,* and *Gertrud,* which I discuss in individual chapters.

I hope that the two approaches to Dreyer's work are complementary. Whether I treat Dreyer's films more generally, with an overview of his *oeuvre,* as I do in the first section, or more specifically, by moving through the portals of three particular works, as in the second, I intend that the focus be equally practical. My overall assumption is that Dreyer's style teaches us new and profound ways of understanding ourselves and our everyday experiences, so my interest in the theoretical underpinnings of Dreyer's style is never merely theoretical in nature.

As we celebrate the 100th anniversary of Dreyer's birth, it is arguable that we have never needed his example more than we do now. Many of the major works of world cinema, especially many of the most sophisticated films of the past thirty years, have embraced an aesthetic of naturalism, realism, or nihilism that could not be further from what Dreyer's films have to offer us. As the following pages will argue, Dreyer's work is implicitly opposed to almost all of the fashionable beliefs about life and expression that have come to be identified with twentieth-century modernism. He is a filmmaker who gives us an entirely different vision of ourselves from what Schlöndorff, Fassbinder, Eisenstein, Bergman, Altman, Antonioni, Godard, or Hitchcock provides. For all of his tough-mindedness and unsentimentality, Dreyer gives us an image of ourselves as powerful meaning makers. Like Shakespeare's tragedies, Dreyer's testify more to our imaginative strengths than to our social weaknesses. His work reminds us of the indomitability of the human spirit and of our powers of creativity under even the most oppressive circumstances.

That is why Dreyer's films are perhaps even more important to us today than they were during his own lifetime. He can give us new ways of knowing, new ways of understanding our lives. His work can teach us truths about ourselves that few other films do. Dreyer is one of

the supreme historians of the post-Romantic predicament that we all live within, and his work, if properly
understood, can help us to understand truths about ourselves, our dreams, and our desires that all too few other
films allow us to glimpse.

Acknowledgments

THIS book was begun during a year in which I was a guest of the Stanford Humanities Center, directed by Bliss Carnochan, where I was honored to be named the William Rice Kimball Fellow for 1986–1987. The text was completed with the support of the innovative interdisciplinary studies program at the University of Texas at Dallas. My good friend Robert Corrigan, Dean of the School of Arts and Humanities, provided leave time and financial assistance for the project.

I also want to express my gratitude to the Stanford University students with whom I screened many of these films. Our class discussions taught me more than they could realize, and they will recognize the appearance of many of their insights in my text.

Tony Pipolo, one of the deepest readers of Dreyer's work I have encountered, generously read the entire manuscript in an early draft and redirected my thinking about Dreyer in a crucially important way. David Lubin of Colby College also read an early version of the text and made many valuable suggestions.

Ruth Southard and Rick Biddenstadt helped to make the frame enlargements that illustrate these pages. Permission to reproduce them was generously granted by Ib Monty, Director of Det Danske Filmmuseum in Copenhagen.

Finally, I owe a special debt of thanks to my long-standing editor and friend at Cambridge University Press. Liz Maguire provided encouragement and assistance above and beyond the call of duty, as she always has.

Ways of knowing

The one thing in the world, of value, is the active soul.

Ralph Waldo Emerson, "The American Scholar"

[ONE]

The active soul:
Approaches to Dreyer's style

> Style . . . is the artist's way of giving expression to his perception of
> the material. . . . Through style, he gets others to see the material
> through his eyes.
>   Style is not something which can be separated from the finished
> work of art. It saturates and penetrates it.
>
>   Carl Dreyer, "A Little on Film Style"

THE challenge that Dreyer's style presents to a viewer is undeniable. The first thing the new viewer notices about Dreyer's work is the emphatic stylization of experience within it. It is impossible to ignore the bizarre camera angles and movements in *Vampyr*, the strange lighting and eerie musical orchestrations in *Day of Wrath*, the protracted panning and tracking movements of the camera in *Ordet*, or the retarded pacing and simplified settings and blockings in *Gertrud*. To view a Dreyer movie for the first time is to undergo a stylistic experience like almost nothing else in cinema. As a friend of mine puts it, Dreyer's style performs brain surgery on his viewers; it re-wires our synapses, changes our bio-rhythms.

Yet, at the same time, no aspect of Dreyer's work has given rise to more interpretive debate and disagreement, not only for viewers encountering the films for the first

time, but even for seasoned "Dreyer buffs" and profes-
sional critics.

Although this is neither the time nor the place for a
comprehensive survey of the critical debates that have
swirled around Dreyer's work, I want to summarize two
contrasting approaches to Dreyer's style that recent critics have taken. I want to describe them not only in order
to suggest some problems with each, but more importantly, to suggest how one might move beyond them, to a
third position beyond both. For convenience of reference, I shall call the first, the traditional (or thematic)
approach and the second, the perceptualist (or formalist)
approach.

Traditional or thematic critics deal with the difficulty
and obliquity of Dreyer's style by reading its strangest
features as being subtly symbolic or metaphoric. Camera
angles, frame compositions, lighting and sound effects,
editorial juxtapositions, and other stylistic effects are in-
terpreted as expressing narrative themes. Since, in the
past decade, Tony Pipolo has been one of the ablest
proponents of the thematic approach to Dreyer's films,
I'll quote a sample of his remarks from a recent article
on *The Passion of Joan of Arc* as an illustration.

Early in his essay Professor Pipolo offers a general
statement of the theoretical premises of the thematic
approach:

[Dreyer's] pronounced concern for the symbolic use of
decor and setting is manifest in film after film. Architecture,

objects of art, even natural outdoor settings are made to reflect and symbolize thematic ideas or aspects of characterization and to create strong bonds between characters and their
social, moral, and psychological milieux. . . . The same control and expressive power extends to formal and filmic aspects
[of Dreyer's films] as well, conveying symbolic or metaphoric
value to lighting, masking devices, camera movement, framing and editing. . . .

My purpose is to demonstrate how such forms are designed to correspond with or parallel the aims of the diegetic
material, thereby creating filmic structures that reflect, or
mirror, psychological and dramatic situations. . . . As this entire essay suggests, the patterns of framing and editing one
can observe in [*The Passion of Joan of Arc*] seem to directly
embody – or in Freud's terminology, "dramatize" – its
themes and situations. . . . The filmic strategies take up certain ideas – for example of psychic stability or harassment –
and adapt them to framing devices – such as "centrality" or
"frameline aggression." In a similar way, analogical structures adapt the dominant tone and direction of the dramatic
interaction between characters and transfer these characteristics to the methods of editing itself.[1]

1 Tony Pipolo, "Metaphoric Structures in *La Passion de Jeanne d'Arc*,"
  Millennium Film Journal, no. 19 (Winter 1987–1988), 54, 66–67. The
  interested reader is also referred to Pipolo's unpublished doctoral dissertation: "Carl-Theodor Dreyer's *La Passion de Jeanne d'Arc*: A Comparison of Prints and a Formal Analysis," New York University, 1981,
  and to his general defense of the use of thematic criticism as a means of
  understanding Dreyer's films in "The Poetry of the Problematic," *Quar-
  terly Review of Film Studies*, vol. 7, no. 2 (Spring 1982), 157–168.

As Professor Pipolo's passing reference to Freud suggests, the thematic reader treats works of art very much the way Freud treated dreams. Events and objects are read symbolically or analogically.

As an illustration of how such a theoretical commitment to the analogical function of style works in a specific instance, I would like to quote an excerpt from Professor Pipolo's treatment of the expressive effect of stylistic events in the early scenes of *Joan of Arc* a few pages later in the same essay. The general thrust of the argument is that the initial "formality" and "impersonality" of Dreyer's editing and photography mimic the ceremonial formality and impersonality of Joan's trial; and that the subsequent disruptions of the editing and photography mimic the emotional insults that are inflicted on Joan in subsequent scenes:

For example, let us consider the first interrogation scene in the chapel. An elaborate tracking shot lays out the spatial planes of the chapel in a precise and detailed manner. The positions of the churchmen and the English military contingent are established clearly and unambiguously. The camera tracks directly behind the tiered platform on which judges, priests, and clerics are seated in the foreground, their backs to the camera, while in the background across the chapel and clustered around its columns stand English soldiers in uniform. The center space, the middle ground between these two, is traversed by a church cleric carrying a stool and placing it down. It is in this center space that Jeanne will be seated during the opening session.

Notwithstanding this meticulous articulation of space and the positions of the characters, we soon realize that the angle and scale of the shots of Jeanne do not represent the way she would be seen by her interrogators; nor do shots of the latter represent the way they would be seen by her. . . . In other words, no attempt is made to represent accurate spatial relationships in the cutting of the shots between the tribunal area of the chapel and Jeanne on her stool. Yet the consistency of this practice suggests that there is a rationale for it. The formalities of the trial are also prominent in this first session, suggesting that the rather abstract spatial distance between Jeanne and her judges expressively reflects the impersonal nature of the proceedings. While Jeanne seems to be spatially isolated from the churchmen, the pretense of formality and the modest security it offers can be sustained.

In contrast, when the churchmen descend from their designated places to confront her more directly, this impersonal framing and editing structure breaks down and is literally shattered into fragments. For example, in the confrontation scene between Jeanne and d'Estivet, when he leans over her and shouts, his spittle falling on her cheeks . . . the composition of images becomes increasingly synecdochic, using extreme edges of the frame and breaking down into large close-ups of d'Estivet's mouth and Jeanne's cheek. (68)

As a final example of the ability of the thematic critic to read stylistic events metaphorically, a brief discussion of *Day of Wrath* from another essay by Professor Pipolo follows. The issue Professor Pipolo addresses here is the significance of the slow pace of the actions and camera movements, and the long duration of the shots in the film. Professor Pipolo relates these stylistic aspects of the work to the massiveness of the sets, and argues that all of them combine to thematize the "medieval" qualities of the narrative:

> Every element in [*Day of Wrath*] – from its dramatic structure and stylized composition of shots to the heaviness of the architecture and the pacing of the action – takes on qualities that reflect a sense of the rigid Christianity of the period. In his brilliant study of Western literature, *Mimesis*, Erich Auerbach analyzes medieval representational forms, citing their emphasis on "starkly creatural realism," "ponderousness and somberness, dragging tempo" and illustrates how this pervading style was well adapted to the importance placed on life after death, to Christian salvation, and to the general devaluation of the physical on earth. All of this characterizes the later period of this film as it is articulated through its formal strategies. On several occasions, for example, the camera's slow and deliberate movement around a designated space is halted on the figure of the "doomed" character. Its gestures are aligned with the powerful impersonal forces at work, signaling the hour of death (*dies irae*) itself. . . . The rhythms of *Day of Wrath* have a great deal to do with historical milieu and atmosphere and the ways in which these affected, even determined, psychological behavior. . . .[2]

Even on the basis of these brief excerpts, it should be obvious that there are several sorts of objections that

2 "The Poetry of the Problematic," 164–165.

might be raised against the thematic approach. In the first place, the translation of a stylistic event into a thematic meaning obviously depends on making some fairly free associations. Why is the particular violation of point of view editing that Professor Pipolo describes in *The Passion of Joan of Arc* an expression of "impersonality" or "formality"? Couldn't another critic assert, just as forcibly, that Dreyer's violations of point of view conventions make the editing in that scene "personal" and "informal"? How would the thematic critic refute that position? Of course Professor Pipolo's choice of metaphors suits his particular reading better than other metaphors do, but that is just to say that his argument is potentially merely circular. Just as in dream symbolism, there is an element of arbitrariness to the choice of initial meanings that won't be dispelled by any amount of elaboration and extension of those meanings.

In short, the thematic meaning attached to a particular stylistic event seems somewhat arbitrary and self-serving. Consider the *Day of Wrath* example. If the slowness of the camera work in that film thematizes medieval "ponderousness and somberness," what does one say about the even more extreme retardation of the camera movement in other Dreyer films like *Ordet* and *Gertrud?* Neither of them is set in the Middle Ages, and neither is very interested in senses of sin, doom, or hellfire. The answer, of course, is that one reads the similar camera movements in those films in entirely different ways, as thematizing other things. But doesn't that then reveal the potential circularity of the whole procedure? One attributes an emotional or intellectual quality to a stylistic event, and then argues that the attribution is not the result of the critic's ingenuity, but is "in" the film itself. It is far from obvious how one makes the leap from a particular stylistic event to a specific thematic interpretation of it.

But there is a still more serious conceptual problem with thematic reading. It is that in attributing metaphoric qualities to a stylistic event, one simply begs all of the important questions about how style communicates meanings. For example, to call a particular editing style "formal" as a prelude to arguing that it thematizes the "formality" of Joan's heresy trial, as Pipolo does in the passage on *The Passion of Joan of Arc*, is actually a way of avoiding dealing with the stylistic issues that one needs explained – in this case, the issue of how, exactly, one communicates something as complex and abstract as "formality" (or "impersonality") in the practical, physical terms of realistic filmic expression in space and time.

Asserting that "every element" in *Day of Wrath* communicates "a sense of the rigid Christianity of the period" begs all of the important questions of how such an intangible thing could ever be communicated by such a concrete, practical medium as a realistic film. How can a movie composed of physical objects and events communicate "the devaluation of the physical"? How can a film make that leap from specific to general, from concrete event to abstract signification? Simply to call certain aspects of Dreyer's style "abstract" is to completely sidestep the question of precisely *how* a style can possibly communicate such a thing – which is, after all, the fundamental question to be answered.

There is an undeniable allure to thematic criticism, however. Students to whom I have presented thematic readings of Dreyer's camera work, sets, and lighting eagerly write them down in their notebooks and imitate them in their papers (though the result frequently is an interpretive free-for-all, when it is performed by a practitioner less tactful and intelligent than Professor Pipolo). Why does such an approach speak so powerfully to so many viewers?

A large part of the appeal of thematic criticism is undoubtedly that it plays into the abstracting appetites of our own minds (especially as we remember events as distinguished from experiencing them). Simplifying abstractions promise easy meaningfulness, ultimate order, and relaxing release from the sometimes disorienting flux of the actual film-going experience. Film viewers (who are no different from viewers of paintings, readers of books, or spectators at any artistic performance) obviously get an immense degree of satisfaction in translating any film-going experience into a simplifying abstraction. How much more they crave such a possibility when confronted with an artistic experience as intellectually relentless and perceptually demanding as that which Dreyer offers. Any interpretation is an act of mastery and power, but abstract, symbolic interpretations are especially comforting for this reason.

Thematic criticism gives us eminently portable interpretations to carry home with us after the film has ended. It gives us the film we recall or reconstruct hours or days after the fact of viewing is complete and after the experience of viewing is almost forgotten. But that is just the problem. Thematic criticism egregiously fails to give us the film we actually experience during a screening: the film in all of its temporal and physical specificity, the film in all of its cognitive bewilderments and perceptual challenges.

The reason for this is that thematic criticism significantly leaves time out of its account of the filmic experience. Thematic criticism makes a film's images and sounds static in their effects and cognitive in their meanings. "Themes" are, after all, conceptual structures removed from the spatial partialities and temporal processes of narrative.

The fundamental fact about narrative is that we receive it in time. We receive it in bits and pieces, the meaning of which is continuously adjusted and changed in the time of our reception. We receive it in emotional pulses. Understanding in time and within the contours of emotional trajectories takes place as a series of continuous revisions of understanding and changes of feeling; yet the thrust of thematic analysis is inevitably in the opposite direction: toward the discovery and presentation of static, virtually spatial, patterns of fixed relationships, images, and sounds.

If thematic criticism overlooks the temporal qualities of the artistic experience, it equally downplays the spatial particularity of the experience in a film. In programmatically substituting abstract concepts in place of particular percepts, thematic analysis invariably leaves the sheer materiality of realistic narrative behind. If there are concepts to be encountered in realistic narrative, the abstractions of thematization forget the importance of the fact that they can never be detached from the concrete events that communicate them. The concepts are embedded in percepts and exist only within them. Even when ideas are spoken in a film, they are spoken by particular actors and characters with particular expressive presences. Even when themes are demonstrably present, they are always mediated in forms of spatial perception.

All of which is to argue that the detemporalizing, departicularizing tendency of thematic analysis inevitably locates the viewer almost entirely outside of the actual experience of viewing a film (especially if the film in question is as experientially demanding as one of Dreyer's). That is why the actual experience of viewing the succession of images, shots, and events that constitute *Joan of Arc* or *Day of Wrath* is very different from the abstractions and allegorizations into which the thematic critic translates the film.

But this is not to put the limitations of thematic analysis strongly enough. The feel, the tone, the style of the actual viewing experience are not merely different from, but positively opposed to, the sorts of symbolic meanings summarized by the thematic critic. By virtue of making events and images cognitively coherent and coolly interpretable, thematic criticism takes the perceptual challenges, emotional assaults, and psychological confusions out of the experience of viewing a film. This is not to argue that criticism must be microscopically phenomenological; but only that in many films (arguably, in all of the greatest films) those revisionary swerves of perception, feeling, and understanding are, in themselves, a significant part (perhaps the most important part) of the "meaning" of the work. Dreyer's films are nothing if not perceptually, cognitively, and emotionally challenging. For someone who feels that those psychological, temporal, spatial, and emotional experiences are at the center of a film, thematic analysis betrays (or to put it more mildly, "leaves out") virtually everything of interest in the film-going experience.

Another way to frame this issue is to say that a thematic reading strongly favors what is systematic, repetitive, or normative in a work's style, and downplays or overlooks anything that is temporally or spatially eccentric or unique. To some extent, of course, every work of art depends on systematic patterns and repetitions, but in its essence, thematic analysis is unsuited for dealing with moments in which a work seeks to shake a viewer out of patterned responses or systematic understandings: the moments of disturbance, sublimity, strangeness, bewilderment, or emotionality – precisely the artistic moments that may be the most important and powerful ones within it.

Although the avowed aim of thematic criticism is the bringing forward of the style of a film as essential to its meaning, the irony is that, in certain respects, the one aspect of the experience of a film that thematic criticism is unable to deal with is its style. In leaving out all of the expressive strangeness, obliquity, and difficulty of style, the thematic critic, in effect, leaves out the "stylisticness" of style. He leaves out everything that distinguishes style from mere statement or conceptualization. Of course, the images, sound effects, and editing patterns in a film "mean something," but what thematic criticism avoids grappling with is why their meanings exist in such an extraordinarily oblique or complex relationship to the characters, events, and settings depicted.

In its faith that one can translate fairly directly and quite unproblematically from style to narrative theme, from style to character psychology, from style to moral significance, thematic analysis fails to appreciate the degree to which style may actually be an attempt to delay or frustrate or complicate the imposition of these sorts of literal, paraphrasable meanings on a scene.

To put it more succinctly still, thematic analysis fails to account for why the act of thematic translation is necessary in the first place. It fails to account for the strange ulteriority and openness of analogy, the meta-phoricity of metaphor. In this sense, one's problems with thematic analysis are less with the particular readings than with the thematic critic's inability to say why these readings are necessary at all. In using concepts like "metaphorization" and "analogical structure," the thematic critic avoids the more important question of why metaphors and analogies are present in the works in the first place. Nature has no metaphors. "Reality" is not analogical. Even most other movies are not so relentless-ly metaphoric as Dreyer's. So why are Dreyer's films so metaphoric? Why are their meanings so stylized? Why do they make things so hard to see? In its activity of metaphoric translation, thematic analysis fails to explain why a work must express itself so metaphorically in the first place.

Artistic metaphors and analogies are expressive events whose very existence needs to be explained, not merely translated into "meanings." But this is precisely what the thematic critic cannot do. Metaphors are shifts out of one mimetic realm and into another. They are acts of imaginative substitution. But why are such obliquities of expression, such indirections necessary? Even if the thrust of the thematic reading of *The Passion of Joan of Arc* that I quoted above were correct, the important questions would still be untouched. Even after every metaphor is explicated, the issue of why a work must express itself so metaphorically remains. In his or her eagerness to translate Dreyer's metaphors (if we agree for the moment that they are metaphors) into meanings, the thematic critic leaves the sheer fact of the metaphoricity of Dreyer's works, what Wallace Stevens would have called "the motive for metaphor," completely unexamined.

What thematic criticism overlooks is the necessity for the enterprise of thematic criticism itself. Thematic criticism is necessary only because Dreyer's means of expression are so hard to see and understand, but in this case the proper question would be why are they that complex, that elusive? In building a bridge from style to meaning, the thematic critic ignores the question of why the bridge is necessary at all. Why is it so difficult to get from the style to the "meaning"?

It is in explicit reaction against thematic interpretations of Dreyer's style that the "formalist/perceptualist" approach is formulated. David Bordwell has been the most articulate and influential exponent of this approach, arguing in three different books on behalf of a rigorously "formalistic" reading of Dreyer's work.[3]

3 One book is devoted to an extended study of all Dreyer's work: David Bordwell, *The Films of Carl-Theodor Dreyer* (Berkeley: University of California, 1981). The other two contain briefer, but similar treatments of Dreyer's work: *Narration in the Fiction Film* (Madison, Wisc.: University of Wisconsin Press, 1985), and *Film Art: An Introduction* (Reading, Mass.: Addison-Wesley, 1979). (For convenience of reference, in subsequent citations I will designate the first book with the initials *FCD*, and the second with the initials *NFF*.) I would also note that Professor Bordwell's work on Dreyer is an application of many of Noel Burch's theories of expression, as presented in his *Theory of Film Practice* (New York: Praeger, 1973).

Professor Bordwell launches an all-out attack upon thematic interpretations of Dreyer's style. His contempt for them is thinly veiled when he argues in the following passage that if thematic readings may be desirable for the explication of "allegory," they are by the same virtue obviously unsuited to the understanding of nonallegorical works:

Granted that [particular] stylistic patterns are present and important, the critic is tempted to "read" them, to assign them thematic meanings. . . . The urge to read stylistic effects in this way must also be traced to a broader tendency, that of assuming that everything in any film (or any good film) must be interpretable thematically. . . .

Interpretation of this sort is wholly appropriate to such narrative forms as allegory, in which abstract, often doctrinal meanings constitute the dominant structuring force of the text. In other forms, however, thematic meaning is only one component in the system, and not necessarily a very important one. The critic who thematizes technique in every film risks banalizing works [like those of Dreyer] which take as their "dominant" the perceptual force of style. For the problem is not just that thematization tends to rely on the clichés of sophomore literary criticism. Even at its best, thematization aims to assimilate the particular to the most general, the concrete to the woolly. . . .

Possessed of a *horror vacui*, the interpretive critic clings to theme in order to avoid falling into the abyss of "arbitrary" style and structure. The critic assumes that everything in a film should contribute to meaning. If style is not decoration, it must be motivated compositionally or realistically or, best of all, as narrational commentary. . . . (*NFF*, 282–283)

Professor Bordwell completely rejects thematic understandings of Dreyer's style. In order to prevent Dreyer's style from simply being absorbed backward into the "themes" of his films, he gives us a Dreyer whose style, especially in his final, most important films, is cut free from narrative or thematic expressiveness. In *The Films of Carl-Theodor Dreyer* his argument is that Dreyer's mature style is liberated from functioning in support of the narrative content of his films altogether. The stylistic systems of Dreyer's major works, in Professor Bordwell's formulation, "make time as well as space relatively independent of narrative demands" (*FCD*, 65).

What Professor Bordwell says about the style of *Ordet* can stand as a succinct summary of his approach to all of Dreyer's mature films. Style "foregrounds" (a favorite term in his argument) its own existence, emptied of thematic meaning and divorced from narrative content:

Ordet uses sound, *mise-en-scène*, camera movement, and the long take to separate text and representation of text. These devices cooperate in pulling staging and filming away from the play text by creating a relatively independent system that foregrounds the duration, the spatial constructions, and the internal development of the shot. (*FCD*, 149–150)

Under Professor Bordwell's fashionably modernist conception of artistic meaning, stylistic fragments are all that the most advanced works of art provide, and we must therefore resist the temptation to unify a work's contradictory of disjunctive expressions around organizing themes.

The contrast between Professor Bordwell's and Professor Pipolo's approaches could hardly be more extreme than in the case of *The Passion of Joan of Arc.* Professor Bordwell begins his discussion of the film with a ringing call for a "defamiliarization" of the text (specifically meaning a movement beyond conventional thematic readings of its style). For Professor Bordwell, the style of *The Passion of Joan of Arc* does not offer thematic harmonies and feats of organization, but rather fragments, dislocations, and disunities:

The need to recognize disunity and contradiction is nowhere more pressing than in the analysis of *La Passion de Jeanne d'Arc.* [The film] plays on representational systems – especially images and language – in disturbing ways. . . . It is time to de-familiarize this classic and to notice its gaps and dislocations, its estranging features. . . . *Jeanne d'Arc* powerfully rejects dominant relationships between narrative logic and cinematic space. (*FCD,* 66)

In *La Passion de Jeanne d'Arc,* the framings are as eccentric as the camera positions. . . . Once the privileged zone of classical screen space has been emptied out, once the characters have been flung to every corner of the frame as if by centrifugal force, areas and gestures can rhyme across the entire film. . . .

Graphic patterns come forward to fill the vacuum left by

the eviction of conventional scenography. . . . A purely decorative overlay serrates and stylizes the screen surface. Even more noticeable are the numerous graphic motifs which, although *in* the scenographic space, are raised to extra-narrative prominence. . . .

Even when perceived movement can be attributed to figure movement, camera mobility can still distort frame space by means of careful synchronization of camera and subject action. . . .

The movements are hardly subordinate to story action; Dreyer calls attention to them [in a variety of ways]. First, the movement is frequently gratuitous by the standards of classical narrative. . . . Secondly, camera movement gains still more autonomy by the fact that a moving shot will unabashedly be interrupted by a static one. . . . Finally (and most radical of all) . . . camera movements . . . split the dramatic space apart, confusing rather than concretizing relationships. (*FCD*, 70–77)

While Professor Pipolo argues that Dreyer uses space and imagery to communicate general, unifying meanings about scenes and characters, Professor Bordwell asserts that Dreyer's use of space deliberately frustrates a quest for thematic meaning, narrative continuity, or psychological coherence. Where the thematic critic found thematic significance, the formalist finds only gaps, dislocations, distortions, and gratuitous stylizations. One of the key concepts in this passage, and more generally in Professor Bordwell's treatment of Dreyer's other films, is the idea of Dreyer's "playing" with styles. In "playing" with representational systems, in *Joan of Arc* and his other films, Dreyer indicates his unwillingness to commit himself to the meaningfulness of any style in particular. His works are, at their very best, deconstructive works, the expressive function of whose style is negative.

To contrast the approaches of Professor Bordwell and Professor Pipolo further, compare the following passage on *Day of Wrath* with the one several pages back. While Professor Pipolo read the so-called slow, heavy style of the film in terms of the ponderousness, somberness, gloominess, and asceticism of medieval Christianity, Professor Bordwell argues the opposite: that the slowness and heaviness of the style of *Day of Wrath* prevents totalizing readings of the sort that Professor Pipolo seeks. The style frustrates the imposition of thematic meanings on the scenes.

The film resists being read. . . . The slowness of events, the catalyses between them, the gravity of the rhythm of the editing, camera movement and sound, all retard the momentum of the film. . . . The result of this device is an extension and heightening of our awareness of the work's aesthetic specificity; retardation aids the text in offering a difficult – Shklovsky says "fractured," "splintered" – perception. . . . *Mise-en-scène* and camera movement are systematically utilized to slow our reading process down and, in an important way, block the flow of narrative meaning. The rhythms of *Day of Wrath* refuse to be unified narratively. We cannot interpret the long walks, the pauses, the camera movements as "significant" in some way (representing psychology, historical setting, atmosphere). Instead, we must recognize that such rhythmic devices are in a literal sense quite empty, barren of significance; they *mean* nothing. (*FCD*, 143)

Professor Bordwell argues that in the course of Dreyer's career his style is increasingly disconnected from thematic or dramatic meaning. Therefore, it increasingly makes itself felt as being "in excess" of narrative needs. As he summarizes near the end of his study, Dreyer's final narratives are "parametric" (adapting a term from Noel Burch), which is to say that they deliberately offer us the vision of style functioning independently of social and psychological expressiveness:

Against the background of the classical model, [the distortions of space and time in Dreyer's] films – in various ways – deflect clear transmissions of story meaning, outrun narrative function, and focus attention on their manipulations of the film medium. For convenience, we can designate as "excess" all these patterns whereby the films systematically escape narrative determination. [By the time of *Gertrud*, Dreyer's final film] narrative events – dialogue, gesture, character confrontations – become swallowed up in cinematic structures, like pennies tossed into a canyon. The film's structuring of space and time creates that excess described by Roland Barthes. "It is this story which here finds itself in some sort parametric to the signifier for which it is now merely the field of displacement, the constitutive negativity, or, again, the fellow traveler." However readable, even in its ambiguities, the film forces us to notice a disparity between narrative and cinematic form. . . . (*FCD*, 176)

41

Now, in comparison with the thematic approach, it should be obvious that there are immediate apparent gains to be reaped from Professor Bordwell's more positivistic, more phenomenological approach. In the first place, formalist criticism acknowledges the sheer strangeness of Dreyer's style as the thematic approach does not. Secondly, Professor Bordwell's descriptive fidelity to the actual perceptual events of Dreyer's shots brings the critical explanation much closer to the true viewing experience of Dreyer's work – its temporality and spatiality. Professor Bordwell's approach is much better at communicating the viewer's ebbing, surging, time-bound processes of perception than the thematic account can ever be. The formalist description gains in perceptual fidelity by liberating itself from the bias toward the expressively systematic, repetitive, and normative that is built into the thematic approach.

Yet it must be acknowledged on the other side of the question that Professor Bordwell's critical methods introduce their own set of problems. In his fidelity to the perceptual disruptions, distortions, and disjunctions of the viewing experience, the formalist critic goes so far in the direction of emphasizing the merely perceptual and logical aspects of the works he describes that he risks understating the cognitive dimensions of the viewing experience as much as the thematic critic understates its perceptual qualities.

As even the brief section that I quoted from the discussion of *The Passion of Joan of Arc* suggests, Professor

Bordwell's spatial and temporal literalization posits a viewer who functions in an almost purely perceptual relationship to the text – a viewer who is oblivious to the text's emotional trajectory and human meanings. It is no accident that Bordwell's Dreyer book is crammed with diagrams of characters' positions, causal relationships between events, itemizations of camera movements, and stopwatch measurements of shot durations. In the formalist's critical universe, a cinematic narrative is consumed and understood almost the way a physicist measures the interaction between subatomic particles or the way a Scholastic philosopher analyzes the logic of a proposition. Narratives are understood as sequences of spatially and temporally organized, causally related events.

The problem is that, however technically correct Bordwell's spatial and temporal measurements and elaborate diagrams of narrative events and logical relationships may be, viewers do not actually experience narratives in such microscopic units – any more than they experience the world as electrons and protons and neutrons just because such things may really exist. I am not arguing that purely perceptual events within a film do not matter, only that they are not the only things that matter. Our lives are continuously affected by the laws of physics and mathematics at the microscopic level, even as they are shaped by wishes and dreams and ideals at the macroscopic level. The viewer does respond to perceptual events in a film; but what the formalist downplays is that he or she also responds to larger emotional and cognitive structures of meaning that perceptual/logical accounts can't include. When we are faced with certain sorts of spatial or temporal distortions in a work, we struggle to put things meaningfully back together in a way that the formalist never acknowledges. Dreyer, like any other narrative filmmaker, not only depends on these macroscopic processes of meaning making being performed by a viewer, he encourages them by interesting the viewer in his characters and their situations in ways that formalists never acknowledge.

When a viewer responds emotionally or intellectually to the expression of a character's eyes, tones of voice, face, and interactions with another character, when a viewer gets upset about or involved with a situation on the screen, the totality of the response will never be strictly ۱educible to the mere camera angles or editing patterns that transmit those experiences to him. In downplaying large narrative structures of meaning – like the meanings communicated by the tones in an actress's voice, the expressions on her face, the emotional resonances and contours of scenes – the formalist fails to account for most of what the most sensitive and alert viewer gets from such scenes. The structures of meaning that the formalist pays attention to are just too microscopic, too merely perceptual and logical to do justice to the actual "look and feel" of a work – especially work as emotionally and intellectually powerful as Dreyer's.

Bordwell's imaginary viewer is lobotomized, and amnesiac almost to the point of being sub-human. He or she has given up normal emotional concerns and intellectual interests in characters, events, and human relationships. He or she has renounced conceptual, emotional, and psychological understandings of the text to become a responder to purely spatial, temporal, and logical effects. He or she has renounced memory to live in the eternal present of the shifts of perspective and time upon which Bordwell so microscopically focuses.

For Bordwell, there are apparently no wrenchingly emotional scenes, no stimulating virtuosities of acting, no plangent human expressions, no laughs or tears worth describing in Dreyer's work. The experience of a film is only the disembodied development of a set of stylistic/perceptual/logical permutations. That is why it is ultimately not surprising that the only kind of assault he can apparently understand, the only kind of effect his criticism can describe is a perceptual or logical one. Since it can't account for them and has nothing to say about them, Bordwell's system of understanding simply leaves out the emotional and personal reactions to characters and events that the ordinary viewer experiences.

The result is that, while for a sensitive viewer *Ordet* may be said to be an excruciatingly painful tragedy presented in a spatially expressive and temporally stimulating way, for Bordwell, the final, astonishing word about the film is that its style "foregrounds the duration, the spatial construction, and the internal development of the shot" (*FCD*, 149–150). Spatial and temporal and logical effects are all that he gets from the film. Relationships between characters and expressions of feeling are so far from being "foregrounded" by Bordwell's analysis that they hardly get mentioned. The best one can say of this bizarre reversal of priorities, this strange, positivistic limitation of one's vision to the formal and perceptual aspects of experience is that it leaves out almost everything that makes a work of art matter to most viewers.

But there are larger issues at stake than how one describes a particular film, or what one pays attention to within it. One has to consider the conception of the function of art that informs all of Professor Bordwell's acts of analysis. After making the strongest possible claims for the importance of Dreyer's work, Professor Bordwell gives his readers a Dreyer who is, essentially, a manipulator of (or "player with") cinematic styles and forms of expression. At its best and most interesting, according to his formalist reading, the value of Dreyer's work is that it "defamiliarizes" both "ordinary perceptual reality" and the expressive forms of "other art works" (*FCD*, 64). This is, of course, a fashionable deconstructionist agenda, and it was applied to other works of art long before it was applied to these films; but still the heart sinks at including Dreyer's work under this rubric. Is perceptual and stylistic "de-familiarization" the noblest, most exalted attainment of which our art is capable? Is "playing" with forms of perception and conventions of representation the highest aspiration to which the human spirit can aspire at this point in the twentieth century? One hopes the answer is no.[4] Bordwell's expressive agenda trivializes both the artistic work and the act of cinematic spectatorship. In the final analysis, the ultimate disservice of Bordwell's book would be for a reader to decide that the formalist's Dreyer is the real Dreyer. The danger would be that he or she would then go on to draw the obvious conclusion: that Dreyer is emotionally too detached, ethically too disengaged, and morally too unconcerned to deserve any further scrutiny.

Bordwell's vision of "de-familiarization" as the supreme achievement of a work of art points to a conceptual fallacy at the heart of all formalist/logical/perceptualist analyses that fatally limits them: an either/or view of style as being ultimately either a mere acceptance of or a mere reaction against perceptual norms and expressive conventions. The problem is not only that Dreyer's cinematic style may not define itself in relation to any of the norms of cinematic "verisimilitude" that

4 This is not to argue that there may not be particular films (avant-garde work from Ernie Gehr or Michael Snow, or feature films from Godard or Resnais, for example) that are almost completely describable in terms of their efforts of deconstruction or de-familiarization. But the same question then must be asked about these works: In their modernist presentations of experiences cleansed of the impurities of social engagement and the messiness of complex psychological and emotional content, do they represent the highest and most interesting expressions of which our souls are capable? Is the very best and most complex thing we can do to "play" with conventions, to deconstruct meanings, to produce works of art "about" other works of art?

Professor Bordwell posits, but that even if Dreyer's style were proved to be cognizant of and reacting to such norms, Professor Bordwell allows it no more complex function than to undermine/deconstruct/play with conventions.

Bordwell's book on Dreyer conceives of only two contrasting functions for style: to maintain expressive norms and conventions or to subvert them.[5] For him, on the one side, conventional Hollywood filmmaking upholds expressive and perceptual norms; Dreyer and other makers of art films, on the other side, "play with" or deconstructively "foreground" the norms. Given this either/or view of the conception of style, the most creative function that one can imagine for cinematic style is a merely negative one: to deconstruct, parody, or play with forms of representation, to indicate their conventionality, their arbitrariness. The problem is that if this is the most complex function of cinematic style that the formalist critic can imagine, it represents an utter trivialization of the possibilities of artistic expression.

Bordwell has many different ways of formulating the two opposed functions of style. When it upholds norms and conventions, style is "realistic;" when it questions

5 Although there is not space here to document the case fully, suffice it to say that Bordwell's entire Dreyer book is structured around this impoverishing either/or sense of style. I would refer the interested reader to pp. 37–38 and 61, and to the entire discussion of *Gertrud* (and especially pp. 186–190), as well as to pp. 162–164 of *Narration in the Fiction Film*, all of which dichotomize style into either supporting the conventions of what Bordwell calls "the classic cinema" or undermining them.

or disrupts them, it is "poetic." In the first case, style maintains representational "verisimilitude;" in the second, it abrogates it. In the first case, expression is "conventional"; in the second it is "artistic." In the first case, style is, in Bordwell's terminology, "motivated narratively"; in the second, it is "motivated artistically" or "parametrically" (in Bordwell's adaptation of a term used by Noel Burch meaning that the style functions independently of the narrative's themes and subjects). In the first case, style functions subserviently to the narrative; in the second, independently of it.

Once one has bought into this dichotomous vision of style as functioning either one way or the other – either in support of expressive conventions or in subversion of them – it becomes obvious why formalist critics like Professor Bordwell are so adamantly opposed to thematic readings of style like Professor Pipolo's. In the formalists' black and white stylistic universe, the thematic understanding of style is the pole of the either/or dichotomy that the formalist rejects as being a merely conventional and normative use of style. To understand Dreyer's style in a thematic way is tantamount to treating his work as if it were expressively conventional and normative – and since that can't be true of this great cinematic stylist, Bordwell prefers to see his style in the opposite way, as "foregrounding" the arbitrariness of its own transformations or functioning "poetically," independently of the narrative.

In the terms of the formalist's either/or dichotomy,

the thematic critic chooses the "either"; the formalist, the "or." For the formalist, the thematic critic absorbs Dreyer's style backward into being a mere expression of the conventional, realistic, verisimilitudinous narrative and psychological themes of a film; while for the thematic critic, the formalist represents a trivial, frivolous, meaningless, foppishly aestheticized conception of style. As long as one defines the alternatives this way, there can be no middle ground.

Now, what is wrong with this picture? The problem is that neither view of the function of style is adequate. What we need to do is to escape from the forced choice itself: the choice entailed by the either/or conception of the function of style. The limitation of both the thematic and the formalistic approaches is that both of them are equally victimized by the either/or view of the function of style that the formalist is himself trapped within. Both the formalist and the thematic critic exclude everything in the middle: everything between the style merely being either an expression of narrative themes (the thematic understanding of style); or being "poetic" and foregrounding" its own manipulations (the formalist reading of style).

My point is that the either/or dichotomy is itself a trap, a logical fallacy. One needs to move beyond *both* conceptions of style, to move beyond style as a mere reflection of theme and narrative or style as functioning independently of theme and narrative. One must move beyond style being either merely normative or merely subversive of norms. One must entertain an entirely more complex vision of the function Dreyer's style than terms like "perceptual de-familiarization," "spatial distortion," and "narrative excess" can comprehend. One must conceive of a much subtler view of style's relation to narrative theme and meaning than seeing it as merely reflecting or illustrating narrative themes. One must entertain the possibility of style functioning in a far more interesting and profound way than that which either the formalist or the thematic critic describes.

Bordwell's argument is right in one respect: Dreyer's style is not merely a repetition of the themes in the films. Bordwell is entirely correct in feeling that this is a simplification and trivialization of the stylistic complexities of Dreyer's films. Dreyer's style is *not* merely a kind of illustration of his narrative. His style *is* at odds with the commonsense understandings of space and time and history and human experience that we have before we come to the film. Dreyer's style *is* strange, coercive, and bewildering at times. It has powerful, often counterintuitive designs upon us. It is designed to push us in entirely new and unaccustomed directions. Dreyer's style is *not* merely giving us the fairly common-sensical, easily understandable, paraphrasable meanings that Professor Pipolo would read out of it.

Yet Bordwell is completely wrong in another respect, and Pipolo right: Even at the moments of its greatest strangeness and unfamiliarity, Dreyer's style is not merely disconnected from his narrative. It is not merely "poetic." It is not engaged in merely "foregrounding" its own effects. It is not merely "playing" perceptual or representational games, or engaged in acts of "de-familiarization." Professor Pipolo is entirely justified in feeling that Bordwell's view of style is a trivialization and simplification of the expressive complexities of the styles of Dreyer's films. Dreyer's style functions in intimate relation to the characters, events, and (what Pipolo would call) the "themes" of the films. It speaks to us humanely about complex situations. It continuously expresses subtle truths about the characters in the films and their predicaments.

In fact, what makes Dreyer's films so interesting is precisely the fact that their style operates much more subtly than the either/or choice between Pipolo's "thematic" and Bordwell's "parametric" sense of expression allows. Dreyer's style is in a much more intricate and complex relation to the subjects, actions, characters, settings, and events of the films than either being a mere reflection of our commonsense understandings of them (the Pipolo version) or being somehow "beyond," "in excess of," or "independent of" them (the Bordwell version).

What we need is a third position beyond either of these views. This alternative sense of style will understand Dreyer's style as expressing (and creating in a viewer) extremely complex states of consciousness and awareness far beyond anything summarizable either as a "theme" or as a mere perceptual disruption or formal "de-familiarization." Dreyer's style must ultimately be appreciated as being an extraordinarily complex form of understanding.

What does that mean? It will take many pages to spell out even a few of the basic functions of Dreyer's style. But one can begin simply by listing some of the various things it does. It can suspend one between alternative interpretations. It can dangle possibilities before the viewer. It can forcibly broaden (or narrow) perspectives. It can encourage meditative movements of mind. It can complicate what might seem to be simple. It can tease, bait, bemuse, mystify. It can deliberately delay understandings or work against reductive formulations. It can direct our attention within a scene in new and unexpected directions (both spatially and emotionally).

In short, far from being either merely a representation of themes or merely foregrounding its own processes, Dreyer's style vigorously makes new ways of knowing and feeling – ways that may be the opposite of our normal, intuitive, commonsense understandings. Dreyer's style forcibly shapes a viewer's awareness of events, characters, and relationships. It induces special states of consciousness and awareness that affect every aspect of how we understand scenes and events. It establishes standards of awareness and sensitivity that the film's central characters will be judged in terms of, and which they must, in effect, live up to (just as the styles of Jane Austen's or Henry James's novels establish standards of performance and expression in terms of which their characters are judged and to which they must live up). Dreyer's style teaches us new ways of seeing, hearing, thinking, and feeling.[6]

Style is the record of Dreyer's labor of weighing, balancing, probing, and entertaining hypotheses within his text. The styles of Dreyer's films represent an enormously complex set of psychological, emotional, and intellectual adjustments of a viewer's attention. It is the trail left behind, as Dreyer makes, expands, and revises meanings and relationships. But there is really too much to say on this subject to summarize it all here and now. I want to reserve more detailed comments about Dreyer's style for the following chapters; I would like to conclude this discussion by offering some fairly broad generalizations about some of the implications and effects of Dreyer's style in all of his work.

6 Let me emphasize that, as complex as they are, the functions I am attributing to Dreyer's style are only the functions of style in any work of supreme genius. Properly understood, the history of the major art of the Western tradition is the history of such stylistic inventions. Dreyer's cinematic style takes its place alongside the styles of Shakespeare, Milton, Beethoven, Henry James, and George Balanchine as a breakthrough to a new way of knowing, a way of understanding our experience as unprecedented as if it were the gift of an alien being descended from the skies or a god suddenly come down to live among us. That should again suggest the limitations of any view of style that can entertain only a reductive either/or function for it: as being either normative or antinormative, thematic or formalistic. It should suggest the fundamental limitation of any view of style that conceives of it either, on the one hand, as repeating preexisting narrative themes or, on the other, as operating independently of themes and merely "poetically" presenting itself for our attention.

The first generalization that one can make about Dreyer's style is that it heightens a viewer's consciousness of time. (For reasons I have already mentioned, a thematic analysis of Dreyer's style is especially misleading in this regard, since its conceptual and spatial abstractions downplay the supreme importance of temporality in the experience of Dreyer's work.) The retardations of editorial and interactional rhythms and the general avoidance of elisions whenever possible in Dreyer's work make a viewer especially aware of time.[7]

Secondly, and partly as a result of its temporal effects, it is of the essence of Dreyer's style that it continuously reminds us that meaning is *enacted.* It is not a quality of an abstract *system* of themes and ideas (as in the thematic approach) nor a more or less fixed *stance* toward other more or less fixed, logical, perceptual, or representational norms (as in the Bordwellian approach). It is the consequence of an activity, a performance, the result of a series of shifting choices.

There are several important conclusions to be drawn from this stylistic state of affairs in Dreyer's work. In the first place, such a sense of style reestablishes the figure of the author as a felt presence in the work.[8] The author is not in a coolly ironic or detached relation to the work.

---

7 It seems not at all accidental that the ticking (or chiming) of clocks figures prominently as background sounds in both *Ordet* and *Gertrud.*

8 For succinctness, I include under the name of "author" all of the various collaborative "authors" of a text: its actors, its writers, its editors, its technicians, its director.

"Intention" is not cut off from the temporal and spatial particularities of acts of execution. Insofar as one feels Dreyer's stylistic choices being enacted and continuously revised minute by minute within the text – the author is felt to be vigorously *in* the text, meditatively moving around in it, adjusting relationships, comparing positions, weighing, discriminating, judging.

The author is bringing humanly valuable meanings into existence moment by moment, shot by shot, in continuously adjusted and readjusted acts of attention and intellect. (This conception of the author as a shaping presence, continuously at work, making decisions, moving around in the text, is absent equally from thematic and from formalist criticism.) The reason that this matters is that insofar as the author makes meanings and relationships in such a way, he gives us a model for all of the acts of making meaning performed by the characters within his text.

Many of Dreyer's principal characters become surrogates for the director in this process of meaning making. David Gray, the central figure in *Vampyr,* is only the most obvious example of a character whose own tentative, laborious processes of searching out meanings and adjusting relationships mirror the filmmaker's. The viewer of Dreyer's work becomes a collaborator in this process as well. One of the reasons that Dreyer's work requires such an enormous effort of attention from his viewers is that the ideal viewer also is asked to participate in this process of searching out and making meanings. The viewer can no more recline into a predictable system of relationships than the filmmaker (or his characters) can.

In short, Dreyer's work gives us a very special sense of what meanings are and how they are made – a sense different from that of most films and a sense that has important consequences on our functions both in our lives outside of the movie theater and in our lives as viewers of his films. To summarize: Meanings are not found or reclined into, but are made. They are the products of specific acts of human performance. They are made in time and with difficulty. And even once made, they are still always in process, up for revision, adjustment, enlargement, correction. Dreyer's style is the record of a labor of making meaning out of otherwise inert sense data – a labor of transformation that ultimately affirms the viewer's power (and the power of Dreyer's most interesting characters) in the face of meaninglessness or confusion. The individual actor (character or viewer) can become a kind of artist of his or her own life, in this sense, Dreyer suggests.

In this respect, *Vampyr* is a textbook lesson in the process of meaning making for the newcomer to Dreyer's work. Dreyer deliberately presents the world of the film so that virtually nothing is known, or can be known, with any degree of certainty, about the "true" or "correct" relationship of the principal characters. Everything must be worked out. All of the meanings must be made. The camera work (never was the second word in that compound construction more appropriate to the description of the style of a film) enacts the work of knowing that Dreyer's style always figures. If we count the director as the first meaning maker in the film, David Gray enacts a second course of meaning making. And the viewer is enticed into a third process of sorting, weighing, and judging relationships, motives, and causes. The three activities of making meanings parallel each other without overlapping.

Dreyer's style in each of his films is the record of this process as it is conducted by the filmmaker and enacted by various characters within the film.[9] It is the record of a series of imaginative exertions, a history of labors of attention and discrimination. Style is the tracks left behind by this continuously renewed and ever-shifting course of work.

This conception of cinematic style does not limit it to an affirmative function. Creativity frequently requires clearing a space through the application of negative energies as well. That is to say, Dreyer's style is often an act of resistance to certain ways in which we might want to understand a scene or a character. Its decreative function is often as important as its creative function. His style is often designed to complicate simple situations and to prevent reductive judgments, to widen narrow views, and to broaden perspectives.

9 After David Gray, I would count as principal meaning makers and surrogates for their director: Anne in *Day of Wrath*, Inger and Maren in *Ordet*, and Gertrud in *Gertrud.*

To understand this is to appreciate an additional problem with the thematic critic's translation of a stylistic event into a portable meaning. Dreyer's style is frequently counterassertive to the very sorts of meanings that the thematic critic wants to read out of the film. In other words, Dreyer's style often seems designed to delay or complicate easily formulatable thematic interpretations. It attempts to slow a viewer down, to retard his or her sense of semantic completion – not only by actually slowing down the pace of events in the films, but, more importantly, by continuously enlarging the possibilities of interpretation around any one character, action, or scene.

That is to say, precisely in the places in which a viewer may want to rush to judgment, to stabilize a reading around a particular meaning, Dreyer's style opens up new views, or qualifies and complicates old ones. Just when we may feel a momentary end point has been reached, Dreyer's lighting, camera work, or editing deliberately forces a changed point of view, a shift of angle of vision. Where we want to hurry to an interpretation that can be lifted out of the particularities of time and space, his style deliberately slows us down or slightly shifts our understanding.

Dreyer's style encourages the same tentativeness about final meanings in his viewers that his most sensitive principal characters demonstrate in his films – *Ordet*'s Inger being the ultimate refinement of this refusal to rush to judgment or to harden one's position into a rigid stance. Dreyer's ideal viewers, like his ideal characters, live in a world in which meanings must continuously be open to being made and remade in the shifting particularities of specific times and spaces. Meanings are on the move, and Dreyer asks that his viewers and most sensitive characters become as semantically mobile and revisionary as his style. But this should suggest again how much is lost when thematic readings of stylistic events take the temporality out of Dreyer's style.

At the same time, as I hope is obvious, this sense of meaning-making in Dreyer's work as resisting thematic excerpting and atemporal stabilization is entirely different from Bordwell's argument that Dreyer's films (*Gertrud,* in the case of the following quote) indulge in a "potentially endless evacuation of meaning" (*FCD,* 188). On the contrary. Far from leaving meanings behind, Dreyer is so concerned with the adequacy of the meanings in his films, so interested in not simplifying them, so intent on their temporal truth value, that he takes great pains with them. They are worked into existence so laboriously, and adjusted so complexly precisely because the meanings matter so much.

This leads to an even larger point that Dreyer's style communicates. Since meanings and relationships are not weightlessly, metaphorically, or abstractly posited or gestured into existence, but are enacted slowly and laboriously within the particularities of space and time, they are never final or ultimate. They are never more than tentative and provisional. If meanings are on the move, it is another way of saying that they are incredibly fragile in Dreyer's work. They are in danger of being eroded, lost, or forgotten. For Dreyer, meaning must be made against the continuous encroachment of confusion or meaninglessness. To paraphrase William James, Dreyer's world is always vulnerable. If relationships can be made in space and time, they are by the same virtue continuously vulnerable to being unmade, to falling apart in space and time. An adequate understanding of style in this sense must communicate the sheer work of establishing, maintaining, and remaking a set of always eroding relationships between characters and between characters and their surroundings.[10]

The final general point to notice about Dreyer's style is that the stylistic events in his work may not have direct

10 Both the thematic and the formalist/perceptual approaches to Dreyer's work depend on an entirely less arduous and less fragile sense of how meanings are created or maintained. For the thematic critic, the abstract images and patterns he or she discovers might be decided upon by the author of the text before filming even begins, and once put there, they stand conceptually above the erosions of space and time. For the perceptual/logical/formalist critic, the filmmaker's ability to "play" with "systems of representation" and to "defamiliarize" them indicates an entirely more slack relationship between the author of the text and the meanings he or she offers. In the formalist either/or formulation, the author can either recline into particular expressive "systems," or disassociate himself or herself from them by "playing" with them. But either way, the author exists in a fairly abstract and relaxed relationship to his or her own expressions — it being just as easy for an author to "play" with systems of expression, as it is for him or her to accept them.

correlatives in the social and dramatic events of the films. The camera may "know" and "show" things that the characters do not. The lighting or sound effects may express imaginative resonances that can't be spoken in lines of dialogue. Costumes, sets, or editorial rhythms may communicate in ways that the screenplay or the figures of the film do not. In a sense, one feels that this recognition is what may have led Bordwell so far astray: in appreciating (correctly) that there was at times what he calls a "discrepancy" between the stylistic and the dramatic expressions in Dreyer's work, he decided that the style simply functioned independently of the narrative. But that is to simplify the complex relationship of the two. The style does represent events of consciousness that the social or dramatic text cannot, but the point to be taken from this is that there is a slight discrepancy – not a decoupling – of the two. Bordwell's decoupling leads him to see style as thematically meaningless, when it is in fact profoundly meaningful precisely because it *is* discrepant.

One of the most powerful meanings the slight discrepancy between Dreyer's style and his narratives communicates is to express some of the ways in which consciousness is not completely or unproblematically translatable into the forms of realistic stage drama or the forms of social interaction between characters. The style exists to express an imaginative and passional residue that won't be completely dramatized. The style evokes possibilities of relationship and feeling that won't be spoken in the forms of social and dramatic expression.

There is obviously much more to say about this conception of style as meaning on the move, of style not as a systematic stance or fixed relationship of an author to a text, but as a labor of imaginatively transformative action, of style as an expression of the vulnerability of meaning making and of the consequent imperative to work at making meanings, of style as an imaginative energy imperfectly translatable into realistic forms of expression. The following chapters will be devoted to spelling out much more specifically how Dreyer's style functions.

But I hope the general point is clear at the outset that Dreyer's style is more than an artistic matter: it is a statement about the purpose and value of possible relationships to experience and expression. It is a declaration of faith in the ability of the active soul (of a filmmaker, a character, or a viewer) to remain imaginatively (if not actually) free from being trapped or imprisoned by certain impinging forces. It is an act of belief in the power of the imaginative individual to stay on the move in daunting circumstances. It is a statement about how we can make meanings in life as well as in film, even as it is also a statement about the tragic consequences of such beliefs when they are not understood or appreciated by the world.

[Two]

The limits of realistic representation

> The cinematic representation of reality should be true [and] realistic,
> but transformed in the director's mind in such a way that it becomes
> poetry. It is not the things in reality that the director should be
> interested in but, rather, the spirit in and behind the things. For
> realism is in itself not art.
>
> Carl Dreyer, "Imagination and Color"

IT would be hard to think of a greater contrast than
that between the work of Carl Dreyer and that of
Jean Renoir. Renoir is an exuberant, happy master at
dramatizing the ways we represent ourselves through
our words and actions. If in Renoir's comedy of manners, the brilliant, shifting surfaces of social and verbal
life are presented as being all we have to express ourselves, they are dazzlingly sufficient unto the day there-
of. His characters are (at least under ideal conditions)
completely able to "speak" their moral, psychological,
and practical relations with each other in terms of their
social, verbal, and physical expressions. Their facial expressions, voice tones, hands, arms, and bodies are brilliantly "legible" in social terms, and knit his characters
into a complex network of subtly shifting relationships.
All that is true precisely because at the heart of Renoir's
work (just as at the heart of his father's painting) is a
fundamental belief in the ability of individuals to express

65

themselves in terms of their physical and social relations with others.

Such a set of expressive values and beliefs represents a distinctive set of culturally and historically defined assumptions about the relation of persons and their expressions. Dreyer's work springs from an entirely different tradition and an opposed set of expressive assumptions. His films (and most of his characters) entirely lack Renoir's faith in the value of social representations, which is why his characters aren't masters and mistresses of social and verbal interactions, and why, even if they could be, they wouldn't trust social and verbal forms of interaction to express themselves.

I only point up the contrast because the consequences of confusing Dreyer's and Renoir's expressive worlds are so serious. A viewer looking for a Renoirian depiction of social events and interactions in Dreyer's work will be doomed to miss the very different sorts of imaginative events and transactions Dreyer offers. To eyes trained in the other kind of viewing, Dreyer's plots seem to be thin. The talk of his characters doesn't seem to get anywhere. His scenes seem maddeningly slow in their pacing and boringly uneventful in their actions.

To a viewer waiting for moments of Renoirian social drama, Dreyer's films seem downright perverse. While Renoir's characters look at each other, Dreyer's as often as not look away from each other. While Renoir's characters are voluble and animated to a fault, Dreyer's frequently drop out of social interaction altogether into states of energetic silence or moments of solitary meditation. While Renoir's characters continuously and inventively succeed an representing even the most ostensibly "private" aspects of themselves and their feelings in terms of their social tones and styles of behavior, the most central aspects of Dreyer's characters are almost never "spoken" in such ways.

It is not accidental that, while Renoir revels in scenes of vigorous social interaction, Dreyer usually simply avoids such scenes. To the degree that Dreyer does present scenes of robust social interaction,[1] he emphatically advertises their expressive limitations or superficiality. Dreyer's work is an exploration of states of feeling and imagination that are essentially at odds with social or verbal forms of expression.

The essence of Dreyer's work is the effort to gesture beyond the sort of social, verbal, economic, or political events and actions that define the drama in Renoirian and most other "realistic" forms of filmmaking. Dreyer attempts to communicate energies of vision, imagination, or desire that will only be expressed in the work's social and verbal text with the greatest difficulty, if at all. If Renoir's characters volubly and fluently "bespeak" themselves in the codes of social interaction, Dreyer's

1 As in the early scene in *Gertrud* in which Gustav's mother stops by for a brief visit with her son and daughter-in-law, or the scene in *Ordet* in which, following the apparently happy conclusion of Inger's medical crisis, the doctor and minister sit down at the table with old Morten Borgen to chat about the relative power of medicine and prayer.

speak something much closer to what Peter Brooks calls "the language of desire."[2]

Dreyer himself argued something very much like this when, over and over again in his writing, public lectures, and interviews, he talked about his films as expressions of what he alternatively called the "spirit," the "soul," or the "imagination." Compare the following scattered remarks from his important 1955 lecture "Imagination and Color":

Reportorial photography has compelled cinema to keep down to earth, so that it has become addicted to naturalism. Only after it cuts these moorings will cinema have the possibility of rising to the heights of imagination. Therefore, we must wrest cinema away from the embrace of naturalism. We must get it into our heads that it is a waste of time to copy reality. . . . Cinema must work itself away from being a purely imitative art. The ambitious director must seek a higher reality than the one he obtains just by putting the camera up and copying reality. His pictures have to be not only a visual but a spiritual experience. . . . It is not the things in reality that the director should be interested in but, rather, the spirit in and behind the things. For realism is in itself not art; it is only psychological or spiritual realism that is. . . . There is a world outside the grayness and tedium of naturalism, namely: the world of the imagination.[3]

2 Peter Brooks, *The Melodramatic Imagination* (New Haven: Yale University Press, 1976), 41.
3 Carl Dreyer, "Imagination and Color" (a lecture delivered at the Edinburgh Film Festival on August 29, 1955, reprinted in Donald Skoller (ed.), *Dreyer in Double Reflection* (New York: Dutton, 1973), 176–186.

Or compare these excerpts from an essay titled "A Little on Film Style":

There is a certain resemblance between a work of art and a person. Just as one can talk about a person's soul, one can also talk about the work of art's soul, its personality.

The soul is shown through the style. . . . In the artistic film it is [the characters'] adventures of the spirit that we want to experience. We want to enter upon and into the lives we see on the screen. We hope that the film will set ajar for us a door into these other worlds. We want to be placed in a suspense that originates less from outside action than from the unfolding of inner conflicts. . . . Realism in itself is not art; it is only psychological or spiritual realism that is so.[4]

The essay in which these last remarks appeared was published shortly after the release of *Day of Wrath*, and was Dreyer's response to the charge that the film was slow and uneventful. The thrust of his reply was that his viewers were, in effect, applying Renoirian expressive standards to non-Renoirian work. His point was that however slow and uneventful the physical and social events of his film, the real events in the film are events of the "soul" – psychological and spiritual occurrences, not words and actions – and that once that was understood, *Day of Wrath* would be seen to be far from uneventful or boring.

It is interesting that Henry James, an artist whose

4 "A Little on Film Style," reprinted in Skoller (ed.), *Dreyer in Double Reflection*, 127–134.

work has profound and wide-ranging similarities with Dreyer's, had to defend his novels against the identical misunderstanding, the same charges that not enough "happened" in them. In the following brief excerpt from "The Art of Fiction," James was responding specifically to Walter Besant's argument on the importance of "telling a good story" consisting of "adventures," by arguing that what such an argument forgets is that (in Dreyer's terms) "adventures of the spirit" are as real and important as voyages along the Spanish Main (if, indeed, they are not demonstrably much more real and important). In self-defense, James writes:

And what *is* adventure, when it comes to that, and by what sign is the listening pupil to recognize it? It is an adventure – an immense one – for me to write this little article; and [alluding to his own *An International Episode*] for a Bostonian nymph to reject an English duke is an adventure only less stirring, I should say, than for an English duke to be rejected by a Bostonian nymph. I see dramas within dramas in that, and innumerable points of view. . . . I have just been reading at the same time, the delightful story of *Treasure Island*, by Mr. Robert Louis Stevenson and, in a manner less consecutive, the last tale from M. Edmond de Goncourt, which is entitled *Chérie.* One of these works treats of murders, mysteries, islands of dreadful renown, hair-breadth escapes, miraculous coincidences and buried doubloons. The other treats of a little French girl who lived in a fine house in Paris, and died of a wounded sensibility because no one would marry her. . . . One of these productions strikes me . . . as having a "story" quite as much [as the other]. The moral consciousness of a child is as much a part of life as the islands of the Spanish Main, and the one sort of geography seems to me to have those "surprises" of which Mr. Besant speaks quite as much as the other.

But, though it may cast some light on Dreyer's general artistic purposes and goals, mere phrase making about "adventures of the spirit" does not answer the question at hand. How does Dreyer make his text a representation of the "soul," "spirit," or "imagination"? How does he represent energies that are at odds with social and verbal representations (the forms of representation that are very warp and woof of narrative film, one would think)?

The short answer is through his style.[5] It will take many pages to explain the function of Dreyer's style in detail; however, one can begin by noticing that Dreyer's style repeatedly limits the claim of one aspect of "reality" on a viewer's attention in order to increase the claim of another aspect. Specifically, his style minimizes the

5 Though there is not space to elaborate the comparison with Henry James, the value of even briefly juxtaposing his work with that of Dreyer is to suggest the deep similarity between the stylistic agendas of these two artists. James's and Dreyer's styles are entirely comparable acts of redirection of the viewer's or reader's attention. Both great stylists are engaged in strikingly similar attempts to change their viewers' or readers' ranges of awareness and sensitivity. Both have radical designs on what we know and see and feel.

pull of naturalistic, economic, and practical concerns within a scene in order to maximize the pull of emotional, spiritual, and intellectual concerns. His style deflects a viewer's attention from external facts or events and toward internal states of feeling and imagination. Or to introduce two useful terms, Dreyer "derealizes" certain social and physical forms of representation in order to "realize" – to make almost tangibly present – movements of mind and desire, fugitive feelings and impulses that would otherwise be lost or invisible within a scene. Dreyer's "derealizations" of, and deflections of attention away from certain worldly, practical events are essential to his "realizations" of and redirections of attention toward other spiritual, emotional, and imaginative events.

But let me be more specific. One can point to several ways in which Dreyer accomplishes this forcible redirection of a viewer's attention in his work, all of which can be classed under the general rubric of acts of simplification and minimalization. In the first place, he deliberately minimizes or downplays the sorts of narrational complexity and scenic busyness that most other films create, precisely in order to encourage a viewer to enter into a different sort of relation with the material from that of a conventional film. Dreyer empties the frame space and simplifies the *mise-en-scène* in every way possible. He eliminates all but the most essential actions and events, radically simplifying the plots of his films.

He reduces the number of props to a minimum.[6] He holds the movements of the characters to a minimum and also often minimizes the number of repositionings of the camera or the number of intercut shots during the course of a scene.

Next there are the various kinds of temporal retardation and the general paring back of social events in his work. Dreyer often deliberately slows down characters' movements, retards the pace of dramatic events (compared with the rhythms of a standard Hollywood movie), and minimizes the amount of dialogue and social interaction between his figures. Frequently characters simply sit or stand in one place during the course of a scene. When they do move, their movements are frequently photographed in their entire duration rather than being "jump cut" from one point of action to another (as was the almost universal practice in Hollywood movies long before Godard flaunted the technique). When a repositioning of the camera is necessary, Dreyer avoids outright cuts or elisions whenever possible and prefers to use a slow panning movement to follow or

6 My reference to "reducing" the props is not merely a figure of speech. When Dreyer decided to make *Ordet*, he ordered that the principal set for the film, a farmhouse kitchen, be furnished and appointed down to every last utensil and implement. Then, prior to beginning filming, he went through the set with his cameraman and removed virtually everything beyond a minimal number of essential props. See Ib Monty's account in the introduction to Dreyer's unfilmed *Jesus* screenplay: Carl-Theodor Dreyer, *Jesus* (New York: Dell, 1972), 6.

lead the character. (*Ordet* provides the best examples of this technique.) Long silences or pauses in characters' speech are not at all uncommon, and when characters do speak, their lines of dialogue are never overlapped.

In lieu of the social fullness and visual busyness of Renoir's sets and the physical animation and prolixity of his characters, Dreyer offers noneventfulness, figures' physical stillness and silence, and simplicity bordering on austerity in his sets. Given the minimalization of action and interaction, the scenic simplifications, and the general retardations of dramatic rhythms, it is not surprising that Dreyer's scenes seem maddeningly slow and bewilderingly uneventful to viewers who come prepared for a Renoirian experience, viewers not willing to resynchronize their viewing rhythms and their attention to the very un-Renoirian experiences that Dreyer offers. For such viewers (including Professor Bordwell also, by his own testimony), films like *Gertrud* offer only the experience of "tedium" or "slowness."

Though many an uncomprehending viewer has mistaken the minimization of exterior eventfulness, the spatial and photographic simplifications, the reductions of social interaction between characters, and the temporal retardations of Dreyer's work as signs of emotional barrenness or imaginative sterility, I would argue that these characteristics are at the very heart of Dreyer's attempt to emotionally enrich and to imaginatively enhance the effect of his scenes. His goal is nothing less than changing how we understand the events in his scenes. Dreyer's acts of narrative economy and rhythmic retardation are in the service of a radical redirection of our attention and awareness. The goal of Dreyer's work is to alter how we process events: to move a viewer to a different range of awareness and sensitivity – to appreciate imaginative events *beyond* or *behind* characters' words, actions, situations, and social expressions.

Dreyer's stylistic project is a double one. His scenes take as their subject imaginative experiences undergone by characters even as they seek to sponsor imaginative experiences in their viewers.[7] Dreyer not only depicts special, imaginatively enriched states of feeling and awareness in his characters, but he attempts to nurture them in the viewer. If he encourages the characters he cares most about to substitute imaginative values and movements in place of social values and worldly movements, he encourages his viewers to enact the same process of imaginative substitution. One of the fundamental goals of Dreyer's style is to shift a viewer's attention from worldly or social events to spiritual or emotional ones.

It is necessary that the plot be slowed (or momentarily stopped) and that dialogue or interpersonal interaction between characters be minimized or downplayed in

7 The doubleness of this narrative project is not unlike what we find going on in the work of Henry James or Nathaniel Hawthorne. Both writers deliberately slow their plots or stop the social or physical interactions of their characters in order to release both them and their readers to special imaginative states of awareness. See my remarks on Hawthorne in *American Vision* (New York: Cambridge University Press, 1986), 193–194.

order to make a time and space for attention to imaginative events. Dreyer pushes the pause button, as it were, on one sort of action, in order that another kind of imaginative action can be allowed to take place.

Immobilizing the characters, slowing the plot (or actually seeming to arrest it, by having characters repeat lines of dialogue or having the film structured around a series of repetitive scenes and parallel blockings, as Dreyer does in extreme cases like *Gertrud,* his final film), and minimizing characters' social interactions are ways of cordoning off a protected space and time for imaginative movements and emotional transactions. Characters and scenes must be protected from the coercions and reductions of external action and eventfulness.

When the characters are temporarily freed from the pressures of practical action and social expression, the real events of Dreyer's work may begin – events of consciousness. The viewer is wooed into attending to "events" of consciousness, distinct from the "events" of realistic action. At such moments of silence or narrative retardation, imaginative energies are released in both the character and the viewer that the requirements of plot and dialogue would necessarily repress or drown out. Like a character at such moments, a viewer is able to move into a realm of imaginative speculations and connections. The viewer shifts into a state of appreciation for spiritual and emotional events, events which can take place even in the absence of a realistic, utilitarian way to express them.

In frustrating or retarding a viewer's narrative appetence, by denying or slowing a viewer's reception of realistic information and events, Dreyer is engaged in a radical act of redirecting our attention from outer to inner realms of eventfulness.[8] Dreyer's silencing of the dialogue, his momentary stopping of the plot, and his slowing of the pace of scenes are in the service of nurturing a special, narratively nonrepressive, imaginatively evocative relationship between the viewer and the text. A viewer is encouraged to enter into an imaginatively sug-

8 In "The Art of Fiction," the essay from which I have already quoted, Henry James argues something surprisingly similar about the necessity of suppressing narrative events at moments in order to move a viewer into a specially imaginative relationship with the text. Commenting on John Singer Sargent's *Madame X*, he replies to the critics who said that in it the painter fails to depict a sufficiently dramatic "incident" by arguing that, in redirecting a viewer's attention from exterior to interior happenings, Sargent redefines the kind of "incident" that can be depicted:

> It is an incident for a woman to stand up with her hand resting on a table and look out at you in a certain way. . . . If you say you don't see it . . . this is exactly what the artist who has reason of his own for thinking he *does* see it undertakes to show you.

James understands that it may require the suppression of attention to the one sort of "incident" in order to make a margin for the other sort of "incident" to occur in a work of art (or in a viewer's consciousness). It is precisely because an "incident" of the practical sort *isn't* depicted in Sargent's painting that an "incident" of the imaginative sort *is* able to be dramatized.

One may still, of course, legitimately ask why social events and verbal interactions are felt to be so problematically related to the expression of characters' (and viewers') imaginative energies. As I have already noted, Renoir, for one, does not feel this problem.

gestive relationship to the experience he or she is under-going. The viewer is teased away from having to attend to social values and physical relationships in order to entertain a more speculative, more meditative rela-tionship to a character or scene. Dreyer frustrates a viewer's narrative appetence, in order to release him or her into a more visionary or meditative relation to what is seen. The result is what in another context I called a "meditative shift" out of mere immersion in events and into an imaginatively enriched appreciation of them, for both the character and the viewer participating imagina-tively with him or her.[9]

The consequences of this stylistic deflection of our attention away from external events and actions, and toward internal impulses and private states of feeling are obvious in all of Dreyer's major films. Precisely because the physical trappings, the plot events, and the social and verbal interactions between the characters are so mini-mized, the stylistic effects in Dreyer's work "speak" in their place all the more powerfully. Precisely because the physical movements of the characters are reduced and the physical pacings of scenes are retarded, we are put in a position to respond all the more vigorously to the characters' and the films' imaginative movements.

The Passion of Joan of Arc is the narrative of a court-

9 Compare my discussion of the relation of narrative arrest and visionary movement in other films in *American Vision* (New York: Cambridge University Press, 1986), 87–88, 155–172, 192–199, 433–445, and *passim.*

room hearing and a trial, obviously, but the film trains us to notice at a deeper level just what can't ever be spoken in these situations, what can't be said or understood in terms of a legal or theological proceeding, what escapes the codes of ideological discourse while transforming them. These imaginative events are expressed only in minute flickers and pangs of emotion on a character's face or in special stylistic effects within scenes.[10]

Ordet is explicitly about practical, social instances of touching, speaking, and moving within a family group – about the ways characters actually and physically reach out and connect up with one another. But the whole stylistic effort of the film is also to educate a viewer to see beyond these physical and social acts of touching, as important as they are, to an appreciation of deeper imaginative and passional ways that characters "touch" or fail to "reach" each other.

Judged by Renoirian standards, *Gertrud* is an "empty" film, and only a series of "sofa conversations" (as it was derisively labeled by hostile critics at its world premiere screening in Paris in 1964), except for the fact that the minimalizations of external eventfulness powerfully redirect our attention to other, more purely imaginative

10 This is also what emphatically distinguishes Dreyer's story of Joan from other films based on the same general events. From Cecil B. De Mille's silent *Joan the Woman*, made in 1916, to Otto Preminger's *Saint Joan*, in 1957, the external events of Joan's life and trial have been put on screen; but only Dreyer (and Robert Bresson in his 1962 *Trial of Joan of Arc*, in a somewhat different way) have conceived of the "story" as a fundamentally interior drama.

events taking place within the film. Because the dialogue and blockings are so simplified and repetitive, our attention is redirected to tones and expressions that would otherwise be inaudible and invisible, that express themselves as pulses of feeling between the spoken lines. We hear the wildness and the plangency of the characters' voices, and feel the almost unendurable intensities of emotion that underlie their deliberately restrained social interactions and anxiously controlled words.

As this last example illustrates, Dreyer deliberately presents what might be called a banal or superficial sequence of social events and practical interactions, in order to encourage a viewer to move beyond it. He presents characters too visionary, too emotionally energetic, or too imaginative for the expressive situations in which they find themselves. The public, outward drama of manners and interactions exists to be punctured by a private, inward drama of imagination and desire.

Having said all of this, I must point out that I have only described half of the stylistic agenda of Dreyer's work. The crucial complication is that – allowing for all of the turns away from Renoirian social expression in the films – Dreyer and the characters he cares most about do not simply renounce the attempt to express their visions and desires realistically. Rather, notwithstanding all of their expressive problems and the difficulties their expressions create, they and he engage themselves with realistic social and verbal forms of expression.

There is thus an essential opposition at the heart of

Dreyer's expressive project that must be understood. On the one hand, Dreyer labors to deflect a viewer's attention *away from* and to encourage his characters' movement *beyond* certain practical forms of action, meaning, and relationship; yet, on the other hand, when properly understood, his work ultimately forces its characters to express themselves *within* those same forms of expression, however frustrating and problematic they may be. In a sense, the acts of derealization in his work – by which social forms are made to seem unimportant or superficial or irrelevant – are ultimately performed in the service of a subsequent re-realization of imaginative impulses *back into* forms of practical expression. Dreams and desires must be socially "spoken" in order to count. One must attempt to enact one's ideals and impulses in the forms of social expression and the structures of realistic narrative filmmaking – however problematic the result may be.

I have been urging a fundamental distinction between Renoirian social forms of expression and Dreyer's more meditative and visionary work, but this last observation should suggest that there is a further contrast that needs to be drawn between two kinds of visionary cinema: Dreyer's socially and dramatically mediated form, and a form of visionary cinema that exists in the mainstream Hollywood tradition (extending from the work of Sternberg and Hitchcock in the thirties to that of De Palma, Kubrick, and Malick today) that is much more purely visionary than Dreyer's is.

If one had to point to one thing that succinctly differentiates these two lines of visionary cinema, it might be summarized in terms of the emphasis on the point-of-view editing convention in the one tradition, and its absence in much of Dreyer's work. Although point-of-view editing might seem to be a neutral artistic convention, the use of subjectivity as the basis for the presentation of experience in Hollywood film represents an acceptance of visionary stylistics as the basis for art, and an acceptance of vision as an acceptable basis for human experience.

Viewers and characters in such works are encouraged to live through the eye in a way Dreyer's cinema never allows. Insofar as Dreyer's films almost entirely avoid point-of-view editing and the cultivation of privileged states of subjectivity that are common in such work, they are expressing a commitment that emphatically distinguishes them from the other tradition – a commitment to the expression of vision within structures that resist it.

Hitchcock is only the best-known practitioner of stylistics in which visual or visionary relationships between characters consistently substitute for social, verbal, and practical ones. In his work, human experience is not composed of the nuanced, extended interactions of a group of individuals speaking and listening to each other, reacting and responding together, complexly enacting their destiny in practical social and dramatic forms of expression, as in the films of Dreyer, but is very largely a matter of seeing and being seen. To see or be seen (by other characters within one's film as well as by an audience watching it in a theater) in a certain way is the major event in all of Hitchcock's work. That is why characters can communicate (both with others and with the movie-going audience) through glances. To "see" is to "know," and all that is really asked of a character is that he or she "see" or "know" something abstractly, intellectually, visionarily, visually. Hitchcock's is a cinema of "mind's eyes." Or to put it most simply, the "eye" defines the "I." The visionary, visual, imaginative "eye" at points almost completely replaces the socially, verbally, and dramatically expressive "I."

How entirely different the situation is in Dreyer. There are no transparent eyeballs; there is no living through the eye. Declining the point-of-view editing convention and states of insulated subjectivity as a basis for dramatic presentation, Dreyer insists that his characters perform their vision, their knowledge, their impulses in the forms of practical social and dramatic expression.[11]

The consequences of this privileging of our powers of

11 The contrast that Dreyer establishes between Johannes and Inger in *Ordet* is his clearest statement of this difference. To frame the difference between Hitchcock and Dreyer in terms of the history of aesthetics, one might say that Dreyer injects the late-nineteenth-century symbolist aesthetic into the realm of twentieth-century realistic narrative. (I would also note parenthetically that Dreyer's *Vampyr* is an exception among his films, in that it alone of all of his work occasionally yields to Hitchcockian modes of presentation and understanding.)

optical surveillance and visionary connoisseurship over our capacities of practical social interaction in the film-makers functioning in the more purely visionary tradition are of enormous ethical and aesthetic importance. The sorts of special effects of photography or lighting temporarily freed from social entailments and consequences that one routinely encounters in the "beauty shots" and in the virtuosity of camera movement and lighting in films by Kubrick, Malick, De Palma, or Toback (as different as these filmmakers may be from one another in other respects) presume the possibility of entertaining an imaginative stance toward experience that avoids the mediations and complications of practical involvements. Such filmmaking reveals the connection between voyeurism and solipsism. It implies that aesthetic stances can replace ethical ones.[12]

I would note that since the criticism that deals with such films is itself frequently premised upon the identical substitution of formal values for social ones, it is no accident that it is blind to the distinctive limitations of the work it treats. Since so many film critics argue (or as-

12 I am limiting my examples to Hollywood filmmaking, for the sake of the general reader. I would only note in passing that the work of avant-gardists like Maya Deren, Michael Snow, Ernie Gehr, Peter Kubelka, and others could be used in place of Hitchcock's to illustrate the same point. What makes this interesting is that the work of Dreyer has been appropriated by many of these filmmakers as participating in "their" expressive enterprise. That should be kept in mind in understanding the potential misreading involved in various avant-garde appreciations of Dreyer's *oeuvre*.

sume) that Hitchcock's visionary stylistics are more "filmic," more "pure," and hence more "artistic" than the more socially and dramatically compromised film-making practiced by filmmakers like John Cassavetes or Elaine May (filmmakers who, like Dreyer, insist on the mediation of vision in social forms of expression), the unlikelihood of their adequately appreciating the achievement of this other visionary tradition is increased. The dominant lines of film criticism in the past thirty years theoretically valorize one very narrow view of experience – in the extreme instance, the view encoded in the relentless subjectivism and point-of-view editing of a film like *Rear Window* – over more socially engaged ways of understanding experience.

This retreat into unmediated vision is just what Dreyer refuses to perform in his work. While the Hitch-cockian cinema entertains the possibility of "pure" (which is to say, verbally and socially unmediated and unexpressed) imaginative relations, Dreyer's vision (his own, that of his characters, and that of his viewers) is invigoratingly "impure" – mediated, compromised, and confronting the endless indirections, substitutions, and repressions of practical social and dramatic expression.

If Hitchcock and Kubrick represent a "visionary" cinema, and Renoir and others represent a cinema of social embeddedness, Dreyer's complex achievement is to attempt to bridge the two realms without compromising either. His films hold vision in solution with all of the forces that resist it. The central narrative project of

Dreyer's work is an exploration of the point at which we attempt (however futilely or tragically) to translate our desires into the practical expressive forms of the world. The very interest of Dreyer's work (not unlike the work of James or Hawthorne in this respect) is the way it straddles that expressive divide.

James used the metaphor of the balloon of the imagination being always tethered to the ground to explain this double allegiance in his own work. Using a strikingly similar metaphor involving maintaining one's "foothold" on reality, Dreyer suggests the same thing in two sentences that I omitted from the conclusion of a previous quote, but that I will now restore:

There is a world outside the grayness and tedium of naturalism: namely, the world of the imagination. Of course, this conversion must take place without the director and his collaborators losing their foothold in the world of realities. Even though he must make reality the object of an artistic transformation, the transformed reality must, however, be rendered so that the viewer recognizes it and believes in it.[13]

But one needn't appeal to Dreyer's statements about his films as evidence of his stimulatingly divided expressive agenda; the division of allegiance is expressed in terms of the divided structures of the films themselves and the divided situations of their characters. Dreyer's texts and his characters are invigorating, expressively divided. Even as the styles of the films try to move us

13 "Imagination and Color," 186.

beyond concerns with practical events and interactions, in all of the ways I have indicated, his films attempt to describe practical possibilities of imaginative performance in the world. Even as they attempt to honor energetic fragments, impulses, and mercurial movements of mind, his films test the ability of such energies to make themselves felt within the forms of chronological, sequential, realistic narratives. Dreyer's characters may be visionaries or dreamers in many respects, but the ultimate test he exacts of them is that they express themselves and their visions in words and actions in the world. That is why they are not allowed to go off on their own, to become transparent eyeballs, to ascend into the solipsistic heaven of the avant-gardists, but are asked to engage themselves practically and energetically with groups of others.

However much a viewer's attention is directed beyond the realm of social expressions, Dreyer and his characters attempt to reinject vision into the world, to express themselves in forms of realistic social interaction with others. Even as his films and characters stand as potential critiques of such forms of expression, they never cease to engage themselves with them. Dreyer never abandons hope in the possibility of speaking emotional and imaginative energies in the forms of social and verbal intercourse.

The excitement of Dreyer's dramas, the incredible energy of his heroines, their unceasing expressive engagement and activity, emerge out of their precarious effort to translate the language of imagination and desire into the language of society, however limiting it may seem to be. The central problem that Dreyer's cinema explores is the relationship between the individual imagination and the forms of worldly (and artistic) expression available to it. The question his major films ask, without quite being able to answer, is: To what extent can we translate our freest impulses and feelings into practical forms of expression?

That is why even as Dreyer's heroines imaginatively gesture beyond forms of social representation, they still continue to interact energetically with the expressive systems around them. *The Passion of Joan of Arc*'s Joan is not a passive visionary (in her life or her trial). *Day of Wrath*'s Anne wittily, playfully, passionately attempts to express herself in a dazzling dance of courtship with her lover. Gertrud tries to "realize" her exalted dream of perfect love in the forms of a practical sexual relationship. Like their creator, Dreyer's heroines are driven by their dream that they can "live" their imaginations in the world, that they can express their most mercurial ebbs and flows of feeling realistically. That dream energizes and troubles Dreyer's work and his most important characters.

Dreyer's most interesting and energetic figures are poised precariously on the margins of social discourse – half within it, half somewhere beyond it. This becomes a kind of visual metaphor in the films. As a shorthand way of cinematically representing their states of expressive marginalization, Dreyer spatially and physically "marginalizes" almost all of his principal figures. (We will see spatial marginalization used as an analogue for expressive marginalization most notably with Anne in *Day of Wrath* and Johannes in *Ordet.*) As they imaginatively turn away from social interactions with other characters, they are frequently moved physically off to one side of a group or to one edge of the frame space as the sign of a simultaneous meditative "turn" out of social values.

The metaphor of Dreyer's figures' "turning out" of society (and the codes of social discourse) is more than a metaphor; it is a literal event in the films. Dreyer's figures "turn" themselves out of ordinary social interactions both imaginatively and physically. Or to put it more precisely, their physical turnings seem to be Dreyer's way of representing their imaginative turnings.[14] The bodies of characters are angled away from each other. Their heads are inclined to one side or turned away from others. Eye contact between characters (most notoriously in the dialogue scenes in *Gertrud*) is sometimes eliminated altogether. The over-the-shoulder photography and shot/reverse shot editorial syntax of a standard Hollywood production that seamlessly knits characters together with a series of eyeline matches is avoided.

Dreyer's most interesting figures are positioned on

14 I describe the operation of a similar visual metaphor in the paintings of Winslow Homer, Thomas Eakins, and Edward Hopper in *American Vision*, 9–25, 55–60, 159–170. Anne's bodily and meditative "turnings" in *Day of Wrath* are the clearest illustration of this event.

the margins of the semiotic systems of both the films that create them and the fictional societies that they exist within. They precariously maintain an expressive stance half engaged with, yet half beyond the repressions of established social and moral categories. Even as the temporal and spatial structures of the films attempt to absorb and channel their energies in the course of the narrative, they attempt to resist incorporation into the systems around them (both those in their society and those in their films).

Needless to say, this position of expressive marginality represents an extremely complex situation for a character (or a filmmaker) to be in. It can be alienating or stimulating. It can represent the prospect of estrangement and loss, yet also the prospect of achieving a newly creative imaginative relationship to experience. That complex state of marginality – being trapped within and yet simultaneously, to some degree, liberated from the expressive systems in place around them – goes a long way toward describing the supremely vexed yet stimulating expressive position of Dreyer's heroines (and the situation of Dreyer himself). In *The Passion of Joan of Arc*, Joan continues to function, excruciatingly yet creatively, within the oppressive linguistic codes of the judicial inquiry within which she is caught, even as she recognizes how irrelevant they are to her authentic expressions of herself. In *Day of Wrath*, Anne and her *doppelgänger*, the witch Herlofs Marte, attempt to express themselves within the world defined by the witch-hunting churchmen of their film, even as they stand as exceptions to all of its normative understandings. And even as Gertrud refuses to subscribe to them and attempts to rise above them, she can never entirely break away from the discursive codes of the society of lovers and relatives that hedges her round.

Dreyer's cinematic project is thus essentially paradoxical. His work and his principal characters are transcendental in aspiration, directing our attention to energies too mercurial and too intense for social forms of organization or control, even as he and they attempt to express themselves, however glancingly and problematically, within the forms of expression that they partially gesture beyond.

This stylistic struggle is crucial to the effect of Dreyer's films. It is enacted in every aspect of his work. His visual and editorial style gestures one way, toward the realm of spirit and imagination, while his dramatic form and the opportunities of expression available to his characters remain doggedly realistic and practical. That is why it is important to observe that, notwithstanding all of his lyrical, poetic, transcendental aspirations, Dreyer is not an avant-garde, nonnarrative, nondramatic filmmaker jettisoning character and plot and realistic dramatic interaction in his films. His stylistic acts of imaginative displacement and derealization are continuously counterpoised against narrative acts of bodily replacement and social realization. His characters' and his own imaginative energies are forced to be expressed practically and physically. That double allegiance generates the essential drama in all of his work. The energies liberated by Dreyer's and his characters' derealizations must be continuously re-realized in practical expressive forms.

Given this state of affairs, it should not be surprising that the most interesting figures in Dreyer's films are themselves caught in a stylistic tug of war in which desubstantiating energies of imaginative derealization are pitted against resubstantiating physical realizations of those energies in particular bodies, spaces, and times. The result is that the most important characters in the late films have an irreducible ontological indeterminateness about them. They shimmer uncertainly between being spirits and being bodies: between expanding imaginatively and emotionally outward beyond all bounds, and contracting inward to inhabit and be represented by their mere physical selves.

Their indeterminacy is the product of Dreyer's divided expressive agenda. On the one hand, the sorts of consistency, predictability, and coherence that we normally associate with character seem entirely too narrow and limiting to answer to Dreyer's notions of the potential plasticity of our imaginative identities, the energetic mobility of our desires, the fluxes and refluxes of our feelings; yet on the other hand, Dreyer can't entirely eliminate from his work the physical beings we call characters either, since his works are committed to structures of practical dramatic interaction and expression.

Dreyer's films stretch the concept of character as far as they can without simply discarding realistic characters (as the works of many avant-garde filmmakers do). Although bodies can never ultimately be left behind or completely forgotten in realistic narrative films of the sort that Dreyer makes, he goes as far as he can in the direction of suggesting that his characters can move beyond the physical and social limits of embodiment. That is why at some point in his narratives Dreyer usually finds it necessary to dissolve or disperse the principal character in some way, or to desubstantiate his or her body, as if to move the figure's actual physical identity beyond limiting definitions to the same extent that his or her imaginative identity is moved beyond them. Joan (in *The Passion of Joan of Arc*) and Inger (in *Ordet*) are made to die and are apotheosized into almost purely spiritual presences at points in their films. Anne (in *Day of Wrath*) is "bewitched" and granted apparently supernatural powers. David Gray (in *Vampyr*) is proliferated into a series of fluxional points of view and dispersed into a sequence of alternative, contradictory visions of himself. Gertrud, perhaps the most complex figure of all in this regard, almost gives up her physical identity altogether, at points in her film, to be transformed into a fugitive succession of ghostlike, desubstantiated images, wishes, memories, and shadows.

The specially heightened styles of the films additionally work to dissolve a viewer's sense of the existence of fixed characters within them. Dreyer's principal characters are so enveloped within the styles of the work, so saturated with the styles, so spoken by them, and their personal styles of performance are so conflated with Dreyer's cinematic styles of performance at various moments, that the characters seem to be mere epiphenomena of the style. At various points in their narratives, Joan, Gertrud, David, Anne, and Inger each seem to be only local, almost accidental manifestations of the all consuming general styles of the works of art within which they are presented. The result is that Dreyer's characters expand beyond anything normally denoted by character in a realistic drama. Their edges become blurred; they imaginatively fuzz into their surroundings (even as, pushing in the other direction, the actual physical presence of the character as a realistic character with a real body keeps reminding a viewer of an undeconstructable physical residue that won't be absorbed into the style).

When Anne's face is turned into a play of flickering, inexplicable, and unlocalizable lights and shadows; when Gertrud's image is projected outward, away from her actual physical body, as a series of floating reflections in the mirrors in her home (or when she is turned into shadows on the wall of her lover's apartment, so that at the very moment that her body is supposedly being revealed it is actually being desubstantiated, or when she is re-represented within her film in photographs of herself); when Inger's movements are synchronized and blended with the movements of Dreyer's camera so that it becomes impossible to say whether she follows it or it follows her, or when her body itself seems almost magically to materialize at the point in space and time at which the camera pauses, as if the movements of the camera created it, and not merely represented it; when it is difficult or impossible to tell whether a particular shot is an expression of David Gray's point of view or merely a reflection of Dreyer's complex stylistic arrangement of events in a scene in *Vampyr* – in all of these situations and many others, the character and the style dissolve into each other. It is as if the character's physical identity had become as mercurial, mobile, and energetically beyond mere realistic, physical specification as his or her imaginative identity.

Even the way in which, in *Vampyr* or *Ordet*, life and death are allowed to interpenetrate, to blend or blur together in ways that most viewers would regard as violating reason, becomes part of this process of moving characters beyond the limitations of character. In becoming partially a stylistic function of the work in which they exist, Dreyer turns the central figures in his films at least in part into *imaginative* presences that are moved slightly beyond what we would regard as unavoidable biological and physical limitations.[15]

15 All of the preceding should suggest why, although the concept of character is indispensable, and the word "character" is almost unavoidable as a shorthand form of reference, I prefer whenever possible to use the word "figure" to describe Dreyer's characters. With its rhetorical, choreographic, and visual connotations, figure more accurately suggests

To the extent that our definitions would limit them, Dreyer works to prevent us from bringing his figures into focus. He works to keep them from being repressively understood – not only by others in their film, but by viewers of it. The deliberate ambiguities of his films involving whether the powers of specific characters originate from supernatural or natural causes are only the most obvious way he suggests that his figures exist somewhere beyond realistic appreciations, yet without having entirely left realism behind. They hover uncertainly between two realms: one in which to imagine something is the same as doing it, and another in which meanings and relationships are enacted practically, in the repressive structures of actual space and time. Their physical bodies (which they can never quite leave behind, without dying out of them) anchor them in the practical realm of human interactions, while their spirits and Dreyer's stylistic transformations, distortions, and intensifications work to make them fluid and fluxional. Shimmering halfway between being mere bodies and

the extent to which Dreyer's characters are not limited by most of the realistic determinants of character. More like a figure of speech, they exist as a temporal process. More like dancers or skaters, they are forms of energy in motion. More like the arc of a curving, irregular line, they free themselves to be deformed by the continuously shifting trajectory of desire. To call an entity in a Dreyer film a "character" is invariably to posit a degree of fixity, coherence, and stability from which Dreyer's principal figures continuously liberate themselves – to their joy and their doom. They are figures of imagination and desire in continuous movement and revisionary redefinition.

pure spirits, they stay just beyond our ability to grasp them – just as far beyond the framework of natural explanations as they are beyond the framework of supernatural explanations. They stay representationally slippery.

As I've already observed, these characters are situated on the margins of the forms of social discourse within their societies: half inside, yet half outside them. The effect of Dreyer's ambiguity about the causes of a characters' powers is to situate these characters in an analogously marginal expressive position *with respect to the audience watching them:* half within and half somewhere beyond realistic understanding. In shimmering between the natural and supernatural, *Day of Wrath*'s Herlofs Marte and Anne, *Vampyr*'s David Gray, and *Ordet*'s Inger stay just beyond our abilities to explain them. For the balance to be tipped in either direction, for a figure to be defined merely as a witch or as a victim of others' fantasies, for example, would be for the figure to give up precisely the representational marginality that Dreyer works so hard to establish.[16]

Yet, as the dialectical tension itself suggests, the ontological vagueness or freedom from predetermination

16 In this respect, as in so many others, Dreyer's work has a deep resemblance to that of Henry James, another artist who frequently suspended his readers uncertainly between supernatural and natural understandings of events. At the heart of both James's and Dreyer's project is the attempt to free the imagination from repressive or limiting realistic understandings in more ways than this one.

that Dreyer's figures participate in or aspire after is a precarious predicament. Energies of disembodiment are pitted against the tangible reality of the characters' bodies. Visual dispersions and imaginative derealizations are counterpoised against focusing and congealing tendencies operating at the same time, in the same works, simply because they are staged as apparently realistic dramas, acted by apparently realistic "characters." Characters' attempts to remain beyond reductive categories of understanding are pitted against the efforts of other characters in their own films to repressively understand them.

As this suggests, a freedom from definition as radical as that which Dreyer's central characters posses ultimately becomes a problem that they must cope with. Since they hold within themselves, in suspension as it were, energies that are too disorganized, intense, or mobile to be pinned down to a character, and yet are at the same time forced to interact within the constraints of realistic dramatic forms, Dreyer's fluxional figures of imagination and desire inevitably get themselves into social trouble with those around them as well as into representational trouble with audiences watching them. They make themselves illegible or incomprehensible not only to other characters in their films, but to the audiences watching them in movie theaters. Just as the other characters in their films attempt to pin down Anne or Gertrud to dependable identities, stable purposes, and responsible social roles, viewers in the movie theater (and most film critics also, it seems) try to pin them

down within one or another repressive, "realistic" understanding: Is Anne "really" a witch? Does she "really" have supernatural powers? What does Gertrud
"really" want?

In this sense, the energy, eccentricity, and stimula-
tions of the acts of revisionary self-figuration of Dreyer's
figures make all acts of realistic self-representation
problematic. His figures are imaginative extremists who
won't be confined within or expressed by realistic structures of narrative and characterization. His figures figure energies that have no expression in the realms of
ideology, theology, or normative social interaction. They
are figures whose flexible, fluxional figurations are not
reducible to fixed categories of understanding, yet who
must somehow express themselves within the social
structures of their societies and the dramatic forms of
their films.

The extremity of their predicament can be indicated by
the fact that even the mere act of "naming" is dangerous
to their ontological health. The plot of *The Passion of Joan
of Arc* is little more than the attempt to "name" Joan as a
heretic, and her answering efforts to avoid being so
named. The plot of *Day of Wrath* turns on the "naming"
of two characters as witches, and their attempts to elude
such naming. Even with characters as apparently gentle
and well-meaning as those in *Gertrud*, "naming" is de-
ployed as a threat to the title figure. By the dozenth time
Gertrud's name has been repeated by one of the men in
her life, it is hard not to feel about the utterance the way

she apparently does: that it is an act of control and normalization that she must resist with every beat of her heart. The struggle of the self in Dreyer's work is to break free of everything that would limit, predict, stabilize, or categorize it, in this case, to resist even the confining tone with which one's name is spoken.

Insofar as they turn out of the forms of discourse around them, it is not surprising that Dreyer's figures seem almost more easily defined in terms of what they are *not* than by what they *are*. They are inevitably doomed to be virtual presences, figures with what Emerson might have called "referred existences" within their own narratives. The enormous expenditure of energy they devote to holding themselves somewhere on the margins of the reigning forms of discourse makes their existence at times seem merely negative. Joan at times seems to be merely everything that *won't* be admitted as testimony at her trial. Gertrud at moments seems to be only what *can't* be lived with the men who surround her. Not out of any mere spirit of negativism, but because they represent such radical critiques of their societies, is why Dreyer's heroines seem better defined as running away from something than as running toward anything. They exist as principles of movement away from, as negations of the present, in search of the possible, the future.

That is why one can't answer the question of what Gertrud or Anne ultimately "wants." (It is a question posed by hostile critics as well as by unsympathetic characters in their films, a question that is meant to disarm and belittle them.) The only answer one might give is to say that they want everything, yet nothing in particular. They are want itself. For their desire to have a destination would be for them essentially to limit themselves imaginatively, to define themselves, in ways they decline to. Or perhaps another way of explaining the representational slipperiness of Dreyer's heroines is to say that they were created not to "want" anything in particular, but to perform the activity of "wanting." They exist in order to affirm not a goal but a process: a process that can never be completed.

Dreyer's heroines function within their films almost as if they were simply a localization of the films' general cinematic styles: They work to substitute fluid imaginative possibilities in place of static social understandings. They offer possibilities of emotional movement in place of worldly fixities. They substitute open-ended speculations in place of worldly definitions. They derealize limiting realities. They indicate imaginative openings out of social or institutional dead ends. Yet, to make the point one more time, it is crucial to emphasize that they, like their creator, perform their acts of imaginative opening and loosening and movement without ultimately losing touch with the limiting realities they are reacting to. Like Dreyer himself, Dreyer's most exciting characters locate themselves precisely on the imaginative margin of repressive social and bureaucratic systems, gesturing beyond them, but also daringly attempting to speak through them. That marginal position is one of the most important things about them.

It is fascinating to realize that, as a filmmaker creating these heroines, Dreyer uncannily (and probably unconsciously) enacts the same process of establishing connections between transcendental imaginative values and practical expressive opportunities that his heroines do within the films. In creating each of his heroines, Dreyer attempts to "embody" disembodied imaginative values. He personalizes states of abstraction. Just as his heroines do *within* their films, their creator attempts to "realize" an unmoored state of imagination in terms of the creation of a "realistic" figure and the making of a "realistic" film.

It is revealing that the particular form of Dreyer's "realization" of the imaginative impulses shifts from film to film. In *The Passion of Joan of Arc*, Dreyer imagines a spiritual and religious figure at the center of the film. In *Day of Wrath*, he imagines a playfully erotic and mysteriously supernatural one. In *Ordet*, he imagines a practical wife and mother. In *Gertrud*, he imagines a grave, ascetic intellectual. The fact that the form of the embodiment continuously shifts from work to work should help us to understand the unimportance of the particular form of the realization at the same time that it helps us to appreciate the crucial importance of the act of realizing imaginative impulses in general.

As if to make this point himself, even within individual

films, Dreyer frequently shifts the particular embodiment of a character's imaginative energies from one practical manifestation to another. For example, in *Gertrud,* Gertrud's eroticism early in her movie turns into asceticism later on. Her stimulating sexuality in some of the early flashback scenes is transformed into a hushed nostalgia in the final scene. In *Ordet,* Inger's down-to-earth care of and practical love for her family before her death turn into a state of beatitude after it. In *The Passion of Joan of Arc,* Joan's religious exaltation gives way to emotional anguish.

Those repeated, fluxional acts of imaginative displacement and worldly replacement are the central events in Dreyer's work. In this sense, *Day of Wrath* is less about witchcraft or eroticism, *The Passion of Joan of Arc* less about religious ecstasy and vision, and *Gertrud* less about an abstract conception of love than all three films are about the substitutional process itself, the process of substituting one figure for another as a temporary and provisional embodiment of abstract imaginative energies – a substitutional process engaged in equally by their central characters and their creator. The narrative pretext for the act of substitution changes from film to film. The specific form of the imaginative displacement is itself displaced from *The Passion of Joan of Arc* to *Gertrud.*

These shifting acts of substitution are Dreyer's answer to the question all of his work poses: How can we speak our fluxional and impulsive dreams of freedom in forms that are spatially and temporally coherent and socially engaged and responsible? The effort is as challenging for a filmmaker speaking such things in cinematic form as it is for an individual speaking them in the forms of life.

Though there are important connections between Dreyer's work and various late Romantic forms of expression in nineteenth- and twentieth-century art, I would note that the dramatic constraints he and his major characters embrace are ones from which imagist poetry, post-Romantic musical compositions, and expressionist paintings are free. His films attempt to express the sort of energies that one associates with a Romantic lyric poem. Yet, in some respects, they embrace a more difficult expressive task than Shelley or Keats did because the films (and the principal characters in them) attempt to express lyrical intensities of feeling and mercurial movements of imagination in the time-bound, spatially constrained forms of practical dramatic structures. They attempt to speak the impulses of Romantic poetry in the prose of life.

That is what it means to say that Dreyer's films are inquiries equally into the limits of their central characters' abilities to represent themselves in their narrative worlds, and into the limits of realistic representation in film itself. As a filmmaker, Dreyer is attempting the same thing as the heroines in his films: to express dreams of ideal freedom and expression in the inevitably repressive forms of social, spatial, and temporal realism.

He is a transcendental filmmaker committed to non-transcendental forms of expression. The vexed, unresolved struggle of Dreyer's central characters against the repressive forms of "realistic" social interaction and relationship is paralleled by the struggle of the filmmaker himself against the repressions of narrative and dramatic realism. His films pit realism against itself.

The central problem Dreyer confronts is the attempt to move realistic depiction beyond realism: How, in short, does one speak the language of desire in the forms of realistic drama? How does one speak the socially unspeakable in a narrative world that renders events in an ineluctably social form? That is the expressive challenge Dreyer embraced. In the largest sense, that is why Dreyer's principal characters risk misunderstanding not only by the characters around them in their narratives, but also by an audience in a theatre. As an expressive experimenter working with forms that resist his visions, Dreyer is as much on the verge of illegibility and incoherence as a filmmaker as they are as characters. He wrestles with the repressiveness of the discursive codes within which he must express himself as fiercely as his characters do. The dream of freedom his characters dream as individuals is embraced by the artist himself in his own expressions. His films stand in the same vexed and troubled relationship to the coercions of narrative as his characters do to the coercions of their societies.

Dreyer's films raise fundamental questions about self-representation in both life and art. What is the destiny of the transcendental impulse? Where does it lead us? How can we express it or "use" it – in life or in art – without leaving behind our commitment to "realistic" relationships and interactions with other characters? The questions pertain to both film and life. Dreyer's style is the record of that expressive struggle.

Figures of imagination and desire

I dwell in possibility . . .

Emily Dickinson

THREE

Day of Wrath
Love on the run

MARTIN: Why are you running?
ANNE (teasing): Don't you know?
MARTIN: No.
ANNE: Because I am longing. . . .

from *Day of Wrath*[1]

No amount of critical reverence about Dreyer's "artistry" can hide the fact that his relationship to his material is entirely different from that of the Flaubertian or Joycean model of the artist as an ironic and detached God of creation, coolly poised above or beyond his work, "paring his fingernails." There is a wild passionateness and idiosyncratic strangeness to Dreyer's greatest work (and to many of his principal characters) that suggests many of his films were less "well-made" works of art than personal nightmares from which Dreyer could never quite awake. Over and over again in the dream, with a nearly obsessional repetitiousness, Dreyer imagines a lone, almost

1 Since the dialogue passages are severely abridged in the subtitled English prints of the films, for completeness of reference, all direct quotations will be taken from translations of the published screenplays, where they are available. See Carl Theodor Dreyer, *Four Screenplays* (Bloomington: Indiana University Press, 1970).

powerless woman pitted against, or trying to make her way within, a hostile (and usually male-dominated) society.[2]

What makes Dreyer's vision most frightening and dreamlike is not the mere power-saturation of his universe, or the fiercely predatory quality of the society within which he imagines his heroines situated, but how *deeply* the forces he imagines to beset us work upon and within us. It is not only the words and actions of Dreyer's heroines that are up for male manipulation and control, but their very definitions of themselves. Many

2 A recent revisionary biography by Maurice Drouzy, *Carl Th. Dreyer né Nilsson* (Paris: Edition Cerf, 1982), suggests that many of the fantasies of victimization in Dreyer's narratives may ultimately be traceable to early events in his life, stemming from his feelings of powerlessness or of not being loved after being shuffled from one foster home to another in the first two years of his life, prior to his ultimate abandonment by his mother and his mistreatment by the family who finally adopted him. But whatever their biographical origins, the important point is that Dreyer's imagination of the predicament of the individual making free and independent meanings in a power-saturated universe speaks movingly to viewers here and now, even if they know nothing about the psychological traumas that may have stimulated it.

Another reason not to place overmuch emphasis on the biographical facts of Dreyer's life is simply that so much of the greatest art in the Western tradition from that of Dante to Milton to Beethoven is apparently traceable to a similar inner wounding or emotional deformation experienced by the artist, a wounding that results in the artist feeling a fundamental misfit or antagonism between his imagination and the expressive forms of the world. Yet comparable woundings in other personalities and other situations result not in works of art, but in various forms of derangement, destructiveness, or wastefulness. That is why what particular artists make of such conditions of alienation is always of more interest than the mere events that may have helped to generate them.

works of art deal with the external compromises forced upon an individual by alien systems of power and expression, but Dreyer's films – from *The Passion of Joan of Arc* to *Gertrud* – focus equally on the *internal* compromises and adjustments we are forced to make.

For Dreyer, our private feelings and understandings of ourselves are regulated by society as much as our public words and actions are. In short, Dreyer is at least as interested in understanding the ways we represent ourselves to ourselves, as he is in understanding the ways we represent ourselves to each other.[3] In this sense, his films are as much psychodramas of inner struggles of imaginative control, as they are studies of the limitations of practical social organizations of expression.

Dreyer gives us a world in which even one's deepest imaginative identity, the story one tells oneself about oneself, is not safe from the predations and manipulations of others. His central characters are continuously in danger of being remade in someone else's image, changed more insidiously and more profoundly than external force or coercion could change them. They are in danger of being altered by the application of others' language and categories, transformed in such deep ways that they are not even aware of it. That is why in Dreyer's artistic universe, even for one to hold on to a free or independent identity requires an unending application

3 In terms of intellectual traditions, if Freud is the patron saint of the one sort of exploration, Marx is the father of the other.

of effort, a continuous labor of self-definition and self-assertion.

The central problem that Dreyer's cinema explores is the vexed relation between the individual imagination and the practical forms of social and artistic expression available to it. The question his major films ask, without quite being able to answer, is: To what extent are we able to translate our finest, freest impulses and feelings into worldly forms of expression? The most frequent way in which Dreyer dramatizes this problem in his major films is in terms of the expressive predicament of a single female character surrounded by a predominantly masculine group of others, a group hostile or indifferent to her expressive efforts. In each of the late films, this central figure embodies a condition of visionary or emotional energy of which it is then the goal of both the character and the artistic narrative to explore the possible expression.

As my conflation of the character's and the text's expressive efforts is intended to suggest, Dreyer's films are not fundamentally dramas of character in the conventional Hollywood sense. In *Day of Wrath*, specifically, the two most important female characters, Anne Pedersdotter and Herlofs Marte, are only, as it were, "embodiments" of problems of expression figured much more broadly by the film's style itself. Their personal expressive dramas as characters are only, in effect, local manifestations of general stylistic dramas enacted within their films. As characters, they are only provisional and

112

partial representations of larger problems of artistic representation resulting from the gap Dreyer posits to exist between imaginative energies and practical expressions.

Dreyer's emphatic stylizations of experience in his work are his vehicle for directing a viewer's eye to these general issues of expression. Just as Jane Austen's or Henry James's distinctive authorial voices, by enveloping their characters in pervasively mediating tones and rhythms, which include the characters' personal voices but extend beyond them, expand our view beyond their personal expressive situations, so Dreyer's cinematic styles of presentation represent standards of awareness and expression by means of which we are sensitized to general expressive issues in his films, issues that extend beyond the specific expressive situations of the individual characters.

Furthermore, the style of the work, when it is brought forward to the consciousness of the viewer so vigorously (all the more saliently through the minimalizations of dialogue and action and the retardations of physical eventfulness that one encounters in Dreyer's work) serves to establish standards of awareness and sensitivity in terms of which even the principal characters are then judged.[4]

---

4 *Ordet*, the film to be considered in the next chapter, is Dreyer's most complex illustration of this point. The consciousness of each and every character within it is implicitly compared with and measured in terms of the purely cinematic consciousness that Dreyer's camera work establishes in the course of the film.

To describe more specifically how Dreyer's style educates a viewer to special capacities of seeing and feeling in the course of *Day of Wrath*, and at the same time defines general expressive issues that both the film and its characters must confront, I want to briefly consider the film's first three scenes. The action is set in an unspecified northern European country during a time of witch-hunting hysteria in the early seventeenth century, and the scenes present a fairly straightforward exposition of the basic situation: In the first scene, we see a hand signing a writ for the apprehension of a suspected witch. In the second, we see the witch herself (an old woman named Herlofs Marte) at home giving another character medicine brewed from "herbs from under the gallows," furtively looking out a window when she hears noises, and then, as witch-hunters approach her farmhouse to arrest her, escaping out a back entrance. In the third, we see a church prelate named Absalon Pedersson at home in the vicarage with his aged mother and his young wife Anne, preparing for the visit of Martin, his son from his previous marriage, who will be meeting Anne for the first time.

In the way of plot, there's really not very much more than that to those scenes. Dreyer's films are never very heavy on action and event. But it is *how* his scenes are presented that forces a viewer to look at things in a special way. Even in these brief, introductory scenes in the first few minutes of *Day of Wrath*, the basic outlines of Dreyer's stylistic project – as I described it in the first two chapters – are visible.

The first thing to notice is Dreyer's labors of simplification and reduction in the *mise-en-scène*. In the signing ceremony all that can be seen is the close-up of the top of a table, a hand, a quill pen, a bottle of ink, and the document being signed. In the scene in Herlofs Marte's house, Dreyer constructs a set almost Spartan in its bareness, deliberately reducing the number of props and objects visible in the foreground and background, and generally lighting the set to further reduce any distracting details or visual busyness that would attract our eyes away from the simply costumed figures and their movements.

The scene in Herlofs Marte's house illustrates Dreyer's process of reducing and simplifying not only the sets, but the actions and events themselves by keeping the movements of the characters as simple and direct as possible, and also keeping the repositionings of the camera and the number of intercut shots to a minimum. (It would be impossible to have fewer repositionings of the camera, or fewer shots, than Dreyer does in the scene at Herlofs Marte's. The entire sequence is done in one uninterrupted shot.)

Further, it is entirely typical of Dreyer's work that social or spoken interactions between characters are almost completely suppressed in both scenes. In the ceremony involving the signing of the document for the

Imaginative movements speaking in place of social interactions –
The signing of the arrest warrant and Herlofs Marte at home,
listening to the mob growing closer and then fleeing through the
barn. Her eyes and movements do all the speaking.

116

apprehension of Herlofs Marte, in presenting nothing more than close-ups of the top of a table, a hand, a quill pen, a bottle of ink, and the document being signed (and not, for example, showing a group of magistrates talking, deliberating, or interacting), Dreyer deliberately prevents a viewer from reading the scene as a practical, social event. (As I have already mentioned, as we watch this scene, we don't see the face of the man doing the signing, and don't really even know who he is.)

Even more emphatically, in the scene at Herlofs Marte's home, Dreyer takes a situation that seems inherently social in its content – the meeting of two women at the home of one of them – and subtly redirects our attention within it. As I mentioned, Herlofs Marte is prescribing medicine for a neighbor, but it is essential to Dreyer's deflection of a social reading of the scene that the neighbor (who is not seen again in the film) is never photographed in close-up or from a full frontal position, and that her verbal and social interactions with the witch are kept to an absolute minimum. Photographed only in long shot, with her body at an angle to the camera for much of the scene, and given only a minimal number of lines in the script, the neighbor is kept almost anonymous. Her very limited interaction with Herlofs Marte is clearly subordinated to imaginative and emotional issues involving not social matters, but matters of witchcraft and the imaginative power of a witch in this world.

The important point is that both scenes encourage the viewer to read into them imaginative meanings and emo-

117

tional values in place of absent social values and verbal interactions. This act of imaginative substitution is the fundamental event in Dreyer's work. In its suppression of practical, social interactions between characters, the document-signing scene becomes, as nearly as a narrative film can render such a thing, a presentation of depersonalized historical understandings and abstract theological beliefs. We are seeing not the practical interaction of particular men, but the imaginative enactment of an abstract moral drama.

The shots of the signing itself are preceded and followed by shots of the vertical scrolling of an illuminated text of the *Dies Irae* (with the shadow of a cross superimposed upon it), accompanied on the sound track with the music of the *Dies Irae.* The slow scrolling of the ominously illustrated text and the romantic orchestration that underscores it impart a powerful emotional and imaginative resonance that is different from anything that could be representable in social terms. The imaginative and emotional energies associated with these images and sounds, energies in excess of or detached from social forms of representation, are the true subjects of the scene more than any practical set of events that could be defined interpersonally or presented socially in terms of witchcraft trials or the interaction of church prelates.

The scene at the witch's house moves us still further away from a social reading of events and toward an emotional and imaginative appreciation of what we see by simplifying the outward actions and retarding their pace. Dreyer presents Herlofs Marte doing and saying very little. As the sound of the voices of the approaching mob rises on the sound track, the witch moves slowly across the room, and toward the window to peek out of it to see if the mob is coming for her. The most prominent "events" that take place are merely Herlofs Marte's shuffling, agitated, sideways walk, and the terrified expression we see in her key-lighted eyes as she stands next to the window. For the imaginative viewer, Dreyer makes those silent imaginative "events" count as much as social and verbal events count in another kind of film.

The radical simplification of *mise-en-scène,* the retardation of the pace of both the characters' movements and the movements of the camera, and the stillness and quietness of the central figure shift the drama inward. With his or her perceptions redirected from social or practical realms to imaginative ones, the viewer becomes an imaginative appreciator of Herlofs Marte's own imaginative appreciations.

Dreyer's composition of the scene in Herlof Marte's house in one stunningly extended shot is not at all unimportant to its effect.[5] The moving camera is one of

5 The shot begins with a view from behind a figure whom we will only subsequently discover is Herlofs Marte. The camera then pans and tracks slowly to the right around the shadowy room, first revealing the figure of the neighbor and then slowly searching the space, as it follows Herlofs Marte's movements at a distance, first moving with her toward the hearth on the back of the left side of the room, then panning rightward into the center of the room, and then to a window on the right.

Dreyer's most powerful expressive instruments. With its sustained panning and tracking movements, it gives us a text the very opposite of the so-called invisibly edited and photographed texts of Hollywood. Precisely because it does not conceal its mediating presence or pretend to be merely functional in its presentation of scenes, Dreyer's photography creates a text that feels profoundly mediated. The camera represents a consciousness not only functioning independently of the personal consciousnesses of the characters within Dreyer's text, but independently of practical forms of social expression. Consciousness (the camera's cinematic consciousness, as well as the consciousness of the characters it photographs) independent of practical forms of expression becomes a felt presence in the drama.[6]

The effect the camera nourishes in this scene is related to a larger phenomenon in Dreyer's work: the "subjectivization" of the cinematic experience. Even when an

6 Another important effect of the slowly panning or tracking camera is one that I mentioned in my first chapter: Dreyer's communication of the fact that meaning is made within his work in the terms of particular spatial and temporal acts. In declining to "cut" events into discrete pieces in the normal Hollywood way and in preventing the elision of intermediate points in his work, Dreyer creates a heightened spatial and temporal awareness in the viewer. The moving camera communicates the fact that meaning is enacted, worked, performed into existence within the particularities of specific spaces and times, from which it can not be released (for both the characters and the viewer). It is not created visionarily or instantaneously out of space and time (as many other films create it).

"objective" series of events is presented, the viewer is frequently aware of receiving events as if they were filtered through a consciousness. (The most obvious examples of this phenomenon are many of the scenes of the trial in *The Passion of Joan of Arc,* the flashback scenes in *Gertrud,* the extended panning and tracking movements of the camera in *Ordet,* and almost all of *Vampyr.*)[7] The subjectivization of experience in Dreyer's work accomplishes at least two things:

First, it generally encourages a viewer to process scenes and interactions less literally and more imaginatively, less practically and more meditatively. Events are slightly derealized. Scenes and encounters are partially (but only partially) turned into the stuff of dreams, the fabric of vision. Consequently, the viewer understands them in a different way from the way he or she understands events in a merely realistic film. The effect is to make a character's state of feeling or awareness of at least equal importance to the practical events and phys-

7 I emphasize that one sees these events *as if* they were filtered through a consciousness to point out that Dreyer's "subjectivizing" is not necessarily a representation of the actual view of any particular observer. It is crucial to their effect that Dreyer's camera movements and visual perspectives are usually *not* reducible to being either optical in their origin or psychological in their meaning. If they were attributable to an actual optical or psychological point of view of a character, they would allow a viewer to maintain a degree of psychological detachment from them. They would less represent the filmmaker's energies of consciousness and less stimulate the viewer's activity of meaning making within the film.

ical interactions depicted. At least in part, events of consciousness become actors in the scene.

Second, similar to the effect of the moving camera in general, Dreyer's photographic subjectivization makes the individual observer of or participant in a scene as essential contributor to its significance. Meanings, perceptions, and relationships are "humanized," in William James's sense of the term. Absoluteness is denied. There can be no view from nowhere in Dreyer's work. There can be no pure experience apart from particular human points of view. Experience is the product of human consciousness (the mediating consciousness of the camera or the director, if not the consciousness of a character), which is the source of all value. In this way, Dreyer votes for the absolute centrality of the particular human being, with his or her particular temporal and spatial relationship to local events, as the source of all value.[8]

The stylistic project enacted in the first two scenes of *Day of Wrath* is made all the more obvious by the stylistic shift in the third scene – the scene set in the rectory with

8 For reasons that I will explain subsequently, in this chapter and the following one, this is far from true of every film. Dreyer asserts the centrality and power of the individual performer as a meaning maker in a way that many filmmakers do not. He is a "humanist" – in William James's sense of the word. (The simplifications of his sets and the minimalization of external eventfulness in his plots contribute additionally to this focus on the potential power of the individual. The figure is never lost in the costume drama or setting. The character is never ground down by the plot.)

the prelate, Absalon Pedersson, his young wife, Anne, and his old mother, Merete. Even if Dreyer hadn't explicitly linked the second and third scenes with a match cut – a visual matching of the shot of Marte's crawling out through a small opening in the attached stable on the back of her hut with a shot of Merete coming in through a doorway into the living room of the rectory – it would still be obvious that he wanted a viewer to contrast the two scenes, and specifically to contrast the principal female characters in the two scenes with each other. The similarity of the initial letters of the names of Marte and Merete, the similarity of their ages and general physical appearances, and, above all, the similarity of their narrative functions as matriarchs ruling their respective realms would encourage a viewer to make formal comparisons and contrasts between the two old women, even if the two scenes weren't stylistically contrasted.

Matched with the shot of Marte fleeing from her home, Merete is shown entering the main room of the rectory through a doorway. From that point on in the scene, it is obvious that we are in an entirely different world from the one with Marte. While the scene with Marte looped a viewer into a stimulating, mysterious, and evocative world of shadowy, secret inwardness, this brightly lighted, visually busy, and socially brisk scene positively bristles with purposeful, pointed words and actions. Merete officiously strides forward, gives Anne instructions about setting the table, confiscates a key

A contrasting world of locks, keys, words, and public interactions –
Absalon, Merete, and Anne in the rectory. Note Anne's "turnings"
even here.

from her, moves to the other side of the room, knocks on
the door of Absalon's study to tell him that Martin may
be there any minute, goes back to the other side of the
room to rebuke Anne for not keeping things locked up,
and then bickers about Anne's conduct with Absalon
when he comes into the room. While Marte's general
quietness and the deliberative slowness and obliquity of
her movements and those of the camera called our attention to an inwardness of thought and feeling that
would not be translated into dialogue or interpersonal
interaction, Merete's brusque busyness, her voluble im-
periousness, as she bustles through space, giving curt
instructions to one figure or another, communicate a
world in which social and institutional orders, arrangements, and maneuvers are everything. Needless to say,
the point of the contrast is the way this world of exter-
nalized, social, and practical organizations of behavior is
opposed to everything that Dreyer's cinematic style in
the other scene is interested in nurturing and enriching.

124

Now when a critic encounters a stylistic contrast of this sort in a film, he or she usually merely proceeds to explicate it. The narrative and stylistic events become the basis for general statements about the characters or the scenes. For example, in this instance, as I have already argued, Marte's quiet emotionality can be contrasted with Merete's officious prolixity to suggest different relations between the two characters and the forms of social discourse. Marte's marginality and furtiveness (as she is forced to flee from her pursuers) can be contrasted with Merete's smugness, comfort, and staidness (as she proudly bustles about the rectory with her keys jangling at her waist). Harassed and frightened on the margins of society, the childless, familyless woman is forced to run from her own home, while the other regally rules over her family, radiating petty bourgeois propriety and confidence. The shadows and darkness of Marte's scene can be contrasted with the bright fill lighting in Merete's scene, to make the point that the witch's hut seems imaginatively stimulating, while the rectory denies the dark mysteries of life.

The conscientious critic would perhaps then go on to comment on the fact that in the contrast between the two scenes Dreyer's own position is not neutral. The true experience of spirituality in the early scenes of the film is identified with the world of witchcraft and solitude, while the rectory and the life of the petty bourgeois family ironically seem to acknowledge only energies of worldly acquisitiveness. Dreyer's own photographic style endorses and cultivates in a viewer imaginative energies that are associated with Marte and not Merete. It is not accidental that the movements of Dreyer's camera in the second scene are conflated with the witch's movements. Her capacities of stillness, rhythmic retardation, and her ability to turn out of social interactions correspond exactly with his narrative stillnesses, rhythmic retardations, and dialogic turns out of social interaction. The imaginative energies Herlofs Marte embodies in the second scene are indistinguishable from the imaginative energies Dreyer attempts to release in all of his scenes.

A metaphoric "reading" of the two scenes might run something like that. The generation of such abstract meanings is important in any imaginative work. If there were only a few such comparisons or contrasts within a work or a scene, one would be perfectly comfortable with merely explicating them: pointing out some of the metaphoric meanings in the film and saying how they affect our understanding of it. I want to spend many of the following pages doing just that. However, Dreyer's work is so insistently, so pervasively metaphoric that simply to explicate it is not sufficient. Its metaphoricity is something that must be accounted for.

So many events, relations, positions, scenes, lighting effects, and physical details in *Day of Wrath* function metaphorically that the function of metaphoricity itself, metaphoricity as a fundamental principle of expression, needs to be considered. To put it most simply: an object, an item of dress, or a beam of sunlight in Renoir's work is frequently (though, of course, not always) just an object, an item, or a beam. In Dreyer's work, such things are almost always metaphoric, analogical, or symbolic. They are almost never merely their realistic selves.

I would argue that Dreyer's processes of metaphorization are continuations and extensions of the general "meditative shift" all of his work attempts to induce. When a viewer is encouraged to read a scene or event formally or metaphorically (for example: to read a character's physical position in a group or within the space of the frame as communicating something about his or her imaginative position, or to read the meaning of events in one scene as being not practically, but abstractly related to events in another), with such consistency, the viewer is put into a less practical relationship to what he or she sees than in the other sort of film. The viewer becomes, at least in part, an appreciator of imaginative relationships and abstract meanings. Insofar as certain objects or events are slightly, but consistently, metaphorized in scene after scene of Dreyer's work, the viewer enters into an imaginative relationship with them that is quite different from the way he or she would respond to such things in a more strictly realistic film. It is a relationship in which the viewer functions less as a passive receiver of events and more as an active maker of meanings about them.

Day of Wrath communicates almost all of its most important meanings abstractly or formally: through comparisons of patterns of light and shadow on characters' faces; through contrasts between the way various characters dress, walk, or stand; through contrasts between the blockings of various figures' movements and their mutual positions; and through comparisons of the formal qualities of spaces and sets within the film.

It is of crucial importance that we understand these specific effects, and I don't want to seem to be saying that they are unimportant. But before proceeding to explicate them, I would note that underpinning all of these local effects is the general effect of the work's metaphoricity itself. Dreyer encourages a pervasive, if subtle, shift of perspective in every scene. His formalism moves the viewer from physical to metaphysical considerations; from attention to practical objects to interpretations of abstract meanings; from following social and verbal interactions to appreciating imaginative relationships that may be virtually unrepresentable in social and verbal forms of expression. Independently of whatever the particular metaphors or stylistic comparisons in his scenes may mean, the fact of the metaphoricity itself subtly nourishes an enriched imaginative relationship between the viewer and the text.

One's attention is continuously directed beyond literal words and actions and settings to ponder imaginative meanings and relations. In the process of making comparisons and contrasts between events, characters, and formal qualities of scenes, the viewer is enticed, almost unconsciously, to change his or her relationship to the sounds and images on the screen from that of being an appetitive consumer of words and actions into that of being an imaginative appreciator of feelings and relations.

Finally, in having one's attention directed to such imaginative comparisons, one is encouraged to remove oneself to a certain crucial meditative distance from the mere events and actions of a scene. Objects, events, and characters are compared and contrasted so relentlessly in Dreyer's work that a viewer is moved to a certain distance from them as mere objects, events, or characters. The grip of reality itself is relaxed to some degree.

This is, I believe, what Dreyer was describing in his lecture at the 1955 Edinburgh Film Festival, in terms of one of the most difficult concepts in his work, when he talked about the importance of cinematic "abstraction":

And now we come to the real question, namely: Where does the possibility of an artistic renewal of film lie? I, for my part, can see only one way: *abstraction* – but, in order not to be misunderstood, I hurry to define the word "abstraction" as an expression for the perception of art which demands that an artist shall abstract from reality in order to reinforce its spiritual content, whether this is of psychological or purely aesthetic nature. Or said even more succinctly: Art shall represent the *inner* and not the *outer* life. Therefore we must get away from naturalism and find alternatives in order to introduce abstraction into our pictures. The ability to abstract is the prerequisite. Abstraction gives the director a possibility to reach outside the fence behind which naturalism has enclosed the film. . . . The ambitious director must seek a higher reality than the one he obtains just by putting the camera up and copying reality. His pictures have to be not only a visual but also a spiritual experience. What is important is that the director share his own artistic and spiritual experiences with the audience, and abstraction gives him this possibility by allowing the director to replace objective reality with his own subjective perceptions.[9]

The abstraction of a character's, scene's, or object's formal relations with other scenes induces what might be called an answering state of abstraction in the viewer of the film.[10] The viewer no longer functions simply to process realistic facts or details, to hurry to keep up with external events and actions. He or she is placed at a certain meditative distance from the practical meaning or utilitarian function of events. In that distance is the birth of a potentially more imaginative and emotionally fertile relationship with it.

The viewer is temporarily freed from the narrative and dramatic coercions of the situations themselves. Reality that is so relentlessly metaphorized is partially de-realized. One is encouraged to move to a certain meditative distance from practical events – a distance at

9 Carl Dreyer, "Imagination and Color" (a lecture delivered at the Edinburgh Film Festival on August 29, 1955), reprinted in Donald Skoller (ed.), *Dreyer in Double Reflection*, 178–179, 184.

10 Artists as different from one another as Henry James, Wallace Stevens, and Emily Dickinson have relied on inducing similar states of "abstraction" in their work. They have employed intellectually abstracting effects to move the reader into a less practical and more imaginative relationship to their texts.

which imaginative values are equally present and salient with practical ones; a distance at which imaginative movements and emotional riches fill in for worldly immobilities and physical impoverishments.

The abstracting devices in Dreyer's films attempt to move a viewer beyond the repressive ways of knowing that are dramatized *in* the films. They offer the viewer of the film an escape from more limited, "realistic" ways of understanding. Such stylistic heightenings encourage him or her to move beyond ideological or sociological understandings of the characters and their experience, in order to appreciate energies of imagination and desire not subservient to or defined by realistic systems of understanding.

Yet it is crucial that one is only moderately (in Dreyer's word) "abstracted" from, and not entirely cut off from those other ways of knowing. Dreyer's style is designed to situate the imaginative viewer of the film (and the imaginative character within it) at a certain meditative distance from practical events and social interactions, while still remaining responsive to them. The state of suspension Dreyer cultivates in his audience and represents in his films locates a spectator somewhere between a realistic embeddedness in events and an imaginative detachment from them.

To put it another way, it is important that the objects and events in Dreyer's narratives are never completely metaphorical in their meaning. They also function practically, realistically, and socially. However formalistically abstracted, metaphorically transformed, or stylistically enriched, the events in his films are never merely formal, metaphorical, or stylistic. Dreyer's stylizations never result in purely stylistic events – as formalists like Bordwell fashionably assert. In Dreyer's derealizations, the claims of reality abate somewhat, but are never entirely erased.[11] In his abstractions, the pressure of events eases, but is not completely lifted.

Dreyer's films nurture that complex state of in-betweenness in both their characters and their viewers. The viewer moves into exactly the half-involved, half-detached state that Dreyer's most important characters occupy in their expressive marginality within their societies. The viewer achieves a degree (but only a degree) of meditative distance from the realistic events and practical expressions on the screen that parallels the moderate alienation, the slight meditative distance from their own experiences, that Dreyer's most interesting characters themselves achieve. One is suspended ambiguously between a state of imaginative distance from the prac-

---

11 Another way to frame this would be to say that, if Dreyer's films have psychodramatic aspects (and deep, personal psychological roots), they never are allowed to become actual psychodramas. Dreyer translates his private fears and fantasies into the forms of realistic narrative interaction and expression.

Similarly, as we shall see in *Gertrud,* Dreyer's dream scenes are never merely dreamed. Vision is never merely visionary. Furthermore, although the quasi-dream sequences represent critiques of social expression, Dreyer embeds them in a realistic narrative and asks that the characters in them express themselves in that narrative as well.

tical, social experience presented in the film, and a state of emotional involvement in that experience. One is suspended between derealizations and realizations of imaginative energies.

Within Dreyer's *oeuvre* there is at least one figure in each of the major films who is the filmmaker's attempt at an actual physical "embodiment" of the issues raised more abstractly by the style. A figure is asked to live the style, to realize it by enacting it verbally and socially.[12] In *Gertrud* and *The Passion of Joan of Arc*, it is the title characters. In *Vampyr* it is the figure of David Gray. *Ordet* and *Day of Wrath* each have two figures, since in each of them the first figure dies partway through the narrative and is replaced by the second. *Ordet* has Inger and, subsequently, her daughter (and double), Maren. *Day of Wrath* has the witch, Herlofs Marte, and her double, Anne Pedersdotter, the rector's wife.

The apparent subject of *Day of Wrath* is witchcraft and witch-hunting, but it goes without saying that Dreyer is not most interested in the historical or costume drama aspects of the story. Rather he is deploying a brilliantly apt dramatic metaphor for the suppression and control of socially threatening or psychologically eccentric aspects of our nature. What vindicates Dreyer's

12 This should in itself suggest how far from being purely stylistic are the stylistic explorations in Dreyer's films—the arguments of formalist critics notwithstanding. Dreyer is fundamentally an explorer of the ways that the imagination may be expressed *in* the world, *in* the realistic forms it begins by turning away from, even as he worries about whether it can be.

choice of witches and witch-hunts as his metaphor is his use of it to explore the relation of free impulses to the forces of repression in society. What ultimately threatens the witch-hunting churchmen in the film is not some supernatural power that can be labeled "witchcraft," "evil," or "heresy," but the imaginative and expressive qualities of both Herlofs Marte and Anne. Their energetic sexuality, their feminine mystery, and their passionateness are what the church elders would extirpate.

The fundamental issue is not whether Anne and Herlofs Marte are witches. Their supernaturalism is as invisible to the church elders as it is to the film's viewers. What *is* visible in both Herlofs Marte and Anne is their passion, their sexual expressiveness, their unrepressed imaginativeness. Anne and Marte figure energies of consciousness that are disruptive of all systematic forms of understanding. They are what violates all rules, escapes from all systems of control, and necessarily defies expressive and institutional normalization.

Day of Wrath is an inquiry into the destiny of free impulses in worlds that frustrate and deny freedom, and the drama of the film is generated by pitting Anne's and Marte's energies against a vast structure of normalizing controls and repressive understandings.[13] However

13 The most obvious of those limiting understandings is simply the act of classifying Anne or Marte as a "witch." The churchmen stand as a warning to any critic who is tempted to join the ongoing debate about whether Anne or Marte is "really" a witch or not. See David Bordwell, *The Films of Carl-Theodor Dreyer* (Berkeley: University of California Press, 1981), 124–129, for an example.

weak Anne and Marte may appear to be, Dreyer votes on the side of their personal power and against the impersonal institutional organizations of knowledge, however impressive they may seem.

The principal representatives of the institutional control of discourse in the film are Absalon Pedersson (in the public world) and his mother, Merete (in the home and family). Absalon, the more important of the two figures, stands at the head of three interrelated systems of power and control that Dreyer clearly wants a viewer to compare: as the rector of the church and a father confessor, he presides over the moral and ethical realm; in his capacity as a magistrate for the punishment of witches, he administers the judicial and legislative activities of the town; and in his situation as a father, husband, and head of a family consisting of himself, his wife, his mother, and his son, all of whom live together at the rectory, he presides over the personal, sexual, and generational relationships of his family.

In *Day of Wrath*, the interrelated structures of knowledge defined by the church, the state, the family, and capitalism in general articulate a complex matrix of codes that regulates both the characters' external expressive behavior and their private feelings and desires. As dramatized by Dreyer, church, state, and the customs of bourgeois family life work together to normalize feelings and beliefs, and ultimately to attempt to suppress or expunge anything that resists their forms of articulation, sorting, and control.

The interwoven capitalistic, religious, and emotional codifications of experience are summarized in terms of three visual metaphors covering three interrelated realms of governance that link capitalism, religion, and bourgeois morality – the regulation and control of bodies, possessions, and emotional energies:

Those associated with the church in *Day of Wrath* are as corseted and controlled physically as they are intellectually and morally. Their bodies are buttoned up in severe, all-enclosing costumes. The covering of the body represents a denaturing process in which individual flesh and blood are hidden from view and replaced by standard items of clothing that signify the individual's impersonal function, rank, and relationship.

Possessions are hoarded and hidden in locked cupboards, closets, and boxes. The bourgeois fetish about accumulation and hoarding of money and possessions behind locks, keys, and doors in the film represents the economic regulation of the conduct of life.

Finally, deviant impulses and feelings are suppressed or regulated by means of religious tests of loyalty and conformity, which attempt to extend the outward control inward to our emotions, intellects, morality, and language.

Within the metaphors of the film, the reigning episteme is a realm of predominantly male intrusiveness and knowingness functioning in the service of violating feminine mysteries and secrecies. Private spaces (specifically, private female spaces) are publicly explored and displayed (as epitomized in the scenes of torture and burning at the stake). Feminine silences are coerced into ritualized forms of masculine speech (in the scenes of ritualized, formulaic confessions). The men preside over a realm of psychic and social hygiene, orderliness, and reasonableness, in which precise codes and laws attempt to govern and normalize all eccentric personal expression.[14]

Given this state of affairs, Anne and Marte represent everything that must be repressed from consciousness: realms of mystery, seductive femininity, and unsuppressed feeling – eccentric expressions of imagination and desire in all of their intensity, unpredictability, and semiotic slipperiness. They represent the opening up of

14 Although *Day of Wrath* (which premiered in October of 1943) is sometimes said to be a thinly veiled allegory about the Nazi occupation of Denmark (with the witch-hunting churchmen representing the fascists), Dreyer correctly resisted this reading of his film during his lifetime for obvious reasons. It narrows a profound exploration of the limits of social and ethical understandings of life into a tendentious political allegory. It makes a work that speaks to the situation of all viewers seem to address only a particular historical aberration. It removes the work from our own lives.

One might note in passing that one of the additional reasons that one has reservations about this interpretation is the profound sympathy with which Absalon, the senior prelate, is depicted. There are no villains in Dreyer's final films, and Absalon is portrayed as an individual deeply conscious of, and disturbed by, the pain he inflicts on others, and profoundly unsure of his own adequacy to judge them. Dreyer's hell is not as far off from our lives as Nazism. It is here and now and forever, and we too, in all of our anguish and doubt, are potentially part of it, contributing to it, victimized by it.

spirits and emotions, the opening of all of the dark compartments and secret depths that the world of the church, state, and family tries so hard to lock up (in the metaphor of the locks and keys that the film associates with Absalon's mother, Merete), to suppress, to systematize, to expunge, or failing that, to burn out of life (in the metaphor of burning at the stake associated with the church). They represent what breaks free from and threatens public controls and institutional arrangements, if only momentarily: the presence of mystery and danger and darkness (whether sexual or spiritual) that resists all normalizing systems of cultural organization. They represent the possibility of an escape from the intrusive, tendentious, probing knowingness of the churchmen of the film.

While Absalon and the other church elders mechanically go through the motions of eliminating the witches and devils in their midst, Marte and subsequently Anne represent free impulses, inviting physicality, highly charged eroticism, and seductive, feminine mysteriousness. They embody the life both of the free spirit and of the uncensored, unrepressed senses.[15]

Since the subject of *Day of Wrath* is expressive free-

15 The expressions of the senses and the spirit are never separated or opposed in Dreyer's work as they are in traditional Christianity. As *Ordet* will demonstrate most emphatically, this is in fact Dreyer's criticism of Christianity: it not only separates our souls from our bodies, but it pits one against the other in a way that his work completely refuses to do. It is too often forgotten that he is one of the great poets of carnal, erotic love, as well as of spiritual, religious love.

dom, it is significant that Anne's and Martin's first act together near the beginning of the film is to play a game. Martin briefly hides from his father to surprise him when he comes into the house, and Anne goes along with the ruse by telling Absalon that Martin isn't home. Nor is it accidental that Anne is repeatedly associated with free bodily and emotional expressions like running through the grass or laughing out loud. Nor that she is given to various expressions of what the others regard as sheer eccentricity or perversity – like her singing on the Sabbath, her giving the "twist" to the spinning wheel comically in front of Merete, her interpreting in a deliberately provocative way the "Song of Songs," and her outrageously adapting of the verse about the apple tree in her drawing of a tree bearing a single enormous apple.

These acts are less immoral than amoral. Such instances of zaniness or playfulness are in their essence expressions of nonnormalized, nonsystematic impulses. Their very significance is that they are caprices not only for the characters themselves, but – perhaps even more importantly – within the narratives in which they are situated. They are moments in which the actress is allowed to follow an impulse, impulsively – to allow herself to get carried away for a second. They are moments in which the performance is allowed to go a little wild. Dreyer's point is that such expressive eccentricities and idiosyncrasies are opposed to *all* systematic understandings – including systems of moral understanding. They are expressions of impulsive, unpredictable, unsystematic energies (on the part of the filmmaker and the actress, as well as the character).

The sheer exuberance (and occasional comedy) of these *jeu d'esprits* disarms all systematic judgment. Merete scowls at Anne's singing and her other forms of impulsiveness; a sensitive viewer is entertained and smiles in admiration of her brashness and energy. The smile that Dreyer induces at these moments is a way of preventing the viewer's attitude from congealing into a repressive moral judgment.[16] Dreyer's humor is a way of keeping our attitudes up in the air, in motion. Humor lubricates and loosens up fixed or rigid positions. It functions exactly parallel to the way that Dreyer uses other expressive devices in his work to keep his viewers and his characters in motion – to prevent attitudes from rigidifying or stabilizing. (After Anne, *Ordet*'s Inger will be one of the great demonstrations of this power of wit and play to keep us free and to encourage imaginative freedom in others.)

There is more that needs to be said about Anne and

16 That is why to proceed to judge these acts in moral terms (as for example moralistically judging Anne to be an Eve figure of temptation, as has been done by more than one finger-wagging critic) is to play the part of Merete or the churchmen in the film. I would also note parenthetically that Dreyer's reputation as a dour Dane has apparently prevented critics from commenting on the importance of humor in his work. Needless to say, Dreyer is not exactly a maker of comedies; yet on the other hand, humor is not at all uncommon in his work and functions quite complexly in many of his films to enlarge our capacities of response, as it does here. Both this film and *Ordet* depend on humor for some of their most interesting effects.

Marte. However, before proceeding further, since I may seem to be talking about them as if they were conventional characters in a conventional drama, I want to emphasize once more the special status of all "characters" in Dreyer's work. In everything I am writing the names of Dreyer's characters function doubly – just as they do in Dreyer's narrative itself. Characters' names mark the difficult intersection of abstract expressive ideals and practical expressive opportunities. It would probably be impossible to write an intelligible account of *Day of Wrath* that didn't use names like "Anne" and "Marte" to signify certain expressive events within the film, but one must keep in mind that those words must be taken in a special, double sense. The way Dreyer's cinematic expressive style overlaps with the styles of his characters and extends beyond their personal expressive styles tells us that those words mark only the problematic point in the text at which ideals and impulses are momentarily realized in the practical expressive forms that we call characters, even as they continuously break the container of character we seek to confine them within and extend beyond each of the local identities we provisionally assign them.

Anne and Herlofs Marte function to realize abstract expressive possibilities. They are Dreyer's effort to perform certain states of emotional and imaginative energy in practical expressive forms. They are acts of concrete "embodiment" of otherwise purely imaginative states. This realizing impulse was a powerful one in all of

Dreyer's work and his creation of these two figures is evidence of it.

Yet, at the same time, Dreyer's derealizing impulses continuously war against his realizing impulses, in every aspect of his work, including his attitude toward characters. Anne and Herlofs Marte reveal Dreyer's deep ambivalence about the acts of expressive realization in his work. As much as he attempts to represent imaginative energies in particular characters' performances, Dreyer is driven by an equally strong belief that such energies fundamentally resist any actual form of worldly representation. The way this manifests itself is in the tendency in his work I have already mentioned to erase or melt or disperse figures away from their actual, physical identities. It is as if, no sooner having "embodied" abstract impulses in characters, Dreyer immediately works to "disembody" the impulses and move them beyond particular characters.

It is not accidental that Anne's initial turning to Absalon's son, Martin, for love and support, occurs at the precise moment at which Marte is exorcised from the narrative (by being burnt at the stake). A literal-minded viewer could argue that Marte's spirit transmigrates into Anne at the moment of her death; a more imaginative one would realize that Dreyer's point is that the energies that Marte figures can never be burnt out of society or extirpated from our hearts, and that they therefore reappear in another figure as soon as they are destroyed in one.

The substitution of Anne for Marte halfway through the narrative communicates Dreyer's ambivalence toward the very acts of realization and embodiment that he wants to endorse. Insofar as the one figure is substituted for the other Dreyer makes the particular figure count for less than the substitutional process itself. The person is rendered less substantial than the abstract energy he or she (apparently only temporarily) figures in a physical form. The exchange value of that state of energy matters as much as any of the particular bodily forms it happens to take. Insofar as Anne and Marte are one person viewed twice, the individual figure is signaled somehow to be less substantial than the abstract energies that are transmitted through the figure. (This point will be made again in *Ordet* in the substitution of Maren for Inger during the course of the film.) The imaginative energy that first speaks through Marte and then through Anne in the narrative is the reality; the personal, physical manifestation is the epiphenomenon. The character realizes energies only for a moment; the progress of the film derealizes the character.

Furthermore, as I argued already, since the characters are only local manifestations of general stylistic phenomena, the actual characters become, as it were, only epiphenomena of the styles. The styles of the films assertively exceed what can be put into the characters or their interactions (overflowing into the lighting and photography of the shots, the musical orchestrations on the sound track, or the movements of the camera). That stylistic surplus tells us the extent to which, notwithstanding his attempts to realize them in particular figures, for Dreyer, these imaginative energies will not be confined within the forms of characterization, dialogue, and realistic social interaction. There is an imaginative excess in all of the major films that remains expressible only as artistic style.

Thus the drama in Dreyer's work is played out on two intertwined lines: in practical social and verbal interactions between persons; but also in abstract interactions between artistic styles. To turn to one of the most obvious ways that the style of *Day of Wrath* exceeds the styles of the characters within it, one notices that paralleling the personal tendentiousness and coerciveness of the institutional representatives of the church, state, and family depicted *in* the film are the expressive tendentiousness and coerciveness in the representations of them performed *by* the film itself. The overdetermined way in which Absalon, Merete, and the other churchmen are expressed by their clothing, the blocking of their movements, and their behavior in specific scenes and shots of the film embodies a form of artistic control that mimics (and at moments outdoes) the institutional control of discourse within the society of the film.

That is to say, Absalon and many of the characters associated with him are as semiotically normalized and expressively confined within the artistic structures of Dreyer's film as they are imaginatively limited and socially placed within the society of the film. They are transformed into abstract semiotic functions within *Day of Wrath* in a way that repeats their status as abstract institutional functionaries in the world imagined by the film. To put it most simply, the schematic quality of their hearts and minds is paralleled by the schematic quality of their depiction. Absalon's mother, Merete, has been objected to in certain critical accounts as being gratuitously heartless or cruelly mechanical in her behavior, but the mechanicalness of Dreyer's representation of her in the film is meant to communicate the mechanicalness of Merete's representation of herself in the society of the film. The artistic world that represents Absalon, Merete, and the churchmen wars against free expression as much as the social world they inhabit does.

In this realm of doubly confining structurings, Dreyer's effort is to find an escape for at least some of his characters – not only an escape from the ideological narrowness of the society they belong to, but, even more challengingly, an escape from the tendentiousness and narrowness of their own film's structure.[17] Dreyer uses

17 This, incidentally, should suggest another reason why formalist analyses of Dreyer's work are doomed to misunderstand it. They are in effect an extension of the enterprise of Absalon and Merete and all of the depersonalizing institutions they represent. The interest of the films begins where formalist accounts end. Notwithstanding all of their formal arrangements of experience, Dreyer's films are explorations of the limits of formalist understandings. They are studies of the points at which deterministic or mechanical systems of knowledge and understanding – including, but not limited to those within the work of art – necessarily break down or prove inadequate.

specific characters and styles within his film to criticize the coerciveness of other aspects of his film's own narrative structurings. The difficult task he sets himself is to find a way for some of his characters (and his viewers) to move beyond the semiotic determinations in which they are at the same time inevitably participating. The effort is obviously difficult, if not paradoxical. How does one escape the tendentiousness of one's own movie? How, even as one remains embedded in and responsive to the formal systems that communicate meaning, does one gesture beyond them? How can one escape the artistic structures of the work of art within which one exists?

Marte and Anne are Dreyer's response to that challenge. To explain that, in what follows I want to attempt to talk simultaneously about the expressive styles of Anne and Marte and the expressive styles of Dreyer representing Anne and Marte, since to some extent their styles of representing themselves in their worlds cannot be disentangled from Dreyer's styles of representing them to us as viewers of his film. In either manifestation – whether they reach us as personal styles of expression through a character or as cinematic styles of expression detached from any particular figure – such styles figure the possibility of levering oneself free from the coercions of formal systems of signification. They figure the possibility of imaginative freedom expressing itself in the most daunting circumstances.

But in order to begin doing that one must first distinguish the two figures. Though Marte and Anne are, in many respects, two aspects of one character, Dreyer also intends that we discriminate between them. While both figures generally represent expressive energies and emotional impulses that escape from abstract semiotic determination or description, in separating them, Dreyer, as it were, analyzes the suppressions of capitalistic Protestantism at two distinguishable levels: Herlofs Marte represents the realm of the body in all of its physicality and sensuousness, and Anne represents erotic and imaginative energies that bourgeois society insists that we organize or eliminate.[18]

In the emphasis on the so-called spirituality of Dreyer's work, it is sometimes forgotten that our physical selves and sexual energies are as important within Dreyer's films as our hearts and souls and minds. It is not surprising that Dreyer should be interested in both aspects of his characters. His films take as their subject practical acts of expression. For Dreyer, our bodies are the way we express our spirits. That is why, despite the fact that he is often thought to be the most chaste of filmmakers, there are sexual encounters, or references to sexual encounters, in each of Dreyer's films from *Vampyr* to *Gertrud.* Our practical sexuality is one of the principal ways we express our emotions in the world, as not only *Day of Wrath,* but Dreyer's next important film, *Ordet,* emphasizes.

18 Though how one "represents" such things – in life or in art – becomes one of the central subjects of the film.

Furthermore, sexual and physical expressions have a very special and diacritical relationship to social forms of discourse in Dreyer's work. If Dreyer is the supreme poet of all of the ways we attempt to rise above or go beyond the limitations of social categories of understanding in our "higher" selves (in our dreams, visions, and desires), he is also the poet of all the ways our "lower" selves equally escape from social structures and repressive understandings. Our sexual and physical selves are as much at war with the repressions of society as our spirits are, and it is not accidental that Dreyer would be interested in those aspects of our being that extend *below* man-made rules and ideologies. To understand "transcendence" in this way – not as a state of pure spirituality, but rather as a capacity to escape from systems of normalization and control – is to realize that our bodies and senses potentially "transcend" limiting representations as much as our souls and ideals do.

One of the ways in which Dreyer asserts an alternative to the semiotic depersonalizations and neutralizations represented by Absalon and the churchmen is through a reinstallation of the actual physical body into a depersonalized expressive system like that of the church's rituals of interrogation and torture. Herlofs Marte's body in particular represents a realm of the senses that is pointedly not accounted for by the theological abstractions involving sin and transgression in the books of the church elders and the confession she is tortured into giving.

148

Reinstalling the body at the center of a depersonalized semiotic system –
Herlofs Marte being tortured and interrogated

The elderly actress who plays Marte, Anna Svierkier, has an extraordinarily interesting body and face, of which Dreyer and his director of photography, Karl Andersson, heighten a viewer's awareness in a variety of ways. The key lighting and modeling of her features encourage an almost painfully overly intimate awareness of her wrinkled skin, her sagging breasts, her disheveled hair, the lines on her face, and the moistness of her eyes.[19] The point is to reinstate a particular, physical body at the center of an otherwise impersonal ceremony of confession. Herlofs Marte will not be made into a disembodied functionary in an impersonal system. While the churchmen and their ceremony attempt to neutralize or deny the body, for the sake of saving the spirit separate from it,

19 In his contribution to the posthumously published edition of Dreyer's unproduced *Jesus* screenplay, Francois Truffaut called Marte's body "the most beautiful female nude in cinema, at once the most erotic and the most carnal." Though Truffaut overstates Marte's eroticism, her body certainly is one of the most lovingly, tenderly photographed bodies in all of film.

Dreyer and Andersson affirm the supreme reality of the realm of the senses.

Reinstalling the human body and senses, in all of their ungeneralizable particularity, at their place at the center of life, and as the fundamental source of all expression, is only one step in a larger expressive project in which Dreyer is engaged in *Day of Wrath*. The larger project is a demonstration that Marte (and later Anne) will not be reduced to being impersonal functions in any system of generalized, formal relationships. As Dreyer realizes, if capitalism depends on the denaturing of commodities to make productive standardization possible, it depends equally on the denaturing of the producers, the abstraction of their identities. Just as Protestantism defines the body as something that must be subjugated or ignored for the sake of the soul, so capitalism reduces the individual to an abstract functionary in an impersonal system.

The passionate expressiveness of Marte's face and frightened eyes, her unpredictably shifting vocal tones, her whimpers, screams, pleas, and sobs, her agitated, impulsive gestures, and her tears represent manifestations of eccentric, fluxional imaginative energies that will never be abstractly summarized by or "spoken within" an abstract system of understanding. They are her reply to the normalizing, standardizing understandings that the church would apply to her. As the churchmen try to categorize her, to repressively understand her as a witch, to subject her to a series of impersonal ceremonies of interrogation and confession, her expressive mobility,

150

eccentricity, and wildness tell us what their systems can never understand or eliminate.

Contrast the ways in which the churchmen who conduct the interrogation are represented. Not only are their vocal tones normalized but the very questions they ask and the answers they record during the interrogation are abstract, depersonalized, dispassionate formulas. In contrast with Marte, who is wearing a rough, ragged, torn dress that reveals as much flesh as it conceals, their bodies are buttoned up from foot to throat and are hidden. They have sacrificed their distinctive expressive identities to institutional systems of signification, while Marte is emphatically what will be "spoken" neither by an abstract system of clothing nor within a formal ceremony of theological interrogation.

In fact, Marte (and later Anne) are nothing less than Dreyer's attempts to imagine escapes from the abstract systems of signification of his own film. In a scene immediately prior to the torture scene, when we see Marte kneeling in supplication before Absalon, Dreyer has his actress have a bit of trouble getting back on her feet and totter for a split second. Marte's difficulty rising might be understood as being a naturalistic touch that reminds us of her age and infirmity, but it also serves a much more important expressive function. It reminds us of the extent to which both the actress and the character she plays will not be abstractly understood as a formal function even of her own film's expressive systems. At the moment she has difficulty rising from her knees, Marte (which is to say, Svierkier) is reducible neither to being an abstracted, depersonalized witch undergoing a formal cross-examination nor to being an abstracted, depersonalized semiotic function within a formally organized film. We are suddenly made aware that she (both the character and the actress) is an old woman with bad knees and a faltering sense of balance, which is what any merely intellectual understanding of her (both the understanding of her as a witch by the churchmen and the understanding of her as an abstract functionary within a film by a formalist critic) forgets.

The point is that the effect of the moment at which Herlofs Marte briefly totters before rising is not explainable in terms of abstract narrative or cinematic structures. Dreyer is calling our attention to the specificity of the particular dramatic moment: the particularity of a scene, as it is acted by a particular actor or actress, in a specific take, at a specific dramatic moment. Such things escape formal schemes of signification or description. That is precisely their value. They represent lucky accidents, creative eruptions of saving individuality and eccentricity within even the most carefully structured narratives.

There is a comparable moment in *The Passion of Joan of Arc*, in which Joan, going through a doorway into her cell, ever so slightly stumbles. Perhaps it was not intended to happen at all; perhaps it was something that simply occurred as the cameras were rolling and his actress tripped on the doorstep; or perhaps it was planned and rehearsed.

Whatever its origin or cause, which is not important, Dreyer's decision to put it in the final film speaks volumes about his interest in maintaining touch with the accidental and particular, with the undeconstructable human being with a real body who is at the center of the role, and who emphatically won't be reduced to being a mere semiotic function of a film's systems of artistic expression – in *The Passion of Joan of Arc,* a specific human being who won't be defined by the codes of the trial.

These apparently accidental, physical events, these almost pure experiences of the senses are some of the most important moments one takes away from a Dreyer film. They are not mere eccentric "touches" or signature piece filigrees in an otherwise formally stringent film. They are among the most important or moving moments in his work precisely because they remind us of physical and (as we will see in *Gertrud*) vocal residues that won't be eliminated or absorbed into the overarching structures of the plot and the style.

In fact, insofar as these particular physical and emo-

Expressive particularities opposed to formal systems of signification –
Herlofs Marte stumbles while getting up

153

tional events won't be made into an abstract (and therefore controllable) semiotic function, the only way to remove the threat represented by them is to remove the body itself. As the torture scenes show, working on the body only makes it imaginatively more present. Herlofs Marte's body can finally be eliminated only by being burned. Yet right down to the final seconds of Marte's life, in which she waves her arms and screams as she is thrown into the flames, Dreyer endows her with an impulsive emotional energy that won't be abstractly understood or controlled.

This leads to a larger point about the importance of acting and the performance of the individual actor as the source of meaning in Dreyer's work. The particularity of the expressions of the human face, body, and voice, and the ungeneralizable specificity of the dramatic moment as it is acted by a particular performer at a particular instant in time are what formalists (whether witch-hunting rectors or structuralist film critics) necessarily leave out of their accounts of experience. The eccentricity or particularity of such events is not generated out of a film's abstract systems, and will not be abstractly absorbed back into them. Which is to say that Dreyer's interest in such performed, acted, fugitive, expressive effects represents his own statement on the limitations of formalism.[20]

20 Everything I've already argued about Dreyer's opposition to schematic systems of expression and understanding, and his attempt to reinstall the specific body, sounds, and movements of the ungeneralizable per-

The individual performer, at his or her best, escapes both from the systems within the society that the narrative imagines and from the systems of the work of art itself. As much as Anne and Herlofs Marte represent an escape from the confining ideological systems in place around them in the narrative, the performances of Lisbeth Movin (as Anne) and Anna Svierkier (as Marte) represent an escape from the formal stylistic systems of *Day of Wrath* itself. The performances of these actresses embody energies that defy systematic understanding or expression – in the society of the film or in the abstract structures of artistic expression that are the film.

As Dreyer insisted at the end of the lecture on abstraction from which I have already quoted, the expressiveness of the actor represents an eruption of imaginative energies that will not be absorbed back into the work's semiotic structures:

I have talked much about image and form and not a word about actors, but anyone who has seen my films – the good ones – will know what great importance I attach to the actors' work. There is nothing that can be compared to the human

former (in *Day of Wrath*, in the figures of Marte and Anne) in a depersonalized system should indicate how radically opposed he would have been to the structuralist aesthetic of some of the critics who have championed his work since his death. Dreyer and his performers attempt to demonstrate that an individual is able to lever him- or herself free from the abstract, impersonal stylistic systems encroaching everywhere by offering meanings too passionate, suggestive, or mysterious to be expressed or understood in such abstract ways.

155

face. . . . There is no greater experience than that of witnessing . . . the expression in a sensitive face becoming animated from within and, under the mysterious power of inspiration, growing into poetry.[21]

That is why it is worse than misleading to make *Day of Wrath* sound as if it were merely the consequence of formal effects of lighting, framing, and camera work; it would turn the meaning of Dreyer's work inside out. Dreyer's formal effects would seem merely mechanical if it weren't for the dramatic performances and imaginative energies they are in the service of expressing. The abstract structures in his films exist principally in order to allow the actors and characters to release energies that fracture them, energies that escape formalistic definition and analysis.

It is the richness of the dramatic performances elicited by Dreyer that ultimately convince us of the possibility of an escape from the mechanisms of the world his figures live in (as well as the mechanisms of the film they function within). It is the emotional expressiveness of the performance turned in by Svierkier and the suggestive, seductive mysteriousness of the performance of Movin that convince us that the language of desire may be expressible in the language of men.

Dreyer votes for the fundamental importance and power of the human performer as the source of value in

21 "Imagination and Color," 186.

his films.[22] This is not merely a truism, and is certainly not true of every film. Filmmakers as different from one another as Eisenstein, Hitchcock, DePalma, Kubrick, and Altman (not to mention a whole school of avant-garde filmmakers from Stan Brakhage to Michael Snow) might be cited as artists for whom abstract structural considerations matter more than the performance of the individual actor. As different as their individual films are from one another, meaning is principally created in their work formally – by means of effects of montage, *mise-en-scène*, lighting, framing – not personally. It is created thematically, abstractly, metaphorically – not dramatically (the way it is created in Chekhov or Cassavetes).

It is not accidental that many of these filmmakers basically end up arguing in their works, in a fashionably "modernist" vein, in favor of the powerlessness of the individual, and about his or her being lost in or "spoken by" abstract, social and intellectual systems. Insofar as the structures of their works implicitly create a Foucaultian world in which the individual dramatic performer has been removed as the source of value, and impersonal cinematic structures have replaced him or her, the final meaning of their works is already contained in their

22 So-called advanced film criticism has traditionally neglected the function of the actor as a creator of meaning and value in a work, to favor the director. The result has been a serious bias both in *what* films are treated and *how* they are understood. For a slightly fuller discussion of the role of the actor as a source of meaning as contrasted with other ways of creating meaning in a film, see my *American Vision* (New York: Cambridge University Press, 1986), 317–340.

initial "structuralist" methods of organization. When their works tell us about the individual's victimization, powerlessness, or puniness in the face of overwhelming systems of understanding, they are only revealing how they themselves have chosen to remove the individual as the central maker of meaning in the work.

That is why it is significant that Dreyer is known for the power of the female performances he elicits in his films (and why he deserves to be even more widely known for them). Movin's and Svierkier's performances take their place as fully equal to the better known performance of Renée Falconetti in *The Passion of Joan of Arc*, and are on a level with the subsequent performance of Birgitte Federspiel in *Ordet*. As Anne, Movin, in particular, seems by turns (to pun on the word) as independent as Dietrich, as emotionally intense as Stanwyck, as mysterious as Garbo, and as suggestively playful and vulnerably girlish as Monroe.

Anne's function in the film bears examination. After Marte's immolation, Dreyer uses Anne, as it were, to continue to excavate the emotional and physical realm that Marte opened to view. In moving fifty years backward, from an old woman to a young one, Dreyer uses Anne to explore the expression of sexual desire in the world.

The imaginative differences between Anne and Marte, on the one hand, and Absalon, Merete, and the churchmen, on the other, are brought out by means of a series of narrative and visual contrasts similar to those that compared Marte with Merete. Parallel to the way that Marte's appearance and positional eccentricities (her crawling, crouching, and kneeling) were contrasted with the appearance and movements of Merete, Anne's movements and bodily image are continuously contrasted with those of Merete and the churchmen.

To consider only physical appearance: While Absalon is buttoned up from his toes to the crown of his head in clerical severity in black (just as are Merete and the other churchmen), Anne, a nimble, animated girl at least twenty years his junior, wears lace collars, alluring garments, and (in a sexually evocative progression in the course of the film) gradually lets down her blonde hair as her sexual involvement with Absalon's son, Martin, progresses. (The only other figure in the film who is consistently bare-headed is, not coincidentally, Marte.)

Yet to say that Anne represents eroticism and sexual stimulation is to frame the expressive possibilities that she represents too narrowly. The contrast is more profound than one involving bodies and sexual powers. Anne introduces mystery, drama, and energy to space itself (and therefore to life) as she obliquely and glancingly moves through the corridors and rooms of the rectory (and what finally makes her even more threatening to the churchmen and more interesting to a viewer than Marte is that Anne ultimately brings such energies into the bosom of the home and family). The churchmen call it witchcraft or demonic power; a critic may say that Anne expresses the free play of imagination and desire; a member of the audience may conclude that she simply brings emotional intensity, imaginative allure, or theatricality into life. But however one describes it, the effect is electric. The energies of consciousness in free and eccentric movement that she figures ultimately threaten all of the fixed understandings and stabilities of the world of the churchmen.

Anne's positions and movements are blocked entirely differently from those of Merete and the group of churchmen. Absalon and the other men in the film are repeatedly photographed statically positioned or visually pinned against a confining, flat background. Arranged in lateral groupings extending right and left on the screen, Dreyer arrays them within what appears to be a virtually two-dimensional representational space (lined up along a wall and immobilized within the cramped spaces and low ceiling of a small room). When the individual churchmen move, their movements (and the movements of the camera that follows them) are also generally confined to a two-dimensional representational space.

In contrast, Anne is associated with a variety of free and eccentric movements in depth. In several outdoor scenes, she is shown impulsively running or walking through vast open spaces. In her indoor scenes, unlike the men, far from being pinned against a wall, she makes sinuous movements in depth, toward or away from the camera, back and forth in space. While Absalon's movements (like those of his mother, Merete) are labored, rectilinear, flat, and lateral (generally either along the plane of the screen or at a right angle to it), as he moves purposefully in a straight line from one point to another, Anne's movements are eccentric arcs or diagonals or zigzags, frequently at an oblique angle to the camera, frequently going nowhere in particular. She slides through space in sidling, enticing, sideways-maneuvering dance steps.

While Absalon's walk, indoors and out, is plodding and straightforward, labored and usually bowed down, Anne prances, skips, hops, or runs from one place to another. It is no accident that the initial "steps" in her game of seduction with Martin are for her to take him outdoors, to entertain the possibility of free, unfettered physical movement by walking or running in the fields, or (in a later scene) by drifting in an untethered boat downstream with him. Anne's distinctive achievement, even in the tightest of indoor spaces, is to maintain her ability to move freely, enticingly, and unpredictably.

Anne's movements speak volumes about her and her situation, and about how far she goes beyond anything the churchmen can fit into their flat-minded doctrines and monotonic moral stances and vocal inflections. Her performative obliquity communicates her state of irremediable marginality and the insecurity of her position. Given her precarious situation in this relentlessly oppressive world, she must not only keep moving in order to survive (while the churchmen stand or sit statically), but must also move around or at an angle to everything she encounters, rather than attempt to directly confront it. Furtiveness is forced upon her. Secrecy is her means of protecting herself. In this respect her obliquities are reminiscent of the crouching, climbing, cowering, and hiding positions forced upon Marte. Imaginatively, spatially, and expressively, Anne and Marte exist precisely in the marginal position – half engaged with a system, half somewhere beyond or outside of it, free to play with it or to move around within it – that Dreyer regards as being potentially the most creative position for his central characters to be in.

There is a crucial difference between the movements and the postures of the two women, however. Even when they vaguely remind us of Marte's, Anne's movements are entirely less fugitive than Marte's. They are less a merely negative, defensive stance. Anne's sinuous, sensuous obliquity demonstrates how a state of enforced marginality can be converted into a condition of positive power. Her capacities of movement represent a state of eroticism and imaginative fluidity that makes the men around whom she dances circles seem clumsy, stupid, and boring in contrast. Their institutionally sanctioned powers are useless in their attempts to grasp (in both senses of the word) her emotional mobility and imaginative slipperiness. Her inward "turnings" elude them.

The way that we know that Dreyer is endorsing the states of emotional fluxion, imaginative animation, and erotic stimulation represented by Anne (and related qualities earlier represented by Marte), and is implicitly pointing up the limitations of the expressive styles of the churchmen, is that his own cinematic styles mimic or repeat, in a finer tone, as it were, the expressive performance enacted by Anne (and Marte earlier). Anne's stimulating, mysterious, turning movements through space are only, in effect, a personal dramatization of the stimulating, oblique, searching movements of Dreyer's camera as, for example, it explores Marte's home and sensitively allows her to display her secret fears in the second scene of the film (the one I described already), or as it follows Anne sideways down the colonnade of the church in the shot sequence that leads up to Anne's eavesdropping on the conversation between Marte and Absalon. Or to shift the terms, Anne's and Marte's range of emotional expressiveness with their evocative tones of voice are only, in effect, the personal manifestation of Dreyer's own evocative use of light and shadow in the film. Those camera movements, that use of sounds, that play of light and shadows, tell us how completely Dreyer is on the side of the mercurial, the imaginatively mobile and stimulating, and how completely he is opposed to the static, mechanical, or codified.

Anne pushes against not only the fixities and limiting definitions of her society, but the rigidifying tendencies of filmic representation itself. She tells even the film's cameraman and lighting crew that they must learn how to follow her and not she them. No more than she will allow herself to be defined by codes of law, theology, or ethics, will she be confined within stagy, two-dimensional blocking or lighting schemes or limitingly defined by the abstract structures of the film she is in. It is in this

Moving on the margins of society "turning out of its codes of discourse – Anne's oblique, lithe movements through space contrasted with the churchmen's stasis and two-dimensionality

sense that Anne's performance is Dreyer's attempt to represent a condition of radical imaginative freedom.[23]

But if Anne's movements through space are evidence of her (and her creator's) success in translating her impulses into forms of worldly expression, another aspect of her presence within the film speaks of an imaginative

23 Compare the similar choreographic parables enacted in more conventional films like *Platinum Blonde, American Madness, Boudu Saved From Drowning,* and *The Crime of Monsieur Lange.* See my *American Vision,* 113–130 and 137–148. I would also call the reader's attention to the fact that Dreyer continues the exploration of the expressive power of cinematic movement that he begins here with the characters of Inger and Johannes in *Ordet.*

residue that will not be converted into a form of performance. I am referring to the evocative play of lights and shadows on her face and the key lighting of her eyes. They suggest how far Anne's imaginative powers and personal energies exceed any possible realistic representational forms.

While Dreyer fill lights Absalon and Merete to wipe out shadows and avoid expressive modeling of their features, he throws a continuously changing pattern of light and shadow on Anne's face by employing moving cutout patterns, scrims, and variously shaped objects in the path of his key lights, and employing pencil-point key effects on her eyes. What makes the patterns of light and dark on her face especially mysterious is that (after their initial appearance in the scene of Marte's being burned at the stake) they cannot be traced to any naturalistic source in the film. Though they metaphorically link Anne with both Marte and forces of nature by reminding us of the shapes and shadows of the tree branches we see in the outdoor scenes, after their first occurrence the patterns appear indoors away from windows, and at moments when they cannot possibly be actual shadows of trees. Additionally, another nonnaturalistic aspect of the shadows is that they seem to be present only on Anne's face, and are not generally visible in the room with her.[24]

24 This is accomplished by photographing Anne's face from an angle lower than the angle of the light from which the shadows are generated. The result is that, while Anne's face is shrouded in moving shadows,

Insofar as the evocative shadiness of Herlofs Marte's home in the second scene was washed out by the fill lighting of the rectory in the third, and Marte was pulled out of the shadow of the attic of the rectory into the light, it is as if Anne, literally and imaginatively, brings Marte's shadows back into the rectory from which they had been expunged. It is not at all a coincidence that the shadows clearly appear on Anne's face for the first time during the scene in which Marte is burned at the stake. At that moment they are the actual shadows of trees, but after Marte's death they cease to be naturalistically motivated, as if the spirit of Marte had mysteriously transmigrated into Anne, and had brought the shadows associated with both her life and her death with it.

However, the shadows communicate much more than Anne's mysterious powers; they express a larger tragic point within Dreyer's film. They show us the final impossibility of living the dream of expressive freedom that Anne figures. To the extent that her imaginative energies are ultimately expressible only in the lights in her eyes, in the shadows on her face (or in her hops and skips and sidelong movements through space), Dreyer is implicitly telling us how unconvertible they are into the fabric of time-bound narrative presentation and development.

the background that the camera takes in behind her is bizarrely unshadowed. Only her features are visibly clouded, not the walls or floor behind her. The effect is to make the shadows seem much more mysterious than if they were naturalistically explainable. It is as if the shadows were not cast upon her face, but somehow originated from it.

To shift the perspective from Anne to her creator, with the shadows Dreyer shows how difficult (or impossible) it is for him as a filmmaker to express the energies that Anne represents in the forms of realistic dialogue, social interaction, and dramatic narrative progression. They remain stylistic effects. They will be rendered only in terms of special effects of light and shadow and music and photography.

In this sense Anne figures a representational crisis for her creator as much as for herself. How does one express the imagination and passion she represents – the unfettered eroticism, the energy, the love – in the structures of ordinary life and in the forms of dramatic narrative? Ultimately, Anne's dreams of love and free expression (as in her fantasy of living alone with Martin and having his child) are forced to stay dreams (and to be rendered cinematically in terms of stylistic effects that remain stylistic). They will not be realized. They will not be converted into the temporal and spatial forms of drama, into the patterned exchanges of dialogue. Energies of conciousness, rendered through assertively stylistic effects, will not be translated into practical biological and social and dramatic destinies for the self.[25]

All of Dreyer's mature work is built around a doubt – a doubt about whether we can represent our finest and

---

25 Insofar as Dreyer's major films were each based upon stage plays, this suggests that he is using film not to affirm, but to criticize the adequacy of the social and verbal forms of representation to which stage drama is committed.

freest energies in the practical expressive forms of the world. In a sense this great realistic filmmaker makes each film in order to deny the doubt. He remains daringly committed to cinematic realism as the means of expressing imaginative energies that war against realism. And yet his films repeatedly seem to tell him otherwise – to tell him that we cannot finally express ourselves in the world. Like Inger and Gertrud later, Anne figures Dreyer's own ambivalence about his vexed expressive project. She figures his fear that her energies will not be lived, or that if lived, they will be destructive of all social systems and understandings.

As we shall see when we get to *Gertrud* (made twenty years after *Day of Wrath*), like his title character in that film, Dreyer ultimately gives up on the possibility that Anne momentarily figures (and that Inger also represents in his next important film, *Ordet*) – the possibility of practically expressing the free movements of the spirit in the form of actual movements in space, time, and

Light and shadow called upon to represent energies that characters' words and dramatic interactions cannot –
Anne and Martin

society. In *Gertrud* the possibility of movement is available only in the imagination and not in the real world of words, actions, and practical relationships with another human being.

The final tragic point of *Day of Wrath* is that the coercions and repressions of social and ideological and dramatic discourse cannot be elided or avoided. Insofar as Herlofs Marte and Anne are indeed successfully turned into "witches," and are exterminated from their societies, Dreyer demonstrates that it is impossible to maintain the imaginative opening out of the repressive forms and structures of society that either one represents. (Even merely to name an individual as a witch or for her to accept the name is, of course, in and of itself a powerful strategy of control.) As Freud was not the first to recognize, civilization fights desperately and to the death against the sort of emotional exposure, erotic vulnerability, and imaginative opening that Anne and Marte figure.

Day of Wrath embraces a dream of the expression of radical freedom in the character of Anne, a dream that one can express one's most passionate imaginations in the bosom of the family and in the forms of ordinary life, a dream that one can act out one's most mercurial movements of desire in society. For a few scenes at the center of the film, Dreyer holds out the possibility that Anne and Martin may be able to form a society hospitable to the expression of desire – even if it is only a society of two. But the flickering shadows on her face tell us otherwise insofar as they communicate energies that cannot be converted into practical expressions, energies that bewilder and overwhelm Martin, and ultimately undo Anne herself.

In placing her in an incestuous relationship with Martin, Absalon's son, Dreyer suggests the degree to which Anne is doomed to fail in her attempt to find or make a society hospitable to the finest, freest movements of desire. Even during the scenes in which she and Martin are intimately together in a community of shared feeling, Martin's conscience bothers him. He has internalized society's codes of understanding and they intrude even into the time he and Anne are apart from the rest of the world.

Martin's deeper problem is that, like the churchmen or like ideologues of all stripes, he would give desire a destination. He is unable to live in the fluxional state of arousal that Anne represents. It is telling that Dreyer's way of indicating Martin's process of drawing away from Anne and falling back into his father's attitudes is to have him increasingly focus on spatial destinations and temporal conclusions. "Where are we going?" "Where will it all end?" he asks of Anne. He would limit the expression of the imagination to the very structures and fixed possibilities that Anne radically brings into question. He would stop the movements of desire.

Significantly untroubled by the need to give desire a destination or a timetable, Anne is content to live in the flux of the moment (in the metaphors of the film, to "unmoor" her experience, to "drift," or go "with the current"). While Martin needs to fix, to pin down, and to locate desire, to cut it to fit the rigidifying temporal, spatial, and social forms of the world, Anne – like Dreyer's cinematic style itself – is willing to live in flux, to live with mystery and mercuriality. If there is a discrepancy between desire and the limiting structures of the world, like Dreyer, Anne sides with desire. While Anne keeps alive and stimulates imaginative energies that may have no worldly realization, Martin literalizes. Her willingness to dwell in possibility, which is ratified by Dreyer's own cinematic willingness to evoke possibilities without weakly resolving or specifying outcomes, or committing her ideologically to any particular agenda, is contrasted with Martin's need repressively to specify, to name. While she stimulatingly derealizes, he repressively realizes. And he, of course, wins in the end since he has the world's repressive realizations on his side.

Martin is a crucial presence in the film. He tells us how hard it is to avoid the repressive codes of moral, social, and psychological discourse – since they are ultimately not outside of us, but in our hearts and minds. They are part of our consciousness. The superego is built into us.

Yet even so, to some extent one can dismiss Martin and his guilt, his need to resolve and conclude. Both as a man in a world in which masculinity has been metaphorically equated with regimentation and control, and as Absalon's son, he has been associated with forces of repression in the film prior to the point at which he has doubts about himself and his relationship with Anne. He is an obviously limited character. That is why the final scenes of the film are necessary for Dreyer to drive home the depth of his profoundly tragic insight. Anne must communicate it.

She tells us that, in the end, even she can't escape society's repressive codes of understanding. The most harrowing moment in all of *Day of Wrath* occurs in its final seconds. At the conclusion of the final scene, as Anne is accused of witchcraft, in an astonishing turnabout, she confesses her depravity to her accusers and hangs her head. She affirms what she has denied up to that moment – that she indeed is a witch.

It is a stunning moment. Even she is unable to stand apart from the reigning codes of discourse. Her final act tells us that the repressions of life and society are not only something that it may be impossible for us ultimately to triumph over, but something that even those who may seem to have made themselves exceptions to them have perhaps internalized. No one can escape them.

What *Day of Wrath* finally and tragically tells us is that the repressiveness Anne (and Dreyer's dramatic narrative) faces is not the result of any particular institutional or social arrangement of knowledge. It is not created by the church, the state, the family, fascism, or any individual. There is no enemy to defeat. No social reorganization can change the world. Repression is built into the codes of all life, all drama, all language, all art.

The lyrical suspensions of eventfulness, the poetic releases from ordinary life, the musical interludes – all of
the visionary and meditative releases *Day of Wrath* offers
into a realm of free imagination and unrepressed feeling
– cannot be sustained indefinitely in the practical forms
of drama (or life). The claim of worldly events, the responsibilities of social interaction, and the requirements
of speech (and of narrative itself) force our romantic
reveries to negotiate the obstacle course of the world.
Our spirits are as inevitably ground down by the responsibilities and repressions of drama as they are by the
responsibilities and repressions of life.

After all, social institutions like the church and the
state (and intellectual institutions like the forms of
drama and narrative) are not handed down to us from
heaven, or imposed upon us by alien forces. They are us
too. They are created by us; they are subscribed to by us
and others like us. This is the profound, tragic recognition of this great masterpiece. That is why it should
come as no surprise that in *Gertrud,* a film that is in some
respects a nostalgic, revisionary remake of this one,
Dreyer should finally and explicitly acknowledge what is
only hinted at tentatively in the final scene here: that
there is no other way for his wonderfully stimulating,
imaginatively mysterious, and bewitchingly alluring central figure to save her soul than for her to give up the
whole world. The tragic fear here, which becomes a
tragic recognition there, is that to live in the world is to
have to give up one's soul.

FOUR

Ordet
Imaginative and social relations

MORTEN: Do you know what the difference is between my faith and yours? You believe that Christianity means pulling a long face and torturing yourself. I believe that Christianity means the enhancement of life. My faith makes me rejoice in life from one end of the day to the other. Whereas *your* faith merely makes you long for death. *My* faith is the warmth of life, your faith the coldness of death. . .

PETER: . . . you are lost souls.

from Ordet

W HILE the films that immediately preceded *Ordet*[1] (*The Passion of Joan of Arc, Vampyr,* and *Day of Wrath*) more or less naturalized the spiritual, *Ordet* spiritualizes the natural. Dreyer's films all explore the intersection of the transcendental and the practical, to focus on the process of translation from one realm to another; but *Ordet* – more than any of his other works – is an effort to realize transcendental impulses in terms of a set of characters, styles, and events virtually indistinguishable from the experiences of many of his viewers in their lives outside of the movie theatre.

Dreyer takes the everyday family life of more or less ordinary people as his subject. He focuses on the day-

---

1 Since the English translation of the title (*The Word*) has for some reason not caught on, I will refer to the film by its Danish title.

175

to-day interactions of three generations of a farm family. The families in Dreyer's other films are invariably somewhat simplified and schematic, but this one is not. It is the most complex social group in all of his work – a family of three generations, in which each person is intimately familiar with the tics and crotchets, the likes and dislikes of every other person. The result is that, more than any of Dreyer's other films, *Ordet* is a close-up study of the practical social and moral negotiations that go on within a group of individuals, living in perfectly ordinary circumstances.

Not only is the social setting unusually complex for Dreyer; the styles of expression within *Ordet* are too. For its effects the film depends on the most detailed registration in all of Dreyer's work of the specific tonal inflections, colloquial conversational rhythms, nuanced exchanges of glances and facial expressions, and reciprocated gestures by means of which individuals practically interact with each other.

The film is set almost entirely at Borgensgård, the ancestral farmstead of the Borgens, presided over by the aged Morten Borgen. Morten (remarkably played by the 81-year-old Henrik Malberg) has outlived his wife and now works the farm with his three sons – Mikkel, Johannes, and Anders.

Mikkel, the oldest son, is married to Inger. They have two children at present – Maren (about age eleven) and little Inger (about age six) – and Inger is pregnant with their third child, which they are expecting at any time.

The second son, Johannes, has not been in his right mind since he had a nervous breakdown as a seminary student, and now goes around the farm spouting biblical prophecies and apparently believing that he is Jesus. The youngest son, Anders, works the farm with his brothers and, as it develops in the course of the film, is courting the daughter of a neighboring farmer.

The whole family lives together in the Borgensgård farmhouse. But however close their manifest social, biological, and physical relationship, the situation that Dreyer begins with is one in which each of these great-souled, hardworking men is estranged from and causes pain to the others: In his state of psychological derangement, Johannes has lost his place in the fabric of the family, and is a burden and concern to everyone else. As he has grown up, Mikkel has turned against the religious faith of his father in bitterness and disillusion, and his father has therefore turned against him to some extent. Even the young Anders risks the wrath of the elder Borgen and emotional exile from the family because the neighboring farm girl with whom he has fallen in love, Anne Petersen, belongs to a rival religious sect.

As a consequence of all of these estrangements, old Morten, the patriarch of the family, feels as alienated from his sons as they do from him. He is not only upset and discouraged by Johannes's madness, Mikkel's loss of faith, and what he considers to be Anders's betrayal of the family's faith by wanting to marry outside of it; in the face of so many personal setbacks and what he considers to be acts of apostasy and betrayal around him, Morten is undergoing a crisis of confidence in his own faith and the meaning of his life.

For anyone familiar with the sexual dynamics of Dreyer's work, however, it will come as no surprise to learn that the key figure for this group of lonely, estranged men is a woman – Mikkel's lovely, young, pregnant wife, Inger. In this family of threatened or actual withdrawals and separations, Inger is a soothing, mediating presence. Dreyer's entire *oeuvre* is an exploration of the power of love, in this case, the lubricating, facilitating power of understanding and kindness, and Inger represents love as an inexhaustible capacity to heal wounds, patch up separations, and accept differences. While, in their pain, pride, and frustration, the men of Borgensgård pull away from one another and withdraw from the family in general, Inger lovingly and considerately puts them into relation again.

A little like *Day of Wrath*'s Anne, who expresses her freedom in terms of her fluid capacities of motion *vis a vis* the churchmen, Inger functions as a principle of lithe, mercurial movement in this world of slow-moving, blockish, brooding men. But the crucial difference is that where Anne's expressions are marginal and imperiled, Inger's are central and appreciated by those around her. And where *Day of Wrath* was negative and pessimistic in its understanding of the relation of imagination and the family, *Ordet* attempts to be ecstatically affirmative.

178

Day of Wrath deconstructed the nuclear family and indicated its repressions and avoidances, suggesting that the energies of the imagination could only be problematically (and never satisfactorily) expressed in the forms of familial interaction. *Ordet* is Dreyer's most optimistic exploration of the possibility of actually expressing the finest movements of the imagination in the world. Anne's sexuality was explosively antinomian. It threatened fixed structures of organization, including the household and the social relationships she was part of. Inger's love, in contrast, represents the possibility of emotional and imaginative states serving not to disrupt everyday routines and ceremonies, but to enrich them. Inger represents the most daring attempt in all of Dreyer's work to find a real home and a responsible expressive function for the truly creative individual.

In this sense, *Ordet* and the figure of Inger within it mark a point in Dreyer's *oeuvre* that he never attained again before or after this one film. Most of Dreyer's other works are, in effect, resigned to the ultimate expressive estrangement and social isolation of the imaginative individual. But in *Ordet* Dreyer attempts to imagine the supremely imaginative and loving individual expressing herself completely within the structures of familial life. Possessing the energy and imagination of Joan, Anne, or Gertrud, Inger is the only one of Dreyer's stimulating heroines not doomed to misunderstanding, homelessness, or alienation.

Inger is a lover, a mother, a wife, a counselor, a conciliator, and, in general, a negotiator who lovingly and tenderly mediates between each of the opposed or alienated figures in the Borgen family. She is deft, gentle, tolerant, and responsive to the multitude of emotional claims competing for her feelings and attention, the diversity and urgency of which rather than intimidating her, seem actually to stimulate her into ever finer actions and subtler expressions. She is a dazzling mistress of ceremonies and a consummate actress brilliantly in control of multiple roles, who finds the process of social and theatrical playing not limiting but exhilarating. She is a figure with the imagination and improvisatory inventiveness of a Henry James heroine, yet without being in the least alienated from practical social expressions.[2]

But it would be a mistake to make Inger sound merely like a brilliantly sensitive social arranger – to make her sound too much like the hero or heroine of a Renoir film. She is a social negotiator, and a masterful one at that, but she connects social performances with spiritual values that Renoir's work is relatively indifferent to. In-

2 Though Henry James's Maggie Verver comes to mind as a literary analogue, the only cinematic figure that, in my experience, can bear comparison with Inger is John Cassavetes' Mabel Longhetti in his *A Woman Under the Influence*. Cassavetes' heroine represents a similarly audacious attempt to imagine a home and role and set of relationships within which a supremely creative individual will not be frustrated in her performances, but rather will actually be able to bring them to finest flower. See my discussion of the expressive role of Cassavetes' figure in *American Dreaming* (Berkeley: University of California Press, 1985), 192–196, 301–304.

ger mediates between individuals as deftly as *The Rules of the Game*'s Christine or Octave, but she also mediates between realms of the spirit and those of practical affairs. One thing Renoir's social arrangers are not in danger of being mistaken for is saints; but down-to-earth saintliness (spirituality expressed in practical actions and words) is the most natural thing in the world to Inger.

That is to say, as much as she brings together isolated individuals, Inger brings together separated realms – abstract realms of the spirit and practical affairs of the farm. She brings together being a mother and being a lover, being a tactful social negotiator and a saintly example of charity and hope. Indeed, it is the doubleness of her character and function that makes Inger's capacities of performance altogether so extraordinary. She is, in her own way, as saintly and inspired in her love and sense of responsibility as Joan of Arc; yet she is also a mother and wife and daughter-in-law holding a household together in mundane ways that Joan (or *Day of Wrath*'s Anne) is entirely spared.

Inger's care for others is expressed in the most practical and prosaic ways, as well as in the most exalted and idealistic ways. She can argue at one moment, abstractly and almost grandly, as she does in a scene with Morten, that all that really matters in the courtship of Anders and the neighbor girl Anne is "that they love each other," and the next moment be equally touchingly concerned that Morten and Mikkel not go out into the chill without

Ingers practical prayerfulness baking cakes and filling pipes
Inger with Anders and later with Morten

their coats, or that Morten have a clean handkerchief when he goes calling on Anne's father, Peter Petersen, the tailor.

Dreyer is imagining the possibility of a love and devotion as great and inspiring and abstract as Joan's being expressed not (as it was in *Joan of Arc*) as an alternative to ordinary expressive opportunities, but *within* them and *in terms of* them. He is imagining emotional expressions as passionate as Anne's that will not destroy the family, but creatively enrich the relationships within it. He is imagining a love as exalted and pure as Gertrud's (in the film following *Ordet*) that will not doom the individual to homelessness, but stand at the very center of a home and function as a bond that holds its inhabitants together.

Inger is, in this respect, Dreyer's most extraordinary creation. He tells us not only that she expresses herself both in her saintly acts of self-sacrifice for her family *and* in her cooking in the kitchen, but, more daringly, that she expresses her saintliness *in terms of* her cooking in the kitchen. Inger can pray to God just as hard as she works at soothing delicate egos and allaying fits of pique or brooding. In fact, her practical interventions are as much her way of praying as her prayers are dedicated to practical tasks. She can bake muffins, fill pipes, do the laundry, and find jackets, as well as love her fellow men and pray to God, or, to put it another way, her domesticity in these respects is a direct expression of her capacities of love and prayer.[3]

The subject of *Ordet* is precisely the ways we convert (or fail to convert) our transcendental impulses into worldly expressions. The film sets up an expressive standard in which abstract ideals and values must be translated into practical forms of social expression in order to count. This represents an important shift in Dreyer's work. A figure's ideals and values are not allowed to exist as abstract states of energy. They are not expressed as lights and shadows on a character's face, as they were in *Day of Wrath*, for example. They are not

---

3 This issue is thematized in the film in many scenes, in a series of running discussions by the men about two subjects: whether religious faith is of any "use" in life; and whether "miracles" can occur in the modern world. At various points in the film, Johannes, Mikkel, Morten, the doctor, and the minister each express an opinion on the relation of spirituality and worldliness by taking sides on these questions. It is indicative of their difference from Inger that, even in discussing the issue, the men express themselves merely abstractly and intellectually, while she continuously and joyously answers the question by actually making the translation between the two realms.

expressed primarily through musical effects or purely stylistic heightenings of experience. Dreyer demands that they be rendered practically in ordinary family relationships.

As in all of Dreyer's major films, experience in *Ordet* is not chiefly visionary or private – or to the extent that it is, it is clearly not adequate to the expressive standards that Dreyer establishes within the film. Inger embodies a standard of practical expression of transcendental impulses that all of the other characters have to live up to. When old Morten distractedly stares off into the distance, or Johannes declaims prophetically, we are meant to see the limitations of their turns out of practical familial involvement and social interaction.

In the service of this narrative project, *Ordet* asks its actors to express themselves even more socially, more practically than most of Dreyer's actors in his other films are required to do. They are asked to represent themselves through their tones of voice, gestures, facial expressions, words, and social interactions with each other. Except for his moving camera (about which I will comment extensively below), Dreyer does not feel the need to intervene to supplement their practical expressions with visual and acoustic effects. He lets the social expressions of his actors stand on their own more than in his other work, and indulges in almost no special lighting effects. He experiments with trusting direct social expression in a way he doesn't in his other films.

It is not accidental, given Inger's practical expressive

responsibilities as well as the overall narrative project of *Ordet*, that, with a specificity that distinguishes it from any of the other work, *Ordet* exposes us to the realistic sounds and tones of ordinary domestic life. Though it may seem trivial, when Inger rolls out dough on the kitchen table, Dreyer makes sure that we hear the sound of her rolling pin as well as the sound of her humming and singing as she works. Birds sing, dogs bark, and horses neigh outside of the farmhouse. Cart wheels reverberate on the road, and the jangle of reigns and bits and livery is audible on the sound track. Laundry hung out to dry blows in the wind, and we both see and hear it.

Yet even more important than the sound of objects and events, are the colloquial, vernacular sounds of voices and the expressiveness of faces and bodies in the film. *Ordet* is a film of complex conversational give and take; of chaff, play, and wryness in interactions between characters; of expressive pauses and silences; of subtle tonal inflections; and of the rich but unspoken language of characters' bodily and facial expressions.

No character more masterfully both "speaks" and "reads" this language than Inger. And no sequence more eloquently summarizes Inger's beautifully complex expressive function than the one in which she tries to persuade old Borgen to accept Anders' courtship of the neighbor girl Anne. In order to ground the moment as concretely as possible in the practicalities of everyday life, Dreyer begins the sequence in the kitchen with Inger making biscuits for afternoon tea. Her husband,

185

Mikkel, is chatting with her as he takes a break from his farm work, when young Anders comes in to ask their help in smoothing the way so that he can announce his engagement with Anne to Morten, whom he knows will object to his marrying outside of his religion.

When, in the next scene, Morten tramps into the dining room an hour or so later, with Inger sitting in a chair next to the table, and we see Inger's baked treat, hot from the oven, along with a pot of fresh-brewed coffee waiting as a snack for him on the table, Dreyer has deftly and comically established Inger's practical mastery of the realm of the senses.

But lest we narrow or trivialize her role (as if she were only a combination waitress and pastry chef in charge of sweetening up the boss) Dreyer begins the scene not with the coffee and sweetbread, but with Morten stomping in on Inger looking heavenward and praying, unaware that he has entered the room. The scene in the film differs only slightly from Dreyer's shooting script, which read at this point:

The living room at Borgensgård. Enter Inger with the coffee pot, which she puts on the table. She is not ready for the encounter with her father-in-law. She sits down in the middle of the room and looks up at the ceiling.
INGER: Dear God, please help me today also.
Old Borgen enters the room from his bedroom. He is carrying a pair of boots in his hand and is in his stocking feet, so that Inger doesn't hear him. Borgen approaches her and follows the direction of her eyes.

BORGEN: It's because the rain has been coming through the roof.

INGER: Oh, it's you, Grandfather? You gave me quite a fright.

BORGEN: I did what?

INGER: What were you saying?

BORGEN: I said the damp patch up there was rainwater. The roof's leaking.

INGER: Well I never – so it is.

It is typical of the density of Dreyer's presentation, that this ten-second interchange indicates at least three different things about the two participants: In the first place, it demonstrates Inger's prayerful spirituality. In the second, even more pointedly, it shows us how Inger's prayerfulness is not a turn away from her practical domestic responsibilities and functions, but is expressed in terms of the most prosaic aspects of her life. (On the one hand, we see that her prayer is put in the service of the most ordinary fence-mending between father and son; and on the other, we realize that the coffee pot and biscuits are as much an expression of Inger's prayerfulness as her actual prayer.) And in the third place, in the touching comicality of old Morten's misunderstanding of her glance, the brief interchange demonstrates how far the demoralized old man is from Inger's state of practical prayerfulness. At this point in his life, for Morten, looking up only means there is a leak in the roof.

In the remainder of the scene, Inger goes on to serve

Morten the coffee and biscuits she has made, to hand him his pipe (which she has thoughtfully filled in advance with tobacco), and to engage him in a gentle, playful, occasionally rallying conversation about his notions of life and love, as a prelude to making her case on behalf of Anders. In short, Dreyer wants us to appreciate the practicality of this saintly woman. He wants us to appreciate not her exalted dreams and ideals as ends in themselves, but the extraordinary social sensitivity, tact, and adroitness she exercises to realize them.

In the scene that follows, Inger alternately teases Morten, lectures him, chides him, criticizes him, and plays with him in what can only be called a supreme display of love not as an abstract emotion, but as a practical principle of social interaction. Verbally, she is a mistress of delicate tonal inflections. Both physically and expressively, she dances circles around the dejected old man as she begs, cajoles, argues, and pleads with him to drop his objections to Anders' union with Anne. I use the metaphor of dancing not only abstractly, but as an expression of Inger's actual physical movements around Morten.[4] She lithely moves toward, away from, and around him in the space of the dining room, maintaining imaginative contact with him, momentarily losing it

4 In this respect, *Ordet* is more than vaguely reminiscent of *Day of Wrath* – with its attention to the physical choreography of the relationship of characters. Inger functions as a domesticated version of Anne Pedersdotter, as if Anne could actually live the fantasy of motherhood and familial community that she only dreams about in *Day of Wrath*.

188

more than once (as he rebuffs her approaches, rudely cuts her off short, turns or walks away from her), and then sensitively reestablishing it.

Like most of Dreyer's major films, *Ordet* was based upon a preexisting dramatic work: in this case, a play of the same title by Kaj Munk. However, Dreyer's transformation of Inger into the central character in his film indicates how completely he has rethought Munk's play. In the play, the deranged brother Johannes was a more important figure than Inger. Moreover, Johannes was taken far more seriously by Munk than he is by Dreyer. Munk intended that a member of the audience take Johannes's railings about materialism and irreligiousness in the contemporary world quite straight, whereas Dreyer wants us to have a much more complex attitude toward his Johannes.

Dreyer's Johannes is a limited and problematic figure. He is hard to get a fix on: one can't really endorse much of what he says, yet one can't entirely dismiss him either. At times, like Munk's figure, he seems meant to be taken very seriously; but at other times Dreyer's Johannes seems quite pathetic and childishly ridiculous. Even when Dreyer seems to want us to take Johannes's words seriously, he gives him gestures and stances that undermine them. Indeed, as Dreyer directs Preben Lerdorff Rye in the part, Johannes's antics as a religious fanatic are made to seem almost comical at moments, without, at the same time, ever quite being ridiculed.

Precisely because Dreyer's Johannes is so strange and

eccentric, unlike Munk's beatific, otherworldly hero, he has given no end of problems to critics approaching *Ordet*. Like Johannes's own father and brothers, many critics don't seem to know whether to laugh or cry when they see him – don't know whether Dreyer wants them to mock him or to sympathize with him. Many get quite impatient with his crazy behavior, and more than one writer has suggested that the whole movie would be much better without Johannes in it at all.[5]

How then does one deal with Johannes? Is Dreyer endorsing his statements or jeering at them? I think the way to handle the complexity of feelings that *Ordet* creates about Johannes is to realize, in the first place, that one can't judge Johannes as if he were in another Dreyer movie (in which he might be taken much more seriously and simply). In a film like *Joan of Arc*, Johannes's biblical quotations, his trancelike homilies about the hazards of materialism, and his rants about how spirituality is being lost sight of in contemporary life would deserve to be taken as seriously as Joan herself is. However, the farmhouse setting and family drama events of *Ordet* establish an entirely different expressive universe from that of *Joan of Arc*, a rhetorical universe in which expression is asked to be practical and pragmatic, as Johannes's ravings assuredly are not.

The shorthand name of the narrative difference is of course Inger. Once one thoroughly understands Inger's

5 See, for example: Tom Milne, *The Cinema of Carl Dreyer* (New York: A. S. Barnes, 1971), 162–164.

narrative function in *Ordet* (and Dreyer's purposes in promoting Inger over Johannes in his reimagining of the play), one can appreciate both Johannes's strengths and weaknesses. His strengths (the qualities he has in common with Inger) are his spiritual commitments; his weaknesses (the ways in which he differs from her) are his utter inability to express himself and his beliefs and feelings in a way that can make them matter within this family.

In short, Dreyer includes Johannes in the film, and at certain moments makes him silly almost to the point of ridiculousness, precisely to indicate the consequences of a state of spirituality cut off from the practical, social forms of expression that Inger embodies. The pairing of Johannes with Inger indicates that visionary purity is the same thing as visionary impotence. For all of his holy sentiments and pious pronouncements, Johannes is powerless and irrelevant to the family around the edges of which he moves. That is why Johannes is ultimately not a means of enlightenment, but only a cause of suffering to it. In the contrast with Inger, Johannes makes us all the more aware of the importance of the engagement with concrete forms of expression and interaction represented by Inger's pragmatic prayerfulness.[6]

6 There is every reason to assume that Dreyer endorsed many of Johannes's pronouncements about the evils of worldliness. Dreyer's own critical statements about the limitations of realism in film and other arts are at times not very different from Johannes's pronouncements about the limitation of lives that are, as it were, governed by realist assumptions

All of *Ordet* tells us that, for Dreyer, beliefs are not sufficient when they are merely abstract. They must be practically expressed. Love is not merely a matter of exalted sentiments and biblical quotations (which is what it is for Johannes), but, as Inger shows us, is a force that can reach the lives of others through particular acts of charity. That contrast is established by means of the juxtaposition of Johannes and Inger – the abstract and abstracted prophet of biblical truths, on the one side, and the homemaker, mother, and provider for others of such mundane things as biscuits, handkerchiefs, and jackets, on the other. If Johannes shows us grace or enlightenment cut off from social interaction and ordinary expression, he makes us all the more aware of the distinctiveness of Inger's expressions of grace and love in the forms of the world and within the relationships of an actual family.[7]

of significance. But what Dreyer does not endorse is the expressive *form* of Johannes's pronouncements. Johannes represents a state of abstraction that has renounced practical expression, while Dreyer embraces abstraction that vigorously engages itself with practical expression.

The difference between Johannes and Inger metaphorically figures the aesthetic difference between making purely abstract and idealistic films (Johannes), and making films that express their abstraction and idealism *in terms of* practical expressive realities (Inger). In the difference between the two characters, and specifically in his endorsement of Inger's position, Dreyer is making a statement about his own decision to make transcendental films that are simultaneously committed to negotiating the obstacles of realistic expression in the same way that Inger is.

7 Though there is no space to go into it in detail, I would mention that Dreyer dramatizes the gap between abstract religious faith and practical

There is one more thing to say about Johannes before
leaving him, however, and that is that the critical debates
he has generated are significant. The confusion of feeling that Johannes generates about to what extent his
idealism is impractical, and therefore not to be taken
entirely seriously, and to what extent it is, impractical or
not, spiritually noble and enlightened represents a confusion of feeling built into *Ordet* itself. But it is a confusion that – far from muddling the film – empowers it.
Even as Dreyer wants to indicate Johannes's general
expressive inadequacy and to use Inger as a foil to him in
the ways I have already suggested, I believe that he himself remains to some extent uncertain about Johannes. In
short, Johannes summarizes an empowering ambivalence about the relation of abstract ideals and practical
expressions that is present in all Dreyer's important
work. One can say without irony that *Ordet* is the product of Dreyer's willingness to admit his confusion, rather
than to resolve it too easily. Kaj Munk was not confused
about his Johannes, and the greatness of Dreyer's film is
a result of his willingness to be uncertain about the
relation of souls and bodies, of spiritual and practical

expression in another way in *Ordet:* through the differences that arise
between Morten Borgen and his neighbor Peter Petersen, Anne's father.
Each one behaves uncharitably toward the other in his practical relations,
all the while professing his abstract, Christian charity toward him. This
theme is also touched on by the passage I quote as the epigraph to this
chapter.

193

matters, of ideals and worldly expressions, in a way Munk was not.[8]

That is why there is no final position on the relation of ideals and realities that can merely be read out of Dreyer's films. Dreyer was committed both to the authority of the imagination, and to the necessity of its translation into worldly expressions. He was never able simply to resolve the uneasy relation of the two impulses in his work. *Ordet* and his other mature works suspend themselves within the unstable mix of unresolved feelings that I am describing, in order the better to explore them. Dare one take Joan of Arc's spiritual absolutism completely seriously? What would the world be like if we actually tried to live that idealistically, that absolutely and unappeasably? To the benefit of all of his work, that was the question Dreyer never finally answered – though *Gertrud* might be taken as one attempt to answer it.[9]

As the preceding should suggest, *Ordet* is no more a

8 Note that Dreyer's confusions tellingly operate only in one direction: He may have doubts about the efficacy of the spirit in the world, but he has none about the sufficiency of worldly values as ends in themselves. In *Ordet* the figure of the doctor (and to a lesser degree, the figure of the minister) represent direct criticisms of materialism or naturalism divorced from spiritual commitments, and Dreyer wants us to have very unambivalent feelings about them.

9 The ending of *Ordet* will revive the question again. It is not for nothing that Inger and Johannes come together narratively in the final scene, or that, in the final section of the film, Inger and Johannes trade narrative places, without one being preferred to the other.

mere character drama than *Day of Wrath* was. Inger, Johannes, and the others (like Anne, Marte, and the others in *Day of Wrath*) are figurations of alternative expressive styles that extend beyond the individual characters. They embody those larger styles and have no identity apart from them; their personal expressive styles overlap with them; and our deepest understanding of them is conditioned by those styles.

An account of *Ordet* in terms of individual characters is fundamentally misleading for another reason as well: more than any of Dreyer's other works, the film is, ultimately, less interested in individuals than in relationships (or, to put it more precisely, is interested in individuals only insofar as they enter or fail to enter into imaginative relationships with each other). In place of the individual as the fundamental unit of representation (as he or she exists in the ordinary Hollywood movie, for example), Dreyer offers the web of relationships between individuals. *Ordet* is a radical experiment in re-representation. The individual actor is dethroned and replaced by the relationship as the fundamental unit of experience.

It is impossible not to be struck by the difference between the framing, camera movements, editing patterns, blocking, and pacing of *Ordet* and those of the typical Hollywood movie. *Ordet* lacks the orthodox establishing shots, the brisk editing rhythms, the alternation of long shots, medium shots, and close-ups (lacking glamour shot close-ups altogether), and the shot/reverse shot editing of dialogue scenes that have been the backbone of cinematic syntax since the days of Griffith. The photography and editing of the film apparently take a step backward to the time before Griffith when stage plays were filmed from the audience side of the proscenium arch in static or slowly panning middle-distance shots, though, needless to say, *Ordet* only appears to be primitive. It is, in fact, a breakthrough into a new form of representation, and by virtue of that, a daring criticism of the adequacy of orthodox Hollywood cinematic representation – a criticism contemporary film has yet fully to profit by. The work of Antonioni, Godard, Sautet, Tanner, and Cassavetes, following in Dreyer's footsteps in the thirty years subsequent to *Ordet*, has not yet exhausted the possibilities opened up by it.[10]

Dreyer avoids cutting his scenes and the interactions of his characters into bite-sized bits and pieces of glances, encounters, and lines of dialogue, as studio photographic and editing practice almost invariably does. In abandon-

10 On the subject of John Cassavetes' related experiments in reimagining representation by situating the individual in a matrix of influences and relationships that he or she is unable to rise above, see my *American Dreaming* (Berkeley: University of California Press, 1985), 96–98, 101–118, 129–132, 196–199, 202–206, and 263–264. It is not without significance that Cassavetes viewed both *Ordet* and the world première of *Gertrud* immediately before he began *Faces*, his first major film.

For examples of how even some classic Hollywood films manage to break away from the elevation of the individual above the social matrix in which he or she exists, see my *American Vision* (New York: Cambridge University Press, 1986), 114–130, 137–147, 259–263, 273–281, and 455–463.

ing the traditional Hollywood syntax of intercut close-ups of talking heads and point-of-view editing conventions, *Ordet* restores the represented world of its characters to a spatial wholeness, interactional seamlessness, and social complexity that Hollywood films abrogate. For much of *Ordet*, the world is viewed in long takes in which a slowly tracking or panning camera, almost always in middle distance, moves from one person or group of persons to another, from one part of a room of the Borgensgård farmhouse to another, from characters on one side of the set to the other.

David Bordwell has calculated that the average shot in the important central scenes of *Ordet* runs over a minute and a half in length, with some shots running from two to seven minutes.[11] That is unprecedented in mainstream studio films, except for special cases like Hitchcock's disastrous *Rope*, which only indicated Hitchcock's inability to employ the long take as anything but an exercise in sterile technical virtuosity. As the example of *Rope* resoundingly proves, the value of such camera work doesn't reside in the mere length of the shots or the intricacy of the camera's movements from character to character. Dreyer justifies his use of the long take and the extended traveling shot insofar as he employs them to suggest complex networks of interdependence between his figures. (It is the absence of complex social

11 David Bordwell, *The Films of Carl-Theodor Dreyer* (Berkeley: University of California Press, 1981), 151.

relationships and emotional involvements in Hitchcock's film that makes his camera work so trivial, that makes it seem so much a merely technical achievement, in comparison.)

Few directors are more opposed to the Hollywood world view in which the narrative, photography, and editing combine to draw ever tighter circles around a central group of characters, to focus more and more narrowly on an ever smaller group, eventually to limit its interest more or less entirely to the isolated consciousness of one or two central figures.[12] Rather than being isolated and excerpted, characters' words and actions are socially, temporally, and spatially contextualized in *Ordet*. Where traditional cinematic practice would contract it, Dreyer's photography and editing forcibly enlarge the context around an event. Instead of moving in on a character or an interaction between a few characters in ever-tighter narrative focuses and progressively more isolating shots, Dreyer proceeds in the opposite direction. He repeat-

12 The typical Hollywood film does this both technically and narratively: both my means of the point-of-view editing convention – which almost invariably proceeds from longer shots to closer ones, and from impersonal points of view to personal ones – as well as by means of the arrangement of its narrative itself, which in the course of a film tends to focus increasingly on the experience and consciousness of one or two isolated characters as the center of interest. The progress of shots from far to near, from large to small, the visual progression of the "establishing shots" that begin most scenes, is enacted dramatically in most films' narratives.

edly moves away from so-called centers of action to peripheries. He spirals out away from central positions and actions to establish controlling contexts impinging on an event. The simplifying centripetal impulse we are accustomed to in most films is replaced by a complicating centrifugal one.

It is no accident that the traditional Hollywood production is identified in the popular mind with the figure of the "star" who is featured most prominently in it. With its elevation of the autonomous, isolated consciousness, the Hollywood film of the thirties, forties, and fifties represented the final flowering of late-nineteenth-century Romanticism. The sentimental, Tennysonian cult of sensibility that imagined the individual poetically swooning and suffering alone was resurrected in the Hollywood star. The Hollywood film represents a structure of meanings and relationships designed to justify and perpetuate the ego's luxurious alienation.

The Hollywood tendency to focus on one or two priviledged points of view (as embodied technically in the use of shot/reverse shot editing patterns and, more generally, in the point-of-view editing convention itself) is replaced in Dreyer's work by a recognition of the irreducible multiplicity of actors and positions to be accounted for at any moment. The other sort of film soulfully elevates the consciousness of one or two characters above others and, with the glamour close-up in particular, encourages a fundamentally sentimental relationship

between the viewer and that consciousness, a relationship in which the viewer projects into it certain reductive fantasies. That is what Dreyer rejects.[13]
Where Hollywood's fixed framing and point-of-view

13 *The Passion of Joan of Arc* might seem to be an exception to this generalization. Certainly, much of the cult that has grown up around the
performance of Renée Falconetti seems to sentimentally understand
her performance in ways not entirely different from the ways viewers
understand Garbo or Dietrich in standard Hollywood romantic films –
as isolated individuals whose essence is soulfully representable in close-
ups.

But if we are responding adequately to Dreyer's peculiar placements
and shifts of camera position in various shots of Falconetti, I would
argue that we are forced to assume a much more troubled and uncertain relationship to his heroine than we usually do to Garbo or Dietrich.
The instability of Dreyer's photographic practice puts us in a very
different imaginative relationship to the image than does the standard
glamour close-up. Dreyer photographs sometimes above her, sometimes to one side or the other of her, sometimes below her, but never
dependably from one consistent position or angle. The effect is to
prevent the accumulated shots from stabilizing into any coherent optical
or psychological point of view on her. Joan won't be brought into focus.
She won't be editorially reduced to a fixed point or position. (At the
simplest, that is why a viewer endlessly shuttles between contradictory
hypotheses about Joan: Is she fatuous, inspired, victimized, innocent,
heroic, oppressed? It is impossible to say.)

Working against every simplifying impulse we bring the film, Dreyer's photography and editing prevent Joan from being "read" tenden-
tiously. She stays rich, unfathomable, and mysteriously opaque. We
look at her from different positions; we see her from various sides and
angles; but we can never quite grasp her. We can't quite read her mind
or heart. Her consciousness remains distant and inscrutable. She remains almost as far beyond a viewer as she stays beyond her judges and
accusers.

editing techniques relentlessly simplify situations and interactions, bring events into focus, and elevate one consciousness above others, in *Ordet* Dreyer keeps his characters embedded in complicating contexts of allegiance and responsibility. Specifically, at no point is one of *Ordet's* characters able to excerpt himself or herself from a complex matrix of mutual dependencies and responsibilities long enough to become a "star." Even a single series of intercut close-ups at a climactic moment would be enough to release a character from the web of responsibilities, which is why Dreyer avoids the glamorizing, isolating close-up as assiduously as Hollywood embraces it.

There are, in fact, only three rhetorically freighted close-ups in all of *Ordet*. All three feature Inger, but each, significantly, functions differently from the orthodox Hollywood tight shot. The first, as if actually to advertise its repudiation of the other sort of close-up, is an inverted close-up of Inger's face as she lies on the kitchen table and a Doctor struggles to deliver her child. The second is a shot of her face as she lies in bed following her death during childbirth. And the final one is a shot of her face as she lies in her coffin during the funeral service near the end of the film.

What makes these shots different from the garden-variety Hollywood glamour close-up is not only the inversion of the first one, but the fact that in all three Inger is passive, victimized, or dead. That is to say, she is so far from having her individual consciousness celebrated by each of these moments, that she is in effect photographed at the times at which she has no consciousness.

Even more importantly, in all three scenes, the effect of the shots is the opposite of communicating the swoony romanticism or visionary autonomy of the star. On the contrary, Dreyer's close-ups make us aware of the community of others depending on Inger (and themselves looking at her at such a moment): the doctor and his nurse assisting with her difficult delivery (at the moment of the inverted close-up); Mikkel and Morten looking at her on her deathbed (in the second close-up); the group of family and friends around her coffin after her death (in the third one). Rather than being isolated or alone, Inger is the object of attention of others in these shots. She is an imaginative link that binds them together. She is the imaginative center of a group, not the representative of a state of released subjectivity in the Hollywood way. In short, the close-ups are not exceptions to but extensions of the acts of contextualization of the film that precede and follow them. They generate feelings of complex relatedness.

While Hollywood photography implicitly endorses the cult of the loner, the outcast, and the alien, a typical scene in *Ordet* is constituted out of movements of the camera that relentlessly link and relate individuals. As Dreyer's camera dollies from one part of the small farmhouse set to another, pausing on one figure or group of figures, before moving on, it weaves together the putatively isolated and estranged men of Borgensgård into a

tapestry of continuously larger and more complex relationships and interdependencies. The spatial and temporal connectedness of the shooting and editing of *Ordet*
becomes the visual expression of the psychological and
social relatedness of this closely knit family. The narrative subject of *Ordet* – the complex relations of an
extended family in a confined physical space – goes
hand in glove with its photographic and editorial techniques.

And yet, as I've already suggested, the fact is that
within this network of visual, social, spatial, psychological, and temporal interconnections, the individuals have
drawn apart or lost touch with each other. The blocking
and photography of *Ordet* eloquently communicate the
double dramatic situation: of individuals inescapably involved physically and emotionally with each other's lives
and destinies, and yet at the same time emotionally estranged from one another or attempting to withdraw into
their own private worlds – always with the exception of
Inger, of course. The shifting relations of these figures
(and Inger's negotiations between them) are expressed
in some of the most complex blocking and photography
of mutual movements in all of film. The choreography of
the camera's movements in *Ordet* is at least as complex a
performance on Dreyer's part as the choreography of
the characters' movements.

Consider the scene I have already mentioned, the one
that begins with Inger praying and Morten comically
missing the point and commenting on the leaking roof –

203

the one in which Inger is attempting to bring Morten around to accepting Anders' courtship of the neighbor girl from a family belonging to a rival religious sect. In one long scene, Dreyer shows Morten and Inger approaching each other, separating from each other, moving to different spots in the dining room, and coming back to a common spot or departing from it several different times. The five- or six-minute scene is done in virtually one continuous shot.[14]

The visual choreography of the shifting spatial and temporal maneuverings of Morten and Inger is as complexly expressive as the choreography of the movements of two figures in a dance work. Dreyer creates an awareness of space and time unlike anything in a more conventionally edited film, which, in cutting experience into bits and pieces (shots and reverse shots organized around personal points of view) and forcing characters to interact within the reductive "space" of the one-, two-, or three-shot frame composition and the "time" of the editing rhythms of the film, destroys the felt presence of space and time in the other sense of the words.

Sometimes, as in the spatial negotiations taking place during the encounter between Inger and Morten, it is the actual space – the real distance between or proximity

14 To be strictly accurate, the shot is briefly punctuated by two other inserted shots: one showing a view of the minister outside when Inger glances out the window at one point, and another showing the entry of Johannes through a door on the far wall of the room in which Inger and Morten talk.

of two figures – that counts in Dreyer's framing and photography; at other times, Dreyer uses the abstract shape and formal boundaries of the frame itself to suggest emotional intimacies or separations between figures. As an example of both uses of space, Johannes's emotional and psychological peripherality in the Borgen family is indicated both by his visual placement on the edge of the frame and by his physical placement outside of the main family group and his sliding, sideways movements along the edges of the set.[15] In the scene I have just described in which Inger and Morten are talking, Johannes comes into the room at one point, and Dreyer uses both the physical space of the set and the formal space of the frame to express the emotional chasm that yawns between father and son. Dreyer photographs Johannes at the extreme right edge of the shot, and then shows Johannes drifting offscreen to the right at exactly the moment that Morten, coming into the shot from the left, attempts to approach him. The father tentatively and unsuccessfully reaches out to his son, moving into the frame space at exactly the moment Johannes retreats from human touch and intimacy in the depths of his madness, by moving out of it. The depiction of their estrangement could not be more powerful.

Some of the most complex visual choreography in all of Dreyer's work comes in the first two scenes of *Ordet.*

15 The spatial marginality of *Day of Wrath*'s Anne anticipates that of Johannes in this respect.

(The initial scene involves the family's discovery in the wee hours of the night that Johannes has wandered off into the fields while they were asleep. The second scene comprises the brief conversation the brothers and their father have in the parlor after Johannes has been returned home, but before they themselves have gone back to bed.) Since they are so important in establishing the basic dramatic and visual texture of *Ordet*, I want to describe them in considerable detail.

The first scene is basically assembled from three extremely protracted shots.[16] The first shot is a slow, combination panning and tracking movement that runs for about a minute. It begins with a view from within Anders and Johannes's bedroom of the youngest brother, Anders, stirring in his sleep and sitting up in bed, pans right to reveal the empty bed of Johannes, and then pans back left again to Anders' bed to show him getting up and looking out the window next to his bed. After a brief

16 Not counting two left to right panning shots of the grounds and buildings of Borgensgård averaging about fifteen seconds each that accompany the title cards of the film, these first three shots of *Ordet* run for something like four minutes of screen time. (The first shot is about a minute in duration; the second is again about a minute long; and the third is roughly two or three minutes in length.)

To be strictly accurate, I should add that each of the three extended shots is punctuated by a brief interpolated shot of an exterior scene (which I will mention as it occurs), but the interruptions are so brief that the effect of the three extended shots is not disturbed, especially since as soon as each inserted shot concludes, the shot into which it is interpolated continues exactly where it left off, with the same camera setup and uninterrupted movement of the characters.

interpolating external shot that presumably shows Anders' point of view as he looks out the window and sees Johannes wandering off into the fields in the middle of the night, the remainder of the scene consists of two virtually uninterrupted shots, each more than a minute in length.

In the second shot of the first scene, Dreyer places the camera out in the room in which most of the rest of the film takes place, the large farmhouse parlor that each of the bedrooms at Borgensgård adjoin. To knit the shot to the preceding one and to maintain as much as possible the illusion of a seamless, continuous space and time within which the subsequent interactions will take place (almost creating the effect that there has been no change of camera position at all, and that we are seeing one continuous four or five minute shot in which the camera has merely dollied back from its previous position), Dreyer begins with a view from the parlor looking into Anders' room as he now gets out of bed and prepares to fetch Johannes. (The camera has, in effect, only moved a few feet backward from its initial position.)

As Anders comes out of his room toward the camera, the camera follows him – tracking from right to left in synchronization with his motion as he proceeds in that direction along the far wall of the parlor and goes into old Morten Borgen's bedroom to wake him up. We watch him rouse Morten, not by a change of camera placement (as would be the Hollywood method), but by looking in from our position in the parlor through the now open door of Morten's room. Then, without an interruption, as Anders comes out of Morten's room and continues walking in a leftward direction, the camera continues to pan and track left with him as he then leaves the house through a doorway that is now revealed by the leftward moving edge of the frame to the left of Morten's room.

Then, in this film of extended camera movements and complex visual choreography, without interruption of the shot, an even more astonishing visual event occurs. Though no one is now visible in the space of the frame (since Anders has just gone outside and old Morten is still in his bedroom preparing to go out), the leftward camera movement continues. The camera continues panning without breaking its stride, now moving through empty space under its own momentum, as it were. It continues moving along the wall to reveal another bedroom door that a viewer did not know was there. It arrives at the door and pauses there at the precise moment that Inger (presumably having been awakened by hearing Anders getting up) opens it and steps out into the parlor to see what is happening. That concludes the second shot. (See the illustration on page 225.)

For the second time, a brief interpolated exterior shot allows Dreyer to slightly change his camera position for the third and concluding camera setup. (I would note again, as in the preceding shot change, that the closeness of this initial placement of the third shot to the final position of the second shot is enough almost to convince a viewer that there has been no change of camera position at all, and no interruption in the shot itself.)

The third extended shot begins looking into Inger's and Mikkel's bedroom from the parlor, as she and the awakened Mikkel talk about Johannes, and Mikkel prepares to join his father and brothers to search for him. Dreyer pans from left to right to follow Inger's movements as she moves toward the foot of the bed to speak with Mikkel. Then the camera pans from right to left as Inger goes to the window to watch Anders and then Morten heading out to the moon-lighted fields. (This is the point at which the third brief, exterior point-of-view shot is inserted.) Then the camera (resuming the shot from the same location) tracks back slightly to include Mikkel in the shot with Inger, as he now gets out of bed to go out in search of Johannes.

Disregarding the three inserted exterior shots, Dreyer has audaciously assembled the first four or so minutes of his film out of what are, in effect, three long takes. With the exception of speciality pieces like Hitchcock's *Rope*, one can say with some assurance that this is an opening without precedent in film.

I want to comment in some detail on the visual choreography in this first scene, but before doing that I want to describe the camera movements in one more scene in some detail, if only to emphasize that these stunningly long takes occur more than once in *Ordet*.

The second scene I want to discuss occurs shortly after the one I've just described.[17] Once Johannes has been found and shepherded back home, the Borgen family gather together in the dining room of the farmhouse before going back to their beds. At this point, Dreyer executes a single, stunningly extended shot arguably even more involved than any of those in the opening scene.

As the scene begins, the camera is set up in the parlor or main room of the farmhouse, looking toward and to the left of the dinner table (around which many of the groupings of characters will take place in the rest of the film). The following is a description of what we see in terms of the movements of characters and the camera:

As old Morten Borgen walks into the frame toward the parlor table, moving from left to right in the room, the camera moves with him in a following panning movement from left to right. As it pans with Morten it gradually includes Inger who stands to the right of the table. (She has apparently just set it for the returning men). So far the relation of actors and camera movements seems not entirely unlike what one might encounter in any other film. Then things become stranger.

As I mentioned, the camera has by this point gradually

---

17 The only scene I'm passing over is the one in which Johannes is discovered by Anders, Mikkel, and Morten preaching out on the hillside, which is itself built out of a series of extended shots that are just as interesting and complex as the preceding interior shots.

moved into a position to be able to include both Morten and Inger in the same shot. But, no sooner having managed to take Inger in, the camera surprisingly lets her drop out of the shot and chooses to follow Morten as he passes by her in the room. That is the first point of strangeness in the shot: Rather than progressively including figures (as one might reasonably expect to happen and as would indeed have happened in almost any other film), the camera has chosen to follow one figure and to pass by another.

But the shot (and the strangeness) doesn't stop with that. After leaving Inger behind, and following Morten alone in its movement to the right, a few seconds later, the camera then leaves him behind also. It continues moving through empty space in its slow rightward trajectory across the room with no one now visible in the frame. The camera then bizarrely hovers in front of a doorway with an open door on the right side of the room. It is as if it had a mind of its own, and furthermore as if it knew that someone would be coming through that door. This uncanny movement corresponds to, and is as distinctive as, the one I have already described in the first scene, in which, after Anders leaves the parlor to search for Johannes, the leftward panning movement continues with no one visible in the shot, until it discovers Inger at the exact instant she opens the door of her bedroom.

Consequently, one should not be completely surprised that, only an instant after the camera pauses at the

doorway, Johannes comes through it. As he then proceeds to walk to the right, goes on to light two candles
sitting on a sideboard along the right wall of the room,
and carries the candles further to the right to place them
in a window, the camera movement follows Johannes,
perfectly synchronized in its pacing with him. (As he
pauses in his own movements to stop and light the candles, the pan pauses. As he picks up the now lighted
candles and carries them still further to the right in the
room, the pan resumes its following movement.) The
movements are so delicately synchronized that it is as if
the eye of the camera were not only infinitely attentive
and patient, but could actually read and react to his
mind and movements even before he knew them himself.

Though Morten is invisible and entirely outside of the
space of the frame at this point (since the camera has
long ago continued on its path away from its view of his
place beside the table to pan to the right side of the
room), we now hear him asking Johannes what he is
doing. As Johannes puts the candles down on a window
sill on the far right side of the room, the shot stays with
him. We next hear Mikkel's voice on the sound track
asking him what he is doing, though just as with Morten,
we can't see Mikkel. We now watch Johannes turn back
to the left and walk off in the direction he came from, as
the camera follows him, reversing its direction and panning now from right to left. Still the uninterrupted shot
continues. At that moment, another uncanny and unex-

pected camera movement occurs. As Johannes walks leftward and exits the room, after following him to the door, the camera then reverses its direction, now panning back where it came from, moving from left to right, with no one visible in the frame for the second time in the shot. Traveling through empty space, it returns to the lighted candles that Johannes left burning on the window sill. At the precise moment that it reaches the window, Inger walks in, unannounced and unexpected, from the right side of the frame to extinguish them. The effect is just as striking as when the camera previously twice before "discovered" a character at the moment the character entered the shot. (See illustration page 236.)

Now that Johannes has left the shot and the room, Inger becomes the focus of attention for the camera's next movements (which, I would emphasize, are still continuing in the same uninterrupted shot). As she walks left, blowing out the candles and replacing them on the sideboard, the camera follows her in a leftward panning movement, first to the sideboard, but then continuing further left, as she returns to the parlor table where the shot began. The shot continues to follow her as, in a fluid continuation of its and her own movements to the left, passing the sideboard to the right of the table, Inger picks up the coffee pot and moves leftward with it, rejoining Morten and Mikkel, who are sitting together at the table on the left side of the room and gradually come into the frame, and pours coffee for them at the table. Dreyer's shot is now in its third or fourth minute uninterrupted by cuts. At this point, the camera temporarily pauses in its movements to hold Mikkel and Morten together in view at the table. (The men, weary with having chased Johannes across the heath in the middle of the night and generally discouraged by his condition, talk about his mental illness and their own state of demoralization.) Within this shot, which is now relatively (but not completely) static for the rest of the scene, Anders momentarily steps into the frame at the left of the table and then exits out of the shot from the same side. After serving coffee to Mikkel and Morten, who sit talking, Inger, having as it were led the shot to the table, now moves out of the frame to the right.

The shot is then slightly readjusted to the right as Mikkel gets up from his seat and moves to sit on a window ledge just to the right of the table. It is then again slightly readjusted to the left as Mikkel bids good night to Morten and crosses in front of the table from right to left (passing directly in front of the camera and between it and Morten) and leaves the frame. At this point Anders again briefly moves back into the adjusted frame from the left to say good night to his father and then exits on the left again.

Since his sons have all gone off to bed, Morten is now alone. Dreyer holds the camera immobile on him for the rest of the scene. He is only alone for a moment, however, as his daughter-in-law now moves back into the shot from the right edge of the frame to try to comfort and console the demoralized old man. Their conversation goes on another couple of minutes, before Inger too exits with her "Good night, Fa-Fa" by crossing in the foreground of the shot from right to left and out of the frame to leave the solitary Morten Borgen finally alone with his thoughts. With that, one of the most audacious cinematic experiments in shot composition in the history of film comes to a conclusion.

That is a fairly dry, mechanical description of the blocking and camera movements in two early scenes from *Ordet*. I have described them in such detail in order to indicate the care that obviously went into the visual choreography of the film. But with his interests so firmly grounded in the human situations and emotions of his characters, Dreyer would be the first to scoff at photographic virtuosity as an end in itself. Dreyer's formal arrangements are always in the service of more than formal concerns.

Dreyer's camera work and editing are telling us a number of things in both of the shot sequences I have described. In the first place, even before we know the names of these individual characters (and these scenes occur so early in the film that a viewer may well still be unsure of who is who in them), the photography and the setting impress on us the sheer density of their involvement with and interdependence on each other. If this is true of both of the scenes I have described, it is especially obvious in the first one. There, in the first minutes of the film, we have little or no idea where the scene takes place, and utterly no information about the individual characters we see in it.

The network of relationships is almost more real than the individuals within it (since we don't even know their names at this point). The device of having the action take place in adjoining bedrooms situated around a common farmhouse parlor room, and the use of a continuously panning and tracking camera to move fluidly from one doorway to another (as the awareness of Johannes's absence ripples from Anders to Morten to Inger to Mikkel), suggest the inescapable mutual involvements that are the subject of the film more eloquently and succinctly than any amount of narrative exposition could have done. Characters' capacities of movement and relationship *vis-à-vis* each other become the implicit subject of the film.

The photography functions in another way as well: not only does it suggest the intimate, intricate interrelationships of the members of this extended family living together in the confined space of this farmhouse, but also it indicates the terrible separations between them, which are all the more noticeable and painful because of their mutual interdependence and involvement. The separations and estrangements are communicated not only by the way Dreyer's deliberative pans seem to measure virtual continents of space separating individuals (as in the second scene I described, in which the camera seems to take an eternity to get from Morten sitting at the table on one side of the farmhouse parlor to his son Johannes lighting the candles on the other side of the room), but also by the way Dreyer's conscientiously panning and tracking camera and continually repositioned frame space inevitably leave behind certain individuals in moving on to photograph others. (The shot/reverse shot syntax of a conventionally edited Hollywood film doesn't communicate a comparable feeling of exclusion.)

In that second scene, when we hear first Morten's and then Mikkel's voice calling to Johannes from the other side of the room but are unable to see either of them in the space of the frame (which has moved from their position at the table to his near the window), Dreyer has summarized the gulf that separates members of this family. Mikkel and Morten can "reach" Johannes emotionally and personally no more than their voices can penetrate his clouded intellect. No matter how tight their little family circle and how confined their farmhouse parlor, the photography makes us aware of the looming separations.

The general absence of eye contact between Morten Borgen and his three sons is a further indication of the disturbing distances between the characters. A character's physical or meditative turn out of society, as represented in a turn of the head or angling of the body, or general declining of social contact with others for the sake of cultivating an imaginatively enriched relationship to experience, is a frequent occurrence in a Dreyer film, and it has a complex significance in all of his work. It often indeed signals a positive state of affairs. At crucial moments, Joan, Anne, and (in the film following *Ordet*) Gertrud each turn (both physically and imaginatively) out of social realms of representation and interaction to entertain less limiting, imaginatively more expansive relations to their surroundings. Dreyer frequently encourages such a meditative turn on the part of both his characters and his audience. His cinematic enterprise might be said to be, in large part, an effort to legitimize such turns away from social values and interactions in order to enrich one's imaginative relationship with experience.

Yet such a turn out of the social realm has obvious negative connotations for Dreyer as well insofar as, especially in his sound work, he asks that the individual ultimately translate his or her imagination into a social form of expression. In the dense social fabric and elaborate matrix of interdependencies established by the long-take photography and the confined physical and familial setting of *Ordet*, even more than in any of Dreyer's other films, such an imaginative withdrawal into a private, incommunicable state of consciousness is troubling. At moments Morten's expressive estrangement from the family verges on being as extreme and damaging as Johannes's. To withdraw into a private state of feeling and awareness as the head of an extended family, as Morten does, is an obviously different matter from doing it in front of a hostile or indifferent tribunal, as Joan does.[18]

But I have yet to deal with the most uncanny and astonishing photographic events in *Ordet:* the times during which the camera seems to pan or track through empty space with no one visible in the frame. At such moments it is as if it were moving under its own volition and searching out events and relationships to scrutinize independently of the movements, the presence, or even the awareness of characters in the frame or the room.

A variation of this same event in *Ordet* is the way even fairly conventional camera movements are not made a function of the point-of-view editing convention. (That is to say: camera movements are not psychologically "motivated" or "justified" by having a character "look" or "think" them into existence.) For instance, the two protracted left to right pans during the title sequence of the film are unassigned to any character's (or any conceivable observer's) point of view. Even more strikingly, following these shots, at the beginning of the first scene of the actual film, in the pans that move between Anders' and Johannes's beds, Dreyer virtually flaunts his abrogation of the point-of-view editing convention by

18 Precisely because of its "family film" status, none of Dreyer's works more powerfully dramatizes the conflict between imaginative and social values than *Ordet*, or is more divided in its allegiance to the two realms of value. But far from being a fault, that is why *Ordet* is Dreyer's most interesting work.

moving the camera in one direction while he shows Anders looking or moving in another. In Anders' bedroom
scene specifically, at the moment at which the camera
moves in the direction of Johannes's bed, it is clear that
Anders is looking another way.

The decoupling of the movement or direction of the
camera from the point of view of any particular individual suggests the way individuals in this film fail to see
(and therefore fail to live) possibilities of connection or
relationship. It is as if they lagged behind the camera in
awareness or sensitivity about their own lives and relationships. The vision of the camera is, indeed, the only
thing uniting them, in the absence of the existence of
actual social or psychological connections to link them.

The point-of-view shot convention in a Hollywood
movie communicates almost exactly the opposite of this.
It implies, in the first place, that the available points of
view of individual participants in a scene are ultimately
sufficient for a complete understanding of it. And it
implies, in the second place, that there can be one or two
"best" or "right" views of a scene (usually assembled
from some combination of the points of view of the
major actors in it). In short, the point-of-view editing
convention implies that "truth" resides in an available
combination of individual views, while Dreyer's explora-
tory pans and probing tracking movements in *Ordet* tell
us almost the opposite. They suggest that no observer
actually present in the scene can necessarily provide an
"ideally correct" (or even a more than marginally ade-

quate) view of the possibilities of human relationship in it. They suggest that the available states of human consciousness (embodied in personal points of view) may well be inadequate to fulfill both the abstract requirements of the imagination and the practical requirements of social intercourse. In dislodging the individual consciousness as the central mediator and authoritative presenter of experience, Dreyer's camera movements suggest that there is a problematic relation between personal imagination and expression, whereas the point-of-view editing convention sees no problems at all. The importance of this distinction cannot be overstated. The problematic relation of consciousness and expression takes one to the heart of his work.

An even more emphatic decoupling of Dreyer's shots from point of view editing conventions occurs in the scene that takes place out in the fields (the outdoor scene that occurs between the two scenes I described at length), at the moment in which Morten, Mikkel, and Anders discover Johannes preaching to the empty heath. Dreyer not only denies us a point-of-view shot when we have every reason to believe that we are getting one, but he reverses the relative spatial positions of the characters involved in the shots to doubly repudiate point-of-view editing conventions.

Out in the fields we first see Morten facing the camera and pointing to his left (out of the right side of the frame beyond what we can see) at what we surmise is Johannes. As Morten and the others then walk off toward the right in pursuit of Johannes, Dreyer follows the shot with a shot of Johannes delivering a sermon standing on a hill. Now, based on standard editing conventions we immediately draw two conclusions: First, that the shot of Johannes is a standard point-of-view shot from Morten's and his sons' perspective. A character gesturing and looking in one direction followed by a shot of another character is a standard editing technique for indicating that the second shot registers the point of view of the character or characters in the first shot. Second, again based on standard point-of-view editing conventions (which involve rigorously maintaining the basic right-left spatial relations of groups of characters), we surmise that since Morten gestured to the right side of the frame toward Johannes, Morten and the others are now looking at him from somewhere behind him and outside of the frame space off to the left of him. But we are wrong on both counts. In the first place, our view of Johannes is revealed by a panning movement of the camera (from Johannes to Morten and his sons) to be from a perspective that not they but only the camera possesses. We are looking at Johannes from directly in front; they from off to one side. In the second place, and even more disorientingly, the rightward pan reveals that Morten and his sons are not on the left side of the frame from Johannes (as they were initially), but are off to the extreme right. Within the space of the frame, Dreyer has reversed the right-left positions of Johannes and those who are searching for him.

The result is, at least momentarily, quite a powerful feeling of disorientation. One had assumed not only that Morten, Mikkel, and Anders shared each other's points of view, but that (as in other films) they gently and benignly directed the viewer's own point of view by allowing him or her to see things through their eyes. But as soon as their view is revealed to be partial, and (more importantly) emphatically different from a viewer's own vision of things, it is as if an ontological abyss had opened between the viewer and the characters, and, by implication, between characters' personal perceptions (and expressions) and some other view of truth or reality decoupled from their views.

Figures whom one had assumed to be perfectly reliable in their vision are revealed to be partial, literally off to one side, at an angle – however slight – from the viewer's vision. At the instant that this shot suddenly swerves rightward, against the grain of standard editing, the alert viewer realizes that he or she will have to go it alone for the rest of the film. There will be no character whose view the spectator can merely adopt, as Hollywood film almost always conveniently provides. There will be no cozy personal perspective figured within the film into which the viewer can merely recline. Dreyer will ask us to work, to piece together an adequate view of things. We will not be able merely to inhale the correct, the ideal view through a privileged character's eyes. Experience will not be delivered on such a silver platter. We will have to labor to attain an even provisionally adequate view of things.

But this is probably putting the expressive force of these camera movements and editing techniques too negatively. Dreyer's abrogation of point-of-view conventions demonstrates much more than the partiality or inadequacy of particular personal points of view; it functions movingly in affirmation of values that would otherwise be lost or forgotten: to affirm the possibility of relationships even when they may be almost completely absent in the world of actual observers. His style makes connections between the separated. It visionarily finds or makes relations that the world has given up. It imaginatively knits together what has come socially unraveled.

Dreyer's camera searches out and reveals complications of involvement or feeling of which the characters themselves are frequently unaware – connections that they themselves can't participate in, or that (because they are so painful and troubling) they may prefer to deny or decline. Precisely because connections cannot be made by the characters themselves (or be made through the merging of their points of view with the viewer's), it falls to the camera work and editing to make them instead, so that they are not lost entirely. The camera work and editing tenderly carry the expressive burden of what can't actually be expressed and shared in the actual society of the characters. The camera work and editing lovingly keep alive possibilities that would otherwise not exist.

When, in the scene in which Anders gets out of bed to go out to search for Johannes, the camera uncannily

The goddess of the camera –
Anders goes out to search for
Johannes, the camera continues
moving to the left through empty space, then Inger appears at
the end of the camera's leftward
movement

continues panning left after Anders leaves the parlor,
bizarrely proceeding to move through the room in the
absence of anyone in view, until it arrives at Inger's door
at the moment she opens it, Dreyer's photography is
doing just this. It is telling us of yet another relationship –
of another individual affected by Johannes's wandering
and Anders' pursuit of him, of which neither Johannes
nor Anders is at the moment even aware.

The sliding, probing edges of the slowly moving
frame represent, as it were, the consciousness (and conscience) of an ideal observer, searching out and revealing dependencies and involvements of which the participants themselves may not even be aware. One calls it an
ideal consciousness because the camera represents a
consciousness that no individual is likely to possess: a

consciousness perhaps more sensitive, more aware, more alert than that of any particular character; a consciousness perhaps unobtainable and inexpressible within the practical realities of the world.[19]

The consciousness Dreyer cultivates in a viewer is a very special one – one that deliberately denies us most of the comforts that other films provide. It is a difficult, even an anxious consciousness in many respects – not an easy or relaxed one. The viewer is kept on edge perceptually and psychologically. The moving camera and mobile, endlessly shifting blockings prevent scenes and interactions between characters from being brought into fixed focus, from congealing into static patterns. The moving frame reveals ever-shifting and ever-increasing complexities of context and relationship. Final positions are denied. Ultimate judgments won't be made. The viewer is suspended in a state of endless process, change, and readjustment.[20]

The continual readjustment of camera and character

19 Though there is not space to go into it here, most of what follows could be applied to Dreyer's 1932 *Vampyr* as well; and, in a more general sense, these observations apply to all of Dreyer's major films.
20 It is this state of endless change, renewal, and discovery that Inger represents throughout the narrative in all of her words and actions. It is a state of commitment to process as an end in itself that the final line of *Ordet* also affirms: "Now life begins." For Dreyer, the only adequate ending is inevitably a new beginning. Only in change, revision, exploration of new positions, is there hope. Inger tells us the same thing the camera tells us.

positions is crucial to Dreyer's narrative project. Dreyer prevents relationships of characters with each other as well as relationships of the viewer with the characters from stabilizing. His style forces a viewer to attempt to live in an invigoratingly fluxional state. It forces us to stay absolutely open – to entertain constantly revised hypotheses and visions.

Like a videotape recorder erasing the last used section of a tape as fast as it records new material on it, Dreyer's moving frame is a machine for continuous, energetic acts of imaginative displacement and replacement. (In the very largest sense, it is not too much to say that the challenges and exhilarations of living in this fluxional imaginative state are the subject not only of this film but of all of Dreyer's work.) The trailing edge of Dreyer's frame leaves behind characters, backgrounds, and relationships as fast as the leading edge discovers new entailments, new involvements.

The result in *Ordet* is an adventure of insecurity for the viewer, a voyage of discovery, an extraordinarily heightened sense of living on a narrow margin between two moving edges – literally living on the existential margin between the material being left behind by the trailing edge and the material being revealed to view by the leading edge. What Dreyer asks of us is a continuous responsiveness. Unable to relax our attention, to recline into inherited relationships, fixed positions, or foreseeable destinations, we must stay imaginatively on the move.[21] To say the obvious, *Ordet* is a film about change, growth, and possibility; but the preceding remarks should suggest the extent to which this commitment is embodied in the very style of the camera work and dramatic blocking itself.

The camera's travels represent a commitment to endless exploration and discovery: a commitment to a continuous expansion of perspectives and a widening of horizons. Like the events in the film itself, Dreyer's camera on the *qui vive* embodies a standard of continuously enlarged awareness and sympathy that is meant to remind us of the fallibility and partiality of all fixed points of view, the inadequacy of all "final" understandings. Dreyer tells us that we must stay as mobile and alive to possibility as this moving gaze in order to see the world adequately. We must learn to live in the fluxions of ever-changing spaces and times. We must remain open and ready to be surprised with what the frame will bring into view.

Dreyer imagines life as a fundamental process of change and revision. Yet he also knows that everything in our linguistic and social categories of understanding wars against this conception. Every tendency of the

21 I would remind the reader that, in *Day of Wrath*, that was Anne's challenge to Martin. He indicated his inability to live up to the fluxional possibilities the flickering lights and shadows on her face represented by needing to give desire a destination and to determine where relationships "led", as well as by attempting to "name" and "fix" his relationship with her with moral and theological labels.

characters and the viewers of his film (always excepting Inger) is to fix, to rigidify, to substantiate and maintain abstract positions. The challenge posed by the film is whether even an ideal viewer can succeed in living in the flux in the way the style recommends. Dreyer's attempt to depict states of imaginative energy in motion is his deepest challenge to the conventions of realistic representation which each of us have unconsciously internalized, just as Anne Pedersdotter internalized the very linguistic and moral categories she had seemed to be an exception to. Dreyer's goal is to keep us (and his finest characters) in motion – perceptually and emotionally – against all of the forces arrayed to stop our motion. Only in that state of motion and that openness to emotion are life and growth for Dreyer and his figures.

Insofar as Dreyer's camera represents a point of view with a superior sensitivity and awareness to particular individual characters, we might be tempted to call it the point of view of a god. But that would be a serious misreading of *Ordet,* since the very point of Dreyer's camera is not the godlike omniscience and effortlessness of this process of knowing, but the all-too-human expenditure of energy and effort that it requires. Dreyer's god of the pan and track is more like a careful, at times an even somewhat careworn, man or woman than a supreme deity.

The camera movements in *Ordet* are not masterful and manipulative like Hitchcock's or Kubrick's. The reframings are not tendentious and virtuosic like Welles's or

Altman's. They are diligent and scrupulous. They are slow and ponderous at times. They are hesitant and tentative. They are deliberate and deliberative. They make us aware of the *work* of weaving separated threads together, slowly, conscientiously, diligently. Dreyer's careful camera does not abstractly "know" or "see" relationships, so much as it gradually, haltingly discovers them, meditates on them, slowly maps them out. Above all, Dreyer's camera does not rise above time and space and human particularities, foibles, and missteps like a god, but makes its meanings in time and space and the mess of human events like a human being. Dreyer's camera is a celebration of the virtues of a doggedly human point of view rather than an Olympian one.

The classic Hollywood film (as well as more recent work by filmmakers like Altman or Kubrick or De Palma) comes much closer to offering what might be called a god's-eye-view of things. Even a filmmaker as committed to the maintenance of a point of view as Hitchcock was frequently comes closer to identifying the point of view of camera (and the point of view of his leading character or characters) with that of an ideal, godlike (if sardonic) observer than Dreyer does here.[22]

If we must identify this point of view with that of an actual observer at all, rather than calling it omniscient

---

22 Hitchcock's doctrine that "actors are cattle," like the chilling ironies and black humor of his films themselves, could only have come from a director who, whether he believed in God or not, believed in the possibility of occupying the throne himself.

and godlike, it would be better to call it the view of the merely human artist who made the film, Carl Dreyer – as long as we understand the filmmaker's own point of view on his material not as being absolute and controlling, but rather as being probing, searching, careful. Dreyer builds his meanings, not above and beyond, but relentlessly *within* time and space and particular events, assembled from the particularities of time, space, and particular events. Dreyer functions as an explorer: an explorer of almost unfathomable intricacies of connection. His openness about his own characters and his curiosity about their relations become the standard by which all of the other intelligences in *Ordet* will be implicitly measured.

To express oneself as Dreyer does in *Ordet* – to insist that all important meanings and relationships be worked into existence in the practical forms of space and time – is to express oneself in a fundamentally different way from the way meanings are made in Hitchcock's, Welles's, Kubrick's, Altman's or De Palma's films. Their cinematic meanings and their characters' relationships are rendered entirely more abstractly, more metaphorically, more statically. Dreyer's are teased, prodded, nudged into existence. They are never released from local specifications and constraints.

Though Dreyer's camera represents a standard of awareness that goes beyond any one character's point of view, as I have been suggesting all along, there is one figure who approaches, and at times perhaps equals

Dreyer's camera in sensitivity. When one compares the consciousness of the camera (or the director) in *Ordet* with the consciousnesses of the individual characters, one intelligence is indeed distinguishable from the others.

In the initial scene that I already described, when the camera astonishingly continues on its own after Anders leaves the room to look outdoors for Johannes, it is no accident that the figure it searches out and discovers at the end of its trajectory is Inger, who herself is at that moment opening her bedroom door to discover what has been going on in the parlor while she has been in bed. Nor is it an accident that, in the second shot sequence I described (the one in which Johannes lights two candles and puts them on the window sill on the far right side of the parlor), after a similar self-motivated excursion by the camera to the far right side of the room, Inger is again revealed as being present at the place the camera has arrived at. Even though the last place we saw her was on the opposite side of the room (or, in terms of the formal geography of the frame space, beyond the extreme left edge of the frame), she unexpectedly and almost magically appears, at the end of the camera's rightmost path, entering the frame space from *even further right*, blowing out the lighted candles and restoring them to their original place on the sideboard. She has apparently not only anticipated, but outmaneuvered Dreyer's camera. (See photos on pages 225 and 226).

Dreyer further underlines the unexpectedness and importance of Inger's entry into the frame at this moment by inserting Mikkel's and Morten's voices (calling futilely to Johannes) on the sound track immediately prior to her entrance. The point is that while Mikkel and Morten don't or can't keep up with this camera (or with Johannes, whose movements it has been conscientiously tracking and diligently staying aware of), Inger can. While the weary, discouraged men are still seated at the other side of the parlor, impotent and uncomprehending, trying vocally to reach out to Johannes, but sadly, painfully failing in their effort, Inger, the mistress of lithe, delicate, considerate movements, shows herself fluidly able to join the separated, to bridge the gaps, to hold things together. She connects up with Johannes both visually and emotionally. She literally picks up the pieces of his life and corrects the mess he has made in their lives. In her commitment to endless negotiations, and to establishing relationships where they have lapsed or failed, Inger is as close to embodying an expressive ideal as any character Dreyer ever conceived.

She embodies a sensitivity and awareness almost as great as that of Dreyer's photography and editing. Like his camera work, she represents a power of negotiation between otherwise separated figures, lovingly maintaining or tactfully reestablishing connections where they would break down or be lost or forgotten. Her expressive capacities contrast emphatically with the awkwardness on these well-meaning, but socially reserved and withdrawn farmhands. While Morten and his sons demonstrate their lead-footed fixity and frequently their

233

downright clumsiness in social situations – a clumsiness that Dreyer, a director who is seldom acknowledged to be capable of comedy, sometimes plays for its humor – Inger is a figure of ever subtle movement and delicate lubrication.

Dreyer's work tests the critic's powers of description in a way that filmmakers like Hitchcock seldom do. Insofar as his films make their most important meanings not metaphorically or symbolically, but practically through concrete examples of dramatic performance and utterance, the language of criticism is pushed to its limits to describe the most important events in the films. One must describe how characters walk or talk or use their faces or bodies to express their emotions in Dreyer's work; because such practicalities resist abstract analysis and description, this is much more difficult than describing the sorts of meanings one encounters in the movies of Hitchcock or many other filmmakers, where meanings are usually created less locally, less concretely, less personally and dramatically, and more abstractly and structurally.[23] Dreyer's work takes as its subject practical ex-

23 The difference between how meanings are made in Dreyer's work and how they are made in the other kind of film is of more than technical interest. It represents a difference between a conception of the function of the individual as, on the one hand, a powerful, practical meaning maker (in Dreyer's work), and, as, on the other, a more or less passive receiver of fairly abstract meanings created by the forms and structures of the work itself (in many other films). Notwithstanding all of the abstracting qualities of its style, Dreyer's work measures its most important characters in terms of their ability to perform eminently

pressive events occurring in specific social situations, and such dramatically enacted physical and emotional events are always the most difficult things to describe. The film critic is in a position analogous to that of a dance critic attempting to describe the performance of Patricia McBride in a Balanchine dance – a performance that has no metaphoric meaning or symbolic resonances. (The comparison is apt insofar as Inger's expressive performance in *Ordet* is quite balletic.) The brilliance of the performance comes down to almost intangible aspects of timing, posture, balance, rhythm, and line. It is not communicated abstractly or schematically, outside of the particularities of specific spaces and times.

Inger's expressive performance is enacted in three related ways in *Ordet*, which I want to consider one after the other: she expresses herself in her movements, in her bodily positions and gestures, and with her distinctive repertory of tones of voice and facial expressions – each of which is contrasted with those of the men around her (just as Anne's and Joan's were with the men around them in the earlier films).

To begin with Inger's virtually balletic capacities of movement, *Ordet* is, in effect, a choreographic parable of contrasted capacities of movement that mark the dif-

practical acts of expression; these other filmmakers, by contrast, frequently make no such expressive demands on their characters. In Hitchcock, in particular, to *see* in a certain way is to *know*, and to know is to *be*. The practical social or dramatic expression of what one sees or knows is usually entirely superfluous.

235

Balletic grace of movement and gesture, powers of practical performance – Inger appears at the precise point the camera reaches, puts the candlesticks back in place, and brings coffee to the men at the table

ference between this light-toed dancer and the heavy-footed men around her. The whole of the film is visible in miniature in the differences between the men's ways of walking and hers, just as it is in the difference between the lumbering noises and heavy movements of the farm carts the men use to get from place to place and the grace and poise of her movements when she rolls out dough for their meals or moves around the table to serve coffee to them.

But even beyond the grace and responsiveness of Inger's movements, one needs to focus on the fact of her movement. In a film that is designed to keep the viewer in motion, Inger is a principle of movement as an affirmation of life in itself. In a world of men who sit still and turn their minds, like their bodies, inward to brood on the past, on what might have been, Inger is a figure of endless mobility. She is an opening to possibility, to the future (as her pregnancy tells us also). She is a figure of constant, changing exploration, of loving inclusiveness, of energetic enlargements of attention.

And this leads to the second area of her expressive repertoire: her mastery of gesture. In her mastery of movement through the space of both the set and the frame, Inger negotiates between the separated and estranged; but even when she is sitting still or standing in one place, the particular gestures and postures associated with her are significantly ones of enlargement, inclusion, and embracing. While the men around her hold their arms and hands fixedly at their sides or in front of

237

them, she uses her arms and hands to touch and reach out and draw in (in both the physical and the emotional senses of the words). She extends her arms to touch them, leans toward them with her body, hugs and kisses them, and generally extends herself to them in gestures and postures of love.

Consider the end of the second scene that I described above – the one in which Inger picks up after Johannes when he leaves the candles burning on the window sill. Her movements and timings are nothing less than balletic in their finesse, as after returning the candles to their proper place, and without missing a beat or a step, she fluidly continues on to the other side of the parlor to serve coffee to the weary and demoralized men sitting at the table (a table that, one notes, she has thoughtfully laid out in anticipation of their return).

At the end of the sequence, after the two sons have gone off to bed, Inger is left alone with Morten. It is hard to do justice to the tenderness of Dreyer's depiction of Inger's physical and emotional turn toward Morten at this moment, as she attempts to comfort the discouraged old man. We realize that she must be as tired as he is, and certainly she recognizes the same painful realities of Johannes's condition and his sons' apostasy as Morten does, but what follows is a demonstration of the reach of her love. She moves toward Morten, sits down on the arm of his chair, and tries to console and calm him. But what I would call special attention to is her posture and gestures. As she talks to this sad old man (her father-in-law, whom she understands better than his own sons do, as Inger herself points out to Mikkel at one point), she leans over him and extends her arm behind him in a virtual embrace.[24]

The conversation with Morten that follows is a virtuoso performance of sensitivity and generosity, but, as if there were almost no limit to Inger's acts of inclusiveness, the

24 It is the same gesture that she will employ at the end of the other scene I have described (when she is attempting to persuade Morten to accept the courtship of Anne and Anders), when she goes out to bring Morten his coat after he tramps off in discouragement to watch over the old sow and her new litter in the barn. Inger leans toward Morten and extends her arm toward him in another virtual caress.

I would add parenthetically that, although I treat the subject fairly briefly, one might say much more about the expressive function of hands and arms in *Ordet*. Between old Morten's unsuccessful reaching gestures toward Johannes, the surgical procedures of the doctor's rubber-gloved hands, Inger's acts of reaching, leaning, embracing, and touching, and her little girl Maren's acts of hand-holding and patting, Dreyer expresses a spectrum of human involvements or failures of relationship in terms of the use of characters' hands.

In a more extended consideration of such a subject, one would also want to raise one of the fundamental issues in Dreyer's work, namely: all the ways the experience of his films is *not* contained in the words characters speak to one another. Dreyer's reliance on nonverbal expressive techniques (in this case, his reliance on hands and gestures to "speak" what words won't) represents a statement of the limitations of verbal and social forms of interaction as ways of expressing the self. One's most profound expressions of oneself and of one's relationships with others are forced, as it were, into the subtext of the film, beneath the manifest content, distinct from the lines of dialogue.

 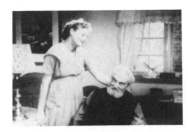

Pulling together, joining what is separated, touching and reaching the discouraged –
Inger imaginatively joining, Morten meditatively withdrawing

next scene shows her back in her bedroom soothing her husband, Mikkel. She touches his arm, then his chin, then strokes his hair, then kisses him and looks deeply into his eyes. (The effect of Inger's eyes is as important as that of her hands and arms in reweaving the unraveled fabric of the family. She reaches out with continuous glances that hold this family together.)

Inger's mastery of verbal tones, in this scene and others, is the third important aspects of her performance (though one that is all too often lost on audiences too busy reading subtitles to allow themselves to hear the tones of voice of the actors in Dreyer's films).[25] Inger uses her voice to move those around her at least as much as she uses her body, arms, or hands. While the men of Borgensgård speak in tones of cynicism or discouragement which draw them apart from each other, Inger's loving voice tones and facial expressions are forms of imaginative generosity and inclusiveness that pull them together. While their voices are manifestations of despair or resignation to forces they feel that they cannot understand or control, as Inger interprets events and characters to each of the others during the film, her voice tones represent forms of enfranchisement and empowerment for herself and others.

More generally, Inger's vocal tones demonstrate that her emotional and imaginative ability to move and to encourage motion in others is at least as great as her gestural and balletic power. Her tones are displays of her ability not to be trapped or limitingly defined by

25 All of Dreyer's films are extremely rich tonally. A non-Danish audience should not allow its attention to the written subtitles of the films to distract it from *listening* to the sounds of the voices in them. If much of the experience of *Ordet* is not to be lost, it is crucial to *listen* to all of the characters, but especially to the tones of both Inger's and Maren's voices in the scenes in which they are present. (Though they may both be translated with the word "father" in the subtitles, there is all the difference in the world between the "Fa-Fa" of Inger and the "Fa" of Morten's sons when they speak to him.)

Gertrud is another work in which tonal meaning is at least as important as semantic (and probably more important than semantic meaning during most of the film).

fixed (and therefore oppressive) attitudes. In Dreyer's cinematic universe, movement is always preferable to stasis, and Inger's voice tones are one of the supreme examples of the power of movement in all of film. With her voice, Inger shows herself able to "play" in the largest imaginative sense of the word. Play is something that Dreyer is not usually acknowledged to be a master of, though we have already seen his use of Anne's playfulness, extravagance, and outrageousness in *Day of Wrath* as a manifestation of her imaginativeness. The men speak largely in monotones that imaginatively figure their fixed positions. But Inger is tonally mercurial, mobile, on the move. The fluidity of her tones is a form of imaginative lubrication. Her playful, teasing tones generate possibilities of imaginative movement. Inger's tonal play thaws frozen positions, lubricates what is stuck. Her loving good humor puts these static men imaginatively into motion. To paraphrase Emerson, she is free and she makes free.

Her tonal powers of movement (and her tonal abilities to stimulate movement in others) are truly impressive: compare the tonal mastery evinced by her various statements about Johannes's madness, Anders' marriage, or Mikkel's atheism. In the largest sense, however, Inger's tonal expressiveness is only a specific manifestation of the general capacities of emotional expressiveness that she displays in the course of the film – from her modesty to her brags, from her daughterly familiarities with her father-in-law to her motherly rebukes of him, from her joking banter to her practical prayerfulness, from her singing to herself to her sighing and crying during labor.[26]

But obviously, in all the preceding, I should have been using the word "Dreyer" everywhere I said "Inger." For there is, of course, no Inger. She is a fiction, an artifact of Dreyer's style. His camera work outdoes even Inger in its power to see and understand and knit together with its movements and observations. His scripting is what gives her her marvelous powers of tonal lubrication and inclusion. Dreyer's tonal shifts, his displays of imaginative mastery and power are even greater than Inger's.[27]

It is not accidental that the functions of "touching" and "reaching" and "moving" (in the imaginative, emotional, and physical senses of the words) are taken over by Inger's young daughter, Maren, at the exact point in

26 The difference between the tonally mercurial Inger and the utterly monotonic Johannes is one more way that Dreyer indicates Johannes's social, imaginative, and expressive limitations. Johannes is tonally much closer to the other Borgens, than he is to Inger.

27 As an example of what this means, one can compare Dreyer's comic capacity to Inger's. Inger delivers the joke punch line ("and they say, miracles don't happen any more") when old Morten runs off to try to arrange Anders' marriage; but the whole of *Ordet* is peppered with wonderful comic scenes orchestrated by Dreyer himself: I have already mentioned the comical leaky roof/prayer misunderstanding, but some of the other comical moments in the film that leap to mind are the comedy of Morten's handkerchief, the comically clumsy first conversation of Peter the tailor and Morten Borgen in Peter Petersen's house, and the comical maneuvers of Peter's wife to keep her daughter and Morten's son separated and chaperoned in the kitchen.

the narrative at which Inger is removed from it. In a series of scenes, Maren (albeit in her childish, immature way) reaches out and touches those around her exactly as Inger did during her own life, continuing her mother's function. Insofar as Johannes was one of the figures Inger worked hardest to knit back into the fabric of the family, it should not be surprising that two of the most moving scenes in which Maren is a participant involve her reaching out (literally and imaginatively), as her mother did earlier, to Johannes.

In the first, in her childish innocence and faith, Maren approaches Johannes to ask him to keep her mother alive. (Inger is lying near death from a difficult childbirth.) The scene – touching and almost comical because of the naiveness of Maren's faith and the sheer simplicity and directness of her argument in favor of her "Mummy" being alive – runs as follows in Dreyer's shooting script (and was changed only very slightly in the final film):

MAREN: Uncle Johannes . . . Uncle Johannes, will Mummy die soon?

JOHANNES: Do you want her to, little girl?

MAREN: Yes, because then you're going to raise her from the dead, aren't you?

JOHANNES: I dare say it will come to nothing.

MAREN: Why?

JOHANNES: The others won't let me.

MAREN: Yes, but what about Mummy then?

JOHANNES: Then your Mummy will go to heaven.

MAREN: (*shaking her head*) But I don't want that at all.

JOHANNES: Little girl, you don't know what it is to have a Mummy in heaven.

MAREN: Is it better than having her here on earth?

JOHANNES: You don't need me to tell you that.

MAREN: (*nudging him*) What nonsense, Uncle Johannes! If we get hurt, then we'll have no Mummy to take care of us.

JOHANNES: Nobody can hurt the child whose mother is in heaven. When your mother is dead, then you have her with you always.

MAREN: But you have that when she's alive.

JOHANNES: Ah, but then she has so many other things to see to.

MAREN: (*looking up at him*) Yes, that's right – she has to milk the cows and scrub the floors and do the washing. Dead people miss all that.

JOHANNES: Of course, of course.

MAREN: (*after thinking it over*) But I'd still rather you raised her from the dead, Uncle Johannes.

JOHANNES: Would you?

MAREN: Yes, because then we can keep her.

JOHANNES: Child of man, child of man.

MAREN: (*ingratiatingly, stroking his cheek*) Won't you *please* raise her from the dead?

In his affecting endorsement of Maren's childish love for her mother and his obviously critical placement of Johannes's position that it is better to be dead and in heaven than to be alive on earth, Dreyer (if there was any

245

doubt about it) shows that, like Maren, he too is emphatically a "child of man," not a son of God. The love that this film lavishes attention on, the love that Inger and her daughter represent the glorious example of, the love that this scene itself powerfully captures, is a love that is expressed not in pious abstractions – however noble – not in the saintly sentiments that Johannes preaches, but in the practical love of a mother for her daughter and of a daughter for her mother.

All of *Ordet* is, in effect, summarized in the difference between the tones of these two speakers' voices, tones that a film-goer can *hear*, even if he or she speaks not a syllable of Danish. One hears the difference between Johannes's use of impersonal tones and formal biblical terms like "little girl" and "child of man" to address Maren, and her own use of warmly familiar and childishly trusting tones to address him. Johannes's problem is precisely that he can't convert his abstract, religious sentiments *about* love into practical expressions *of* love. Like Inger's, Maren's love is not at all heavenly or biblical or abstract in Johannes's sense. It is rather, as Maren puts it, an eminently prosaic matter of milking the cows, scrubbing the floors, and doing the wash.

The mention of the wash refers us to one of the significances of the intercut shots of the lines of laundry that Dreyer uses as punctuation marks between scenes throughout the film. The sheets blowing in the wind function as beautiful objects in themselves, objects imbued, as only Inger's (and Dreyer's) workaday spirituality could imbue them, with an almost visionary significance, but they remind us that in this particular film such beauty is the result not of idle wishes and dreams, or of world-forsaking spirituality, but of practical *labors* of love on the part of Inger. The sheets show us that vision – as Inger (and Dreyer) represents it – must, in this world, be *realized,* must be worked into existence. In short, even this admittedly minor photographic detail refers us to the fundamental tension that energizes *Ordet,* the difficult translation of visionary idealizations into practical expressions of love that the film takes as its subject.

Love in *Ordet* is not something that one feels abstractly or waits for one's arrival in heaven to express; it is not a matter of disembodied, weightless spirituality, but is expressed in terms of actual physical bodies and practical, social acts of touching and reaching and moving between figures.

But even if one weren't attending to the specifics of the conversation between Johannes and Maren in this scene, or responding to the larger issues of the film and the general way dozens of scenes and interactions in *Ordet* are presented so as to ratify the importance of practical exertions of love in preference to abstract theological statements of faith, Maren's gestures, tones, and movements during this conversation with Johannes would communicate its meaning. She virtually caresses Johannes (both tonally and physically) as she gently begs, pleads, and argues with him to bring her mother back to life if she dies.

One can't help but be reminded of Inger's comparable acts. In her childish way, Maren does exactly the same thing that her mother did with Morten in the scene in which she attempted to get him to accept Anders' engagement. It is not accidental that both ultimately succeed in their respective acts of persuasion.

That is the importance of something apparently as trivial as Maren's childish "patting" of Johannes at several points during this conversation. As the scene transpires, she touches his chair, strokes his hair (reminiscent of the scene in which Inger stroked Mikkel's hair),

Maren takes over Inger's expressive functions after her death –
Inger with Mikkel and Morten, Maren with Johannes and Morten

touches his back, leans in toward him (almost bringing them together into the position of a lover's whisper and embrace), puts her right hand on his shoulder, puts her left hand on his shoulder, pats him, leans in again in a virtual hug, kisses him, and lets him pick her up at the end of it. The touching that Maren does here, and again in the final scene in which she walks alongside Johannes, takes his hand, looks up and smiles at him, and generally encourages him with her looks and gestures in front of Inger's dead body – like the leaning, embracing, and verbal caressing that Inger does with Morten and Mikkel in other scenes – represents the tangible conversion of spirit into fleshly expression.

In this scene, and even more obviously in the final scene of the film, in her gestural weaving, within the childish limitations of her ability, Maren, like Inger previously, knits up what has come unraveled; she sews Johannes back into the fabric of the family. (The final scene in particular is a *tour de force* of reestablishing relationships of interdependence that were in danger of being lost or forgotten at various points in *Ordet*.)

The last aspect of this scene to which I would call attention is the distinctively temporal dimension of its development. Like the other important scenes in *Ordet*, it represents a conception of meanings and relationships as emerging in a continuous process of temporal adjustment and negotiation. As the scenes with Morten and Inger have illustrated, meaning in *Ordet* is brought into existence gradually and practically in the give and take of an argument, in the time of a relationship, a scene, or an argument that ebbs back and forth between two characters.[28]

The temporality of the encounter is emphasized by the mutual movements of the characters and the camera during it. As Maren negotiates with Johannes – tenderly and tactfully, but persistently and practically – she moves around him. And as she moves, Dreyer's camera itself slowly moves from left to right in approximately a 120-degree arc around the pair. The camera patiently explores, probes, and observes the interaction from different angles, just as Maren herself patiently explores, probes, and observes Johannes as she tries to follow his argument, and negotiates with him for the life of her mother. The camera's tracking movement represents, as it were, an answering photographic response to Maren's tonal maneuvering. The camera movements here and elsewhere figure the endless mediations, the patient, practical labors of care and understanding that Dreyer is endorsing in the characters' performances.

In the largest sense, *Ordet* is an attempt to imagine the expression of the spiritual in terms of the physical and

---

28 If this statement seems merely rhetorical, I would contrast the abstract, schematic ways in which meaning is created in films by Hitchcock, Altman, Kubrick, or Allen. Dreyer, like Cassavetes or May in the American tradition, sees meaning as emerging from practical dramatic interactions between characters, not as abstractly imposed upon characters by the abstract (which is to say, atemporal) and overarching semiotic or metaphorical structures of the work itself.

temporal, to imagine the expression of the most exalted and transcendental states of love and faith in terms of the most practical, prosaic aspects of our expressive existences. In the figure of Inger (and to a lesser degree, that of Maren), Dreyer suggests how the realms of the body and the world need not be in conflict with the spirit (as they are in traditional Christian practice), but can be an expression of it. Inger's worldly labors of love are expressions of her spirituality.

In the structure of *Ordet,* if Johannes, on the one hand, represents a state of spirituality estranged from social involvements and practical, worldly expressions of its ideals, and, Morten and Mikkel (along with the doctor and, to a lesser degree, the minister), on the other, represent conditions of human caring and involvement that have largely lost touch with, or faith in, spiritual realms, then Inger and Maren alone represent the possibility of drawing together the realms of the spirit and the body, the realms of love and the practical world of men and affairs.

Inger's (or Maren's) act of translation across realms is an expression of Dreyer's narrative project in *Ordet* specifically, but it is also an expression of the general narrative project of his other work. That is why, in this respect, Inger and Maren might be called the summarizing and culminating figures in Dreyer's *oeuvre.* Dreyer's filmic output rests on the same paradoxical attempt that they figure here. Dreyer is a transcendental filmmaker who, as much as Inger, chooses to express himself in terms of realistic forms and structures of relationship.

As an artist Dreyer chooses to translate across realms in the same way Inger does as a character. Both he and she are committed to the expression of transcendental states in the forms of practical, dramatic expression between characters. For all of its transcendentalism, Dreyer's chosen means of artistic expression is not in terms of the nondramatic abstractions, poetic effusions, or the atemporal lyricism of the avant-gardists. He and the characters in which he is most interested do not express themselves in terms of abstractions, metaphors, reveries, or visions – but dramatically, locally, and specifically, in terms of the interplay of social relations between individuals, in worldly achievements embodied in the forms of dialogue, social interaction, and the endless negotiations of love as it works its real destiny in the world.

But, as I earlier suggested, the relation of vision and practical expression is ultimately a vexed, troubled matter to Dreyer, which is why it is not finally resolved in his work. He and his characters – and none of them more than Inger – may aspire to translate their transcendental impulses into the practical forms of dialogue and social expression (in life and in film), but there is always something flawed or frustrated about their attempt that reveals Dreyer's own uncertainty about it.

Notwithstanding all of its aspirations to link bodies and spirits, social expressions and ideal feelings together, *Ordet*, like Dreyer's other works, ultimately reveals Dreyer's profound uncertainty about the possible achievement of such a union.[29] However noble and self-less and inspiring her attempts must be judged to be, Inger ultimately fails as a practical, social negotiator. Her efforts to intercede on behalf of Anders' courtship of Anne, to patch up the quarrel between Peter Petersen and Morten Borgen, and to help her husband, Mikkel, back to the faith of his fathers, all finally come to nothing during her lifetime.

It is significantly only in her death that Inger finally succeeds. She succeeds as a spiritual and imaginative influence on others in a way that she couldn't succeed as a real mother, daughter-in-law, and lover. In that respect, however different she started out, she is a figure finally not all that distant from Joan of Arc. With her death Dreyer shifts Inger from being a figure of social expressiveness to being one of almost purely imaginative impressiveness. This beautiful mover is immobilized and confined within the walls of her coffin. This leaner and toucher is put flat on her back. This wonderful speaker is silenced. This affirmer of life and the possibility of life-affirming change is killed. Inger's function shifts from a practical to a purely imaginative one.

The best way to tease out some of Dreyer's conflicts of feeling about the relation of bodies and spirits, about the sometimes tenuous connection between transcendental impulses and social expressions is to look at the conclusion of *Ordet*. There are few more powerful mo-

29 That is why one finally feels that a viewer's ambivalences about Johannes are ultimately Dreyer's ambivalences too.

ments in Dreyer's work than the scene of Inger's resurrection. Despite the best efforts of the doctor, Inger has died in childbirth, and at the end of the film, during the course of her funeral service, she returns to life.

Dreyer offers a radically revisionary reading of Christianity that argues not only that the resurrection must be substituted for the crucifixion as the central Christian event, but further that, to truly count, the resurrection must be a resurrection to the physical body with all of its needs and cravings. Dreyer said as much in an interview with Michael Delahaye. Asked about the reason he wanted to make *Ordet*, Dreyer said that it was the attitude of Kaj Munk (the author of the play on which the film is loosely based) toward bodies and spirits that motivated him:

I was so much happier doing *Ordet* when I felt myself very close to the conceptions of Kaj Munk. He always spoke well of love. I mean to say, of love in general, between people, as well as love in marriage, true marriage. . . . And for him there was no difference between sacred and profane love. Look at *Ordet*, the father is saying, "She is dead . . . she is no longer here. She is in heaven. . . ." And the son answers, "Yes, but I loved her body too. . . ." What is beautiful, in Kaj Munk, is that he understood that God did not separate these two forms of love. That is why he did not separate them either. But this form of Christianity is opposed by another form . . . which establishes a divorce between thought and action.[30]

30 Carl Dreyer, "Interview with Michael Delahaye," reprinted in Andrew Sarris (ed.), *Interviews with Film Directors* (N.Y.: Bobbs-Merrill Co., 1967), 114.

Dreyer's (and Munk's) final scene, in effect, reverses Christian doctrine since it represents not a leaving of the earthly body behind by the spirit (with the suggestion of the body's ultimate unimportance), but the opposite: an emphatic return of the spirit to it.[31] As all of *Ordet* has suggested, Dreyer tells us that the word must be made *flesh* to dwell among us. Dreyer's resurrection to the flesh emphasizes the impotence or irrelevance of the spirit when it lacks a body to express it in a practical, human form.

In his funeral oration over Inger's coffin, the minister argues as ministers always have, in the tried-and-true way, and in defiance of all of our human feelings, that the conversion to pure spirit and the translation to heaven is not a loss but a gain. Mikkel, on the other hand, grief-stricken and convulsed with the sense of his loss, naturally enough cannot resign himself so easily. He cries out that he can't live without Inger and that her mere spiritual presence is not enough. In one of the most memorable lines in Dreyer's work, in reply to Morten's request that he dry his tears and say his farewells since Inger's "soul is with God," Mikkel cries out

31 The reading of Christianity that Dreyer rejects is the one articulated by Johannes in his conversation with Maren that I quoted above. It is the same reading of Christianity that Dreyer rejected in *Day of Wrath*. In its place, Dreyer ratifies Maren's sense that spirits are expressed in and through bodies and practical acts, not beyond or outside of them. Dreyer clearly also rejects the Christianity practiced by the congregation led by Peter the tailor. *Joan of Arc, Vampyr,* and *Gertrud* similarly link bodies and spirits, and urge their unity.

Joining together socially, emotionally, and spiritually –
Maren and Johannes in the scene of Inger's resurrection

passionately: "But her body – I loved her body too."
What makes the moment so powerful is that it is clear
that, to a large extent, Dreyer endorses Mikkel's cry of
the flesh. He is arguing that having the spirit is not
enough – that the body and the practical relations of
bodies define crucial aspects of love.

But one doesn't really need Mikkel's outburst to tell
us this. As I've suggested, the whole preceding film documents Dreyer's commitment to the expression of the
spirit, not beyond the outside of, but in and through the
body. It is of a piece with the rest of *Ordet* that when
Inger is finally brought back to life, in the kiss she gives
to Mikkel she herself communicates a sense not of disembodied spirituality, but of passionate craving, physical
hunger. It is a kiss that could, in its physical tangibility,
almost pass for a bite out of *Vampyr* – a kiss that reminds
us both of bodies and of souls, or more accurately, of the
necessary relation of bodies and souls that is argued by
the film.

Inger has always represented the importance of the body in the world. That is not only why she is associated with touching and reaching, with practical tasks like baking and washing, but, above all, with sexual intercourse (in a conversation with Mikkel), and with pregnancy and children. Dreyer's film is quite explicit about the sexuality of Mikkel and Inger's marriage. As the presence of their children only emphasizes, theirs has assuredly not been a platonic relationship. Our consciousness of that is what gives point and poignancy to Mikkel's final cry that he "loved her body too." Dreyer further emphasizes the biological reality of Inger's pregnancy by having Birgitte Federspiel, the actress who so sensitively plays her, costumed in a thin cotton dress in most of her scenes, to remind us that this actress is a real pregnant mother with a real swollen belly – as different from the sanitized fifties Hollywood version of a pregnant woman as possible.[32]

If it seems that I am making too much of Dreyer's interest in bodies here, I would remind the reader of the focusing on the skin and body of Herlofs Marte in the torture scene in *Day of Wrath*. There, as here, an awareness of the presence of an actual physical body, as distinguished from whatever merely spiritual facts the body represents, is essential to an understanding of the film.

32 It is of some relevance that Birgitte Federspiel was actually pregnant when she played the part. The state of her body would have had a reality and salience to herself and the other actors on the set that no mere costume pregnancy would have simulated.

In both *Day of Wrath* and *Ordet*, Dreyer's narrative project clearly involves restoring the physical body to a viewer's awareness as a necessary corrective to more abstract or intellectualized views of it.

At the same time, it goes without saying that Inger's body represents more than the realm of the senses. The intertwined spirituality and physicality of Inger's body are deliberately contrasted with the mere physicality and despiritualization represented by the harrowing shots of the doctor's hands and surgical instruments as he works on her during her delivery. In a similar vein, Inger's (and Morten's) prayerfulness and faith are contrasted with the chilling materialism of the doctor's attitudes in the scene in which the doctor, the minister, and Morten sit around the parlor table together.

But Inger's death complicates our attitude considerably and tells us how far from settled Dreyer's own feelings were about the relation of flesh and spirit. Inger ultimately fails to embody the balance between the spiritual and practical realms that she abstractly figures. She does not in the end represent a completely adequate practical, biological, or social expression for abstract ideals.

In the first place, the death of her child is crucial to our final understanding of the film. As her final lines remind us, Inger is not able to embody (the pun that was applicable to Anne in *Day of Wrath* is equally appropriate here) her desires in the production of a biological child any more than *Day of Wrath*'s Anne was (and, in this respect,

258

at the end of her film is not as different from Anne as Dreyer obviously attempted to suggest she was at the beginning of it). In the end, her feelings and imaginations will not be given practical expression.

In the second place, and more importantly, it is significant that the community of feeling and imagination formed around Inger at the end of *Ordet* is not created through her practical powers of social example and moral suasion. The resurrection scene tells us that Inger finally fails as a practical social negotiator, and only succeeds as a transcendental object of awe and love. Whatever is achieved by Inger in the final half hour of *Ordet* is done only through her death, and through the purely imaginative effect it has on everyone around her. As an abstract influence, a sublime visionary presence, Inger ultimately accomplishes what she cannot achieve as an actual biological creator and a practical social mediator. She draws the family together. But she does it not as a practical social community, but as a visionary company – in its contemplation of her death and subsequent resurrection.

This is an essential point precisely because in all of his work Dreyer hovers uncertainly between a faith, a hope, that the finest energies of the imagination can be expressed in the world and a near despair that they cannot. If *Day of Wrath*'s Anne figured his fears that the enriched consciousness is finally alone and cut off from the social representation of its most important dreams and desires in the forms of the world, Inger is clearly an attempt to imagine the possibility of an imaginative individual's survival in the sort of nonrepressive family that Anne was denied, in a family within which an individual can actually express his or her most daring conception of human relationships and possibilities in the practical forms of interaction with others. Yet the function Inger performs (or attempts to perform) before her death is reversed by the function she performs after it. If Dreyer intended to use her as an example of the practical social expression of spirit, Inger's visionary function in the final scenes of *Ordet* reverses the intention that preceded them.

To extend the comparison between *Ordet* and *Day of Wrath:* in the first half of her film, Inger might be said to merge the possibilities separately represented by Herlofs Marte and Anne in the earlier film even as she domesticates them. Like Herlofs Marte, she shows us a world in which bodies and biological realities have a real physical presence and importance; and like Anne, she represents the expression of realms of emotional openness and accessibility that the men in her world have repressed from their lives. Inger shows that such energies can be expressed in practical family life.

But if *Ordet* entertains such possibilities in its initial hour or so, its final hour forces one to see that Inger succeeds only by dying to the world of practical, social expressions. She ultimately moves much closer to the expressive situation of Anne in the earlier film than she had been. She finally brings the various individuals around her together in a community of understanding and appreciation only in her concluding function as a transcendental object. In her death she is transformed from a practical expressive reality to a visionary or spiritual presence, a sublime object eliciting fear and wonder from those around her (as well as from the viewer of the film).

The fragile balance between flesh and spirit, between transcendental ideals and practical social expressions, a balance that was unstable in any case, tips at the end in favor of transcendental spirit. Did Dreyer realize what he was doing? I think it is impossible to know. Suffice it to say that the tremulous oscillation *Ordet* illustrates between the claims of practical social expressiveness and transcendental presence brings one to the frontiers of Dreyer's imagination. The figure of Inger is the closest he ever came to fully believing in the possible conversion of vision into practical expression. With the title figure in *Gertrud*, he will, as it were, return to Anne and the world of *Day of Wrath* in despairing of the translation of our finest impulses and desires into practical forms of relationship.

FIVE

Gertrud
Speaking love's dreams

GERTRUD: Oh, Erland . . . will we never speak the same language?

from *Gertrud*

O*rdet* was the closest Dreyer ever came to believing that the imagination could be domesticated. In the figure of Inger he created an individual who was – at moments – able to express her most exalted spiritual aspirations in the verbal and social forms of everyday life, a figure who was able to express her most mecurial movements of desire in terms of actual physical movements and verbal expressions. Unlike Anne's, Inger's expressions did not threaten society but enriched it. And yet, as I have indicated, Dreyer's ultimate spiritualization of his heroine, and his reliance on a stylistics of shared vision in the final scenes of the film tell us once again how far beyond social representation Dreyer felt our central selves to be.

The expressive crisis that is finally figured by Inger's death is suggested earlier in *Ordet* by the expressive problems of the men in the film. Even as, in the figures of Inger and Maren, Dreyer explores the ways the imag-

263

ination may be translated into the forms of practical social interaction, virtually all of the other relationships and interactions depicted in the first half of *Ordet* emphasize a gap between the imagination and all available forms of social and dramatic expression. That is to say, even as Inger tries to show us otherwise, Dreyer's film itself shows us that the only authentic "speech" of *Ordet*'s characters is a silent one: a "speech" of visual images, of fleeting gestures, of glances – a silent speech forced underground, underneath public forms of expression.

In his essay "A Little on Film Style," written shortly after the completion of *Day of Wrath*, Dreyer justifies the quietness of his dramas in terms of the quietness of tragedy generally:

And isn't the truth that the great dramas are played quietly, that people try to cover their feelings and avoid showing on their faces the storms that are really raging within themselves? The tension lies beneath the surface and releases itself the day the catastrophe takes place. It is that latent tension, that smoldering discomfort . . . that I have so urgently been trying to bring forward.

It is perhaps not enough for those who might have wished a more violent unfolding of the action. But let them look around their own circles and notice with how little of the dramatic the greatest tragedies take place. This is perhaps what is most tragic about these tragedies.[1]

1 "A Little on Film Style," reprinted in Donald Skoller (ed.) *Dreyer in Double Reflection* (New York: Dutton, 1973), p. 134.

That may be true about both art and life, but there is more to it than that. The quietness of Dreyer's tragedies has to do with the nature of expression in his work. Precisely because passages of dialogue and social interaction so frequently will not bear the burden of meaning in Dreyer's work, his films are forced to rely on nonverbal, nonsocial forms of expression to communicate what cannot be translated into words and social relationships. Since social forms of expression are almost invariably frustrating, limiting, or repressive of the imaginative energies Dreyer is interested in depicting, the expressive burden of his films and his characters' interactions must be shifted into subtextual forms of expression. His undertexts communicate impulses that won't be represented (by the film or by the characters within it) more directly or demonstratively.

This is undoubtedly one of the biggest sources of confusion about Dreyer's work. For someone looking for the sorts of expression that one finds in the work of Renoir, for instance, it may seem like nothing at all is happening even at the occasions of the greatest momentousness in Dreyer. Expression is fugitive and oblique almost to the point of invisibility. In *Ordet*, the way Morten Borgen walks across a room, or sits down, or inclines his head to one side, or pauses in his conversation, or stares into the distance is of more expressive importance than almost anything he says or does in the course of the narrative. That is why things like *how* Inger and Maren move through a room, or lean toward, or touch another character's hand or body are frequently of more expressive importance than *what* they say or do. Similarly, the physical position and bodily posture of Johannes in relation to other characters and within the space of the frame or the set "say" more about his situation than the dialogue or actions scripted for him. Unscripted subtexts of silences and pauses, small gestures and tonal inflections are more important than the scripted text of actions and statements.

Of course, Renoir's work also communicates its meanings by means of characters' tones of voice, body language, movements, and relative positions, but the crucial difference between the work of Dreyer and Renoir is that in the work of Renoir such elements of expression are part and parcel of a more or less universally legible and publicly interpretable sign system by means of which one effortlessly "speaks" oneself in public (both to other characters in one's film and to the viewers of it in the audience).[2]

In Dreyer, these subtextual events are withdrawals from expression. They communicate a felt gap between

2 Consider, by way of contrast, the expressive differences between Dreyer's farm family and Renoir's in *The Rules of the Game*. Dreyer's family of quiet, reserved men has none of the verbal facility and social glibness that even the servants and gamekeepers in Renoir's film so brilliantly display. Dreyer's father and sons are wracked with pains, self-doubts, and anxieties that won't be converted into social and verbal performances. While even Renoir's most emotionally upset characters are able to express themselves outwardly in their pain, Dreyer's figures at times withdraw from speech and social interaction altogether.

one's feelings and one's ability to "speak" them. The most important tonal and gestural events in Dreyer's work (the silences, the stillnesses, the stares) represent a recognition of what cannot be "spoken" socially and verbally. They figure undercurrents of imagination and desire that don't enrich and inform, but rather undermine linguistic and social expression. They express how much is always lost in translation from one realm to the other.

In this sense, the major expressions in *Ordet* and Dreyer's other most important films are not contained within the general contours of the plot or defined by the social interactions between the characters. In Dreyer's work, such larger narrative structures and social interactions are, almost always, not expressive, but *repressive* of our finest imaginative energies and emotional impulses. That was Anne's problem in *Day of Wrath*. Her problems as a character paralleled Dreyer's as a filmmaker: She was unable to create a "plot" and a series of "dramatic interactions" that would adequately express the energies represented by the flickering lights and shadows on her face. The energies Dreyer is interested in evoking are essentially opposed to the forms of social and psychological control that dramatic plots and interpersonal interactions represent. They break any container that would stabilize them. They are disruptive of all forms of organization and control.

Consequently, Dreyer's films honor fragments, not wholes: moments of vision, sudden accesses of imagination and movements of feeling that won't be knit seamlessly into the overarching contour of the plot or that won't be responsibly spoken in the forms of interaction between characters. That is why the responsive viewer leaves even *Ordet* (which works much harder than *Day of Wrath* to domesticate the sublime) remembering not some intricate, Renoirian trajectory of personal interactions, but bits and pieces, fragments of scenes and expressions that won't be knit together into the seamlessness of a "well-made" plot or subtly patterned interchanges of dialogue.

One recalls the plangency and desperation of Morten's voice as he calls Johannes's name out on the heath; the discouragement in Mikkel's voice as he says of Johannes following Inger's death: "No father, that sort of person doesn't die." One remembers Maren's fleeting reference to Inger's having changed the children's sleeping arrangements when she felt herself going into labor for all it tells us about how Inger's performative mastery is displayed even in the scenes that take place off camera, in the scenes Dreyer doesn't even dramatize in the film. One remembers the way Peter the tailor touches the coffee pot to indicate that he doesn't want any more during Morten's visit; the way Inger leans toward old Morten in the pigsty to console him; or the way Morten turns to Mikkel, grins, and touches his arm when at one point during the difficult delivery he thinks that Inger is out of danger. Or, to cite one of the supreme moments in all of Dreyer's work, one recalls

Morten's tone of voice and the way he tramps across the farmhouse floor at the moment he asks Mikkel to help him to assist the doctor, while Inger is lying near the point of death on the kitchen table and her dead baby is about to be put in a bucket. (It is a moment fully as profound and as moving as anything in *King Lear*, and one that equally exposes us to the depths of pain to which we can be brought.) As in *King Lear*, at these moments we glimpse or hear almost inexpressible imaginative and emotional depths underneath the most prosaic acts, under the most mundane surfaces of life.

Such small, evanescent events in *The Passion of Joan of Arc* as the way Joan pauses before answering the judges, the glances she casts at her interrogators, the way she walks alongside her guards, or her stumble as she goes through a doorway speak more powerfully and eloquently about her vulnerability, innocence, strength, and idealism than does the written text of her spoken words.[3]

Similarly, in *Gertrud*, Gabriel Lidman's pace and

3 One reason to cite *The Passion of Joan of Arc* is to suggest that insofar as Dreyer's texts and characters communicate in such nonsocial, nonverbal ways, his sound films can employ many of the same expressive devices as his silent work. This is not by any means true of most other directors. Renoir, Hawks, and Capra (to cite a range of examples) came into their own as filmmakers only with the advent of sound, precisely because of their reliance on social and verbal interactions between their characters. Chaplin and Keaton, on the other hand, are examples of the complementary phenomenon: in their different ways, they were both unable to make the transition to sound films because their work depended on avoiding or minimizing social and verbal interactions.

slouch, the tones of his and Gertrud's voices when they speak together at his birthday banquet, and the pause of a beat or two that they take as they shake hands in their final farewell all communicate what their words and actions with each other could never "speak."

There is no better example of how an audience prepared to attend only to the social and verbal surfaces of events will be doomed to miss or misunderstand everything that is of interest in Dreyer's work than the reception given his final film, *Gertrud.* At the conclusion of its world premiere screening, in Paris, on December 19, 1964, it was greeted with a chorus of boos, hisses, and catcalls from the audience of French critics, press, and high society. Or from what was left of the audience, since many of the opening-nighters had left during the course of the screening.

There are only nine scenes in the film, most of them consisting of nothing more intrinsically "cinematic" (as the jargon goes) than conversations between the title character and one of the four men with whom she is associated in the course of the work. Unsympathetic critics, unprepared for its economy, jeered in articles over the course of the next week that Dreyer had made a film entirely of long, boring "sofa conversations."

The hostile reviewers were right in a way: The drawing room settings in *Gertrud* are austere. The acting is restrained. The photography is unrhetorical in the extreme. The scenes, are, in any purely visual sense, static. There is none of the visual virtuosity (however hollow) of lighting, framing, and camera movement that Welles, Hitchcock, De Palma, and Kubrick have accustomed us to expect in a "masterpiece." But that is to examine only the surface, and *Gertrud* consists not of surfaces, but of depths. Thrilling imaginative events take place under the static social surfaces of the film.

Indeed, as I argued in the second and third chapters, the stillness and placidity of the social surfaces, the reductions of narrative action, the simplifications of the sets, the abstractness in the presentation of scenes and interactions, the metaphorizations of objects and events are attempts to induce a new way of knowing and feeling, a special state of consciousness that Dreyer is after. Dreyer redirects the viewer's attention away from social and verbal surfaces to imaginative agitations in the depths. It is necessary that the events in the film be slowed and the verbal interactions between the characters be made almost ritualistic in order to encourage the mediative shift that Dreyer wants to take place in his viewers. The social and verbal text of the film is deliberately simplified, in order to encourage the viewer to move into another kind of relation to the characters and events. Scenes are paralleled, and lines of dialogue and interactions between characters in various scenes are formally compared and contrasted, in order to induce a special state of abstraction in the viewer and to encourage a reading of the film in a specially abstract way. Repetitions (of events and lines of dialogue) are deliberately used to frustrate the narrative appetitiveness of the viewer and to induce in its

271

place a state of meditativeness. In short, Dreyer's narrative and visual impoverishments are in the service of nourishing an extraordinary imaginative enrichment of the viewer's relationship to what is on the screen.

What most of *Gertrud*'s first audience failed to understand was that Dreyer was making a film as different as possible from the Renoirian cinema that his audience was primed to appreciate. If we (or Dreyer's characters) were busier keeping up with narrative events, physical movements, and verbal interactions, if we were busier attending to the gaudiness of sets or the virtuosity of the photography, we might be distracted from paying attention to the imaginative movements and emotional interactions that are the real subject of the film. Dreyer makes a special cinematic time and space, distinct from the time and space of worldly interactions, within which the viewers' attention is released to new ways of knowing.

Furthermore, the much criticized drawing room settings, the stasis of the narrative, and the physical immobility of the characters represent an essential commentary on the difference between the title character's practical expressive situation and her soaring Romantic dreams. Gertrud Kanning is a former opera singer with a vision of freedom and self-expression as exalted as the sense of life in Italian opera. Though, at times, Gertrud attempts to treat life as if she were a character in an Italian opera, the drama of the film is generated around the fact that Dreyer absolutely denies his heroine the luxury of living in a world as responsive to her desires as that of Italian opera.

To summarize the film in one sentence, one might say that all of *Gertrud* is devoted to showing us (and showing its heroine) why life cannot be lived as if it were opera, even while simultaneously honoring the impulses that make us keep going to operas and keep imagining our lives in terms of them. Gertrud dreams of absolute, unconditioned love and tries to live her dream. "I want love without bounds," she says early in the film. Her imaginative glory and her ultimate tragedy reside in her refusal to compromise her operatic ideal, even in the face of her own final recognition that she cannot live it off the stage.

Thus, far from being an artistic miscalculation, or an unfortunate carry-over from the stage play source of the film, Dreyer's Victorian parlor settings and static groupings remind us of (and eventually bring home to Gertrud as well) the non-operatic environment her operatic sense of expression must negotiate. Dreyer embeds Gertrud in a world that relentlessly and overwhelmingly resists her dreams and ideals. The thrust of Dreyer's "sofa conversation" format is that, no matter how grandly Gertrud imagines herself, she must sit still in a drawing room and express herself in the language and forms of polite society. Utterly denied the set speeches and grand theatrical gestures of the forms of nineteenth–century stage melodrama she steps out of, she must talk quietly and undemonstratively. If she would express her operatic imagination, she has no arias or duets with which to do so. Dreyer's point is that she must express herself, if at all, within the incredibly repressive forms of ordinary social language and practical action.

Gertrud is one of the most poignant examinations of the practical social and expressive complications of the High Romantic commitment to an ideal of absolute personal freedom and expression in all of film. The title character attempts to bring into existence an actual social relationship that will live up to her ideals of love – not simply to imagine it in the form of a lyrical poem or an imaginative extravagance. Henry James brought these doomed heiresses of the High Romantic tradition to their finest and most tragic flowering, and Gertrud is a figure who, had Dreyer not brought her into existence, could only have been imagined by another James. Like Dreyer in this film, James took the imaginative heightenings and intensities of Romantic poetry and nineteenth–century stage melodrama and attempted to translate them into the language of society and the realistic novel. The drama that results in both James' novels and Dreyer's film is made out of the fierce discrepancy between the two realms.

To locate *Gertrud* within the trajectory of Dreyer's career, it might be said to cross *Day of Wrath* with *Ordet*. Insofar as it takes the absolute commitment to free self-expression as its subject, *Gertrud* has much in common with *Day of Wrath* (and Gertrud has much in common with Anne). *Gertrud,* as it were, brings *Day of Wrath* into the twentieth century. Gertrud is, in effect, Anne Pedersdotter as she might have been two or three centuries later in history, and ten or twenty years later in life. (To extend the parallel between *Gertrud* and *Day of Wrath* a bit further, one might say that Gertrud's husband, Gustav Kanning, takes the place of Absalon, and Gertrud's affair with a young poet, Erland Jansson, replaces Anne's liaison with Martin.) Both Anne and Gertrud are committed in a specially uncompromising way to the authority of desire against the authority of social and verbal forms that work against the expression of desire. Both are absolutely committed to emotional and imaginative energies no matter how explosive of social and ideological structures they may be.

But the difference is that the heroine of *Day of Wrath* was freer to express herself (if only in the lights and shadows on her face or her eccentric movements through space) outside of social constraints and definitions than Gertrud ever is in the parlors, parks, and drawing rooms of her film. Anne could run through the fields, she could drift in a boat, she could lie in the grass, she could fantasize and dream freely, if only for a few minutes, with her lover in ways that Gertrud is almost completely denied. Thus it must be said that *Gertrud* brings to bear against transcendental impulses the forces that *Ordet* (and Inger) distinctively acknowledged. Though she has a completely different repertory of gestures and words than Inger, Gertrud is constrained and her expressions are mediated socially in ways that bring Inger back to mind.

The parallel between *Day of Wrath* and *Gertrud* can also clarify an important point about the earlier film that I have already touched upon. It is possible to interpret *Day of Wrath* as being about the limitations of particular institutional arrangements of knowledge or power. Thus, the film can be taken specifically as being a parable about the German occupation of Denmark, or more generally, as being a condemnation of the tyranny of particular religious institutions, or most generally, as being about male domination of females. The first reading makes it a response to a particular political situation; the second and third suggest that specific institutional, cultural, or sexual arrangements of power are the focus of Dreyer's concern.

However, the relationship of *Gertrud* with *Day of Wrath* helps us to see how all such readings are too superficial. They represent a fundamental misunderstanding of Dreyer's work. Insofar as *Gertrud* completely omits ideological structurings of experience from its text (and stays relentlessly in the realm of "domestic drama"), it allows us to appreciate the degree to which not only it but all of Dreyer's earlier work is essentially nonideological – even when (as in *Day of Wrath*) it might appear to be ineluctably ideological.[4]

4 As strange as the comparison of Dreyer's work with that of a Hollywood studio director might seem, I would call attention to the similarity within their directors' canons of Dreyer's *Gertrud* and Capra's *It's a Wonderful Life*. Both are "nonpolitical" or "nonideological" works within *oeuvres* generally thought of as being fundamentally "political" or "ideological"

Or, to put it more accurately: the nonideological nature of *Gertrud* helps us to appreciate the extent to which Dreyer's earlier work uses the limitations placed on expression by ideological arrangements of discourse and knowledge only as a metaphor for the fundamental repressiveness of *all* discourse. *Day of Wrath* is indeed a critique of the repressions of Nazism, fanatical Protestantism, and male chauvinism; but it is much more than that as well. It is a critique of the repressions of all bourgeois life and capitalism. It is a critique of the frustrations of all social interaction. It is a critique of the repressions of all psychological and moral categories of understanding. It is ultimately a critique of the limitations of all realistic forms of self-representation – in life and in art.

Dreyer's vision of the frustrations of human expression is more radical (and more tragic) than an ideological approach to his work can comprehend. What *Gertrud* makes clear (though one might equally well have taken the lesson from *The Passion of Joan of Arc* – except that it also is too often understood in limiting ideological terms) is that Dreyer depicts the limitations of particular institutional arrangements of knowledge (like those of

in their interests; and by that virtue both indicate the *essentially* nonpolitical nature of their creators' visions, even in their apparently most ideological works. For more on the use of *It's a Wonderful Life* as a correction to this common misreading of Capra's career, see my *American Vision* (New York: Cambridge University Press, 1986), 427–428. Compare also Capra's *Forbidden*, a film strangely similar to *Gertrud* from this perspective.

the church and state in *Day of Wrath*) not as portrayals of actual problems in those institutions, but as metaphors for expressive problems that reach beyond any institution or ideology.

Though it may sound paradoxical, the problem with an ideological analysis of Dreyer's work is that it is fundamentally too optimistic and superficial.[5] Insofar as ideological criticism locates expressive problems in particular social arrangements and institutional structures of knowledge (which may be changed and corrected), it proposes possible resolutions of problems for which Dreyer sees none. Dreyer's films represent the conviction that there is a radical and tragic gap between desire and the expression of it under *any conceivable arrangement* of human relations and institutions. The limitations on the "realization" of our desires that Dreyer is interested in exploring are ones we are born into, not ones imposed on us by individual oppressors or oppressive cultural systems.[6]

5 This is, as far as I am concerned, the problem with ideological analyses of most other works of art as well.

6 Perhaps the example of a nonideological author like Henry James can be helpful here. The fact that his work (so irresponsibly, his critics would charge) neglects "downtown" workaday realities for the sake of depicting "uptown" social gatherings is actually evidence, not of the superficiality, but of the profundity of his expressive critique. James's recognition was that we serve life sentences in the prison house of society, language, and thought; no particular ideology or cultural system imposes them on us, and therefore no particular ideological or cultural transformation can release us from them. That tragic recognition cuts deeper than ideological analysis can plumb.

Whether one takes an ideological or nonideological approach to Dreyer's work affects how one understands his whole *oeuvre*. Insofar as Dreyer's style is an attempt to validate energies of imagination and feeling that represent criticisms of the limitations of all "realistic" or "ideological" understandings of experience, an ideological approach to his work fundamentally misunderstands it. An ideological analysis is grounded in a description and analysis of specific systems of discourse, and in comparisons of one system with another; but the energies Dreyer presents in his films are opposed to all systematizations, including those of ideological analysis itself.

The specific reading I am trying to defend Dreyer and *Gertrud* in particular against is a fashionably "feminist" one. A reading of *Gertrud* that was based on a "feminist" understanding of Gertrud's situation as a woman in a man's world would not only trivialize, but essentially misread the film (just as a feminist interpretation of Isabel Archer's situation in James's *The Portrait of a Lady* would trivialize and misunderstand James's novel). Like Isabel's, Gertrud's transcendentalism represents a more radical expressive critique than a political or social analysis of specific institutions and relationships can comprehend.

Furthermore, the basis of realistic or ideological analysis is a set of normative assumptions about what constitutes expressively adequate behavior, assumptions that Dreyer refuses to accept. Because of its essentially normative definition of what constitutes reality, realist criticism always at least implicitly represents a more conservative position than Dreyer's. Insofar as it intrinsically limits the possibilities of human expression to the conventional and normative, ideological criticism is implicitly opposed to art that is transcendental in aspiration. That is why an ideological analysis is fundamentally repressive of (or blind to) the very energies that Dreyer's work attempts to release.

Precisely to the extent that figures like Joan, Anne, and Gertrud are expressively exorbitant, emotionally unappeasable, or imaginatively inordinate (in other words, precisely to the extent that they interest Dreyer), they are doomed to be misunderstood or to be judged adversely by ideological or socially engaged critical methodologies (which necessarily value systematic understandings, normative stabilities, and conventional standards of expression over an allegiance to the exceptional, the extreme, and the transcendental).

That is why it is only to be expected that Gertrud, Dreyer's most expressively daring and transcendentally committed character, should be regarded as a prig, a bore, or a bluestocking by critics with a realistic social agenda in their work. Many critics have commented negatively on the excessiveness of her expressive positions, as if that were a limiting judgment on her, rather than being the most interesting thing about her. To call Gertrud extreme is a little like calling Hamlet too intense, Lear overwrought, or Cleopatra excessive. The only appropriate reply to the criticism that these characters are "too much" is not to deny the charge but to concede it. Of course Hamlet and Lear and Cleopatra are imaginatively extravagant (and to this degree, are – judged by normative, realistic standards of expression – "exaggerated" and "unrealistic"). But to notice that is to criticize neither them nor their creator. Their imaginative unappeasability is the point of the work.

Gertrud, like Joan and Anne in this respect, takes her place in a long and venerable expressive tradition[7] – the theatricality, performative extravagance, and expressive extremity of whose members are not evidence of artistic miscalculation, irresponsibility, or self-indulgence. These figures in search of worldly figuration communicate the limitations of all normative understandings of expression and experience. They are their creators' attempts to honor impulses that fracture the structures within which so-called realistic life and expression are organized. They represent – in however fugitive a way – intensities and mobilities of feeling that won't be rendered in the fixities and stabilities of normative styles of performance or narrative presentation.

But even this is not to characterize the full complexity of the expressive predicament of these figures. For all of their expressive exorbitance and performative extrava-

7 In drama, the tradition includes Shakespeare's Lear, Hamlet, and Cleopatra; in literature, Henry James's Eugenia, Isabel, Charlotte, and Maggie; in film, Elaine May's Lenny Cantrow, Mikey, and Nicky, and John Cassavetes' Lelia, Mabel Longhetti, and Sarah Lawson.

gance, these characters are not allowed simply to move outside of the systems that oppress them. No more than Shakespeare's Coriolanus are they free to move into the "world elsewhere" of their dreams and desires. Insofar as they are situated as characters in "realistic" works – that is to say, in works that honor the requirements of temporal presentation, gradual narrative progression, coherent characterization, consistent behavior, and interpersonal interaction by means of patterned exchanges of dialogue – these characters' transcendental impulses are injected into hostile or alien environments. These figures must express their dreams of freedom not outside of, but within "realistic" forms of intercourse. Though this social side of Dreyer's work is most complexly detailed in *Ordet,* and reaches its finest artistic flowering there, expression is socially and realistically mediated in all of his films.

Insofar as he makes "realistic" movies, Dreyer builds into his works implicit criticisms of the very impulses his characters embrace.[8] The linguistic and dramatic forms of Dreyer's works themselves require his most exalted

8 Just as Shakespeare builds into his plays, James into his novels, and Cassavetes into his films forces that war against the energies they and their characters seek to release. Not only does Lear have his daughters, Hamlet his Polonius, and Antony his Rome, but, more importantly, Lear, Hamlet, Antony, and their creator have the repressive forms of language and dramatic presentation itself that continuously mediate their expressions.

characters to negotiate the obstacle course of social interactions and repressive influences that they would attempt to leave behind or rise above.

This is not to unsay what I have just argued about the inadequacy of realist or ideological understandings of such works, but rather to indicate a second level of deficiency in such criticism. The forms of the narratives in which these works force their transcendental characters to function, in effect, raise the same criticisms of their exorbitances and extravagances that a realistically biased critic does, before the critic ever comes on the scene. In effect, they reply to the realist position, before it is even offered. Shakespeare, James, Dreyer, May, and Cassavetes have already defined the limitations of the realist position in their works, in ways of which realist criticism is apparently unaware.

In the specific case of *Gertrud,* this means that Dreyer not only entertains a transcendental expressive stance in the style of the work and the figure of his title character, but that he simultaneously criticizes and "places" his own (and his character's) transcendentalism. Notwithstanding its transcendental aspirations, Dreyer's style in *Gertrud* is one of inescapable immanence of all life and experience, an immanence that encloses, circumscribes, and resists transcendental impulses. The resistance of his narrative forms and structures to Gertrud's expression of her dreams makes itself felt in the course of the film as solidly and substantially as the Victorian furniture that she sits on and moves around in the staid, sober drawing rooms in which most of the scenes are set.

This inclusion of a counterimpulse, a resistance to the central character's acts of imaginative expansion in the film is what I described as crossing Anne with Inger. On the one hand, Gertrud is called upon to represent the most exalted ideals of love and free expression of the emotions imaginable, and certain stylistic aspects of the film she is in are designed to endorse her state of imaginative absolutism. On the other hand, in the majority of the scenes in the film,[9] she is required to express herself to characters and in settings and forms of discourse that inevitably frustrate the expression of her operatic ideals. Even as she attempts to leave social valuations behind, she is embedded in a society that everywhere imposes them on her. At the very moments Gertrud strives most sublimely to articulate ideals that would rise above the limitations of ordinary expressive realities and the tangled web of human relationships, Dreyer's polite, reserved, sedate social gatherings and dramatic forms embed Gertrud and all of her expressions in contexts that resist her dreams of ideal freedom and love.

Characters in Italian opera never had it so hard. But the hardness is Dreyer's goal. To create the expressive hardness is why, notwithstanding all of the transcendental aspirations of Dreyer's aesthetic, he chose to make

---

9 The flashback and flash-ahead scenes are exceptions to the "sofa conversation" format, as are certain other moments, which I will comment on below.

realistic films – films that proceed by means of social interactions between characters, temporally structured sequences of events, and spatially coherent settings.

It is another reason why this celebrator of High Romantic consciousness has virtually no glamour close-ups in his work, beyond those I already adduced in my discussion of *Ordet*. For all of their visionary power, his characters (and his viewers) are almost never allowed the luxury of relaxing into states of pure vision or dream. It is crucial that Gertrud (like Joan, like Anne, like Inger) is never released into a state of pure reverie or vision. A glamour close-up or a sequence of "beauty shots" (as such things occur in Hollywood films), would grant her a visionary autonomy, a costfree capacity of transcendence that it is precisely Dreyer's effort to worry and question. To allow a character (or a viewer) a static moment of reverie or vision, as a close-up (or even a point–of–view shot) invariably does, would be to allow vision to be detached from the forms of practical expression in terms of which Dreyer insists that it express itself. Considered as visionary or transcendental documents, Dreyer's films are radically, savingly impure in that the visionary impulse is always visually, socially, and dramatically "placed."

As he does in all of his most interesting work, Dreyer pits the vision of his principal characters *against* the social responsibilities his scripting, his photography, and his realistic dramatic forms exact of them. Society hedges individuals round. Dreyer's long takes and middle-distance camera setups keep the characters in *Gertrud* embedded in a matrix of relationships that the photography prevents them from rising above. This is what he was getting at, I believe, when he told Børge Trolle in an interview that he had rejected the shot/reverse shot syntax of most other films, and deliberately replaced it with shots in which he held the faces of two or more actors in view at the same time:

[In *Gertrud*] the idea has been to have the actors' faces in focus all the time so that the audience can read their thoughts, eventually one character's thought while the other speaks. Why must a dialogue scene be bound to the idea that one either sees the people in profile or sees one actor with his back turned around? That way the *interplay* between the actors can easily be washed out.[10]

Yet if the social embeddedness of *Gertrud*'s characters is indicated by the "sofa conversations" they are trapped within, their simultaneous meditative turn out of the realm of social values is suggested by their avoidance of eye contact with each other, the angling of their heads away from the vertical, and their sometimes dreamy or abstracted tones of voice – all of which suggest that their "conversations" are as much with themselves as with one another. If they are Jamesian figures in many respects, not the least Jamesian quality of their drama is

10 Børge Trolle, "Interview with Carl Dreyer," *Film Culture* (Summer 1961), 59.

that it is generated out of the felt *discrepancy* between their capacities for dreaming and the oppressive social and expressive realities within which they must represent themselves. That discrepancy generates the fundamental drama in Dreyer's work from *Joan of Arc* to *Gertrud*.

But a discrepancy can be a stimulation toward renewed effort, not a reason for abandoning it. However great the discrepancy between ideals and realities, however yawning the chasm between love's dreams and practical realities and social expressions, Dreyer's greatest films (and his heroines) attempt to bridge the distance. They attempt to reach across the gap. Gertrud's (and her film's) fundamental effort is to translate her exalted ideals into practical forms of expression and relationship.

As a way of summarizing the expressive compromises asked of her, Dreyer surrounds Gertrud with men each of whom, in one way or another, has abandoned the attempt at translation and encourages her to do so also. Each of them, in different ways, asks her to cut her ideals to fit actual expressive realities. Each of them represents an expressive compromise to which she refuses to yield:

Gustav Kanning is Gertrud's husband. He is, by the standards of cultivated society, a well-meaning and reasonable man and an earnest and conscientious civil servant. On the day of the film's first scene, he has apparently just reached his life's goal of attaining a prestigious ministerial appointment in the government. He communicates the good news to Gertrud, and, in so doing, holds out before her the prospect of all of the social glamour and worldly admiration attendant on being a minister's wife. Needless to say, such things are absolutely unimportant to Gertrud. In the opening minutes of the film, on the day of Gustav's grand success, Gertrud announces her irrevocable decision to leave him.

Gertrud and Gustav represent opposed conceptions of expression. As Dreyer subtly demonstrates throughout the film, Gustav is a master of ceremonies and social interactions. He is thoughtful, earnest, and sincere. He might be the best and most well-meaning character in a Renoir movie. But Gertrud, again, is out of Italian opera, which is to suggest how far from comfortable she feels in the expressive world of Renoir. As a statesman, expressive compromises are Gustav's *forte;* but, as a lover, expressive compromises are what Gertrud refuses to entertain.

Dreyer goes to great lengths to show us that Gustav is not evil, not insensitive, not cruel, not callow. He demonstrates Gustav's Renoirian tact and delicacy in scene after scene. For example, in his brief visit to a performance of *Fidelio* one evening to look for Gertrud, Dreyer shows how Gustav is able to tactfully tease information about the whereabouts of his wife from the usher, and then deftly tip him for his information at the conclusion of their encounter, without insulting him or embarrassing either of them. Yet Gustav's very limitations (from Gertrud's point of view) are that he is so masterfully the possessor of Renoirian expressive virtues. He is so expressively moderate and reasonable. He is a master of expressive tact and consideration. He is, in short, the perfect choice for Cabinet minister.

The expressive difference that looms between Gustav and Gertrud is summarized in one moment near the end of the film when Gustav, driven to distraction by the impending loss of his wife, proposes to Gertrud, in a spirit of desperate abjection, that she take Erland Jansson as her lover if she must, but that he and she in any case continue to live together as man and wife for the appearance of it. She takes his remarks, not as an excruciatingly painful concession (which they are), but as the ultimate expression of the difference between them: as proof that he doesn't even remotely understand the expression of love in the way she does.

The second man in Gertrud's life is Gabriel Lidman. He is a now-celebrated poet with whom she lived many years before, and who, in the course of the film, proposes love to her once again. Dreyer shows us that if Gabriel once believed, as Gertrud still does, in the ideal of perfect love, he has now abandoned his dreams at least in part because his relationship with Gertrud turned out so poorly. Gabriel is weary, disillusioned, and tired. Even as he proposes to Gertrud that they begin again, he urges that she trim down her expectations to realistic dimensions: "Earth is small; people are small."

But cutting one's dreams down to the size of the available expressive opportunities is just what Gertrud refuses to do, and she turns her back on his proposal.

It would be hard for Dreyer to be more explicit about how his film is about an individual's relation to expression that he is in making Gabriel a love poet who has, in effect, abandoned his belief in the possibility of actually living his poetic ideals in the world. As the banquet scene (which I will discuss in some detail below) makes clear, Gabriel has erected a wall between abstract, poetic values and practical worldly realizations and, forced to choose, has given up on the ideal, in order to live out his life on the side of the real.

The third man in Gertrud's life is a young composer named Erland Jansson. Though he proves himself in the course of the film to be callow and unfeeling, at its start, Gertrud is deeply in love with him. The evening of the first day of the film (the day on which she announces her intention to leave her husband) she sleeps with Erland. But, as Gertrud discovers, Erland apparently sleeps with the former opera singer only as an act of bravura. He is manipulative, self-pitying, ironic, and cool. In the expressive dynamics of *Gertrud*, Erland is completely cynical about the expression of ideals and feelings. He is merely using Gertrud (and as is subsequently revealed, has used another woman as well). He only pretends to feel what she feels. He is merely using her faith in the possibility of living one's ideals in the forms of practical relationship against her. In short, he divorces his expressions from his feelings completely. Cynically saying or doing whatever is convenient at the moment, and abandoning ideals and beliefs altogether, he has no awkward acts of translation to make across realms.

The differences between Erland's attitude toward expression and Gertrud's are succinctly summarized in their initial conversation in the park. Gertrud attempts to convince the composer to write, to work, to perform his feelings into a tangible expression for the world – in a symphony or a piece for the piano. But Erland indicates that he would rather wallow in a sentimental and self-absorbed state of pure feeling and do nothing. That is to say, while Gertrud urges – and believes in the possibility of – translating feelings and values into expressions, Erland feels no need at all to make the translation from one realm to the other.[11]

The fourth and final man in Gertrud's life is Axel Nygren. He alone offers Gertrud nothing more than a platonic relationship. (As such, he is the only one of the men in Gertrud's life whom she continues to see at the end of the film.) He is a former psychology professor of

11 I can't resist pointing out the contrast between Erland and Dreyer himself, insofar as *Gertrud* uses the figure of Erland to raise issues about the purpose and value of artistic expression. Dreyer obviously believes what Gertrud herself does about the imperative to convert one's feelings into practical artistic expression, or he wouldn't have made this film, or any of his others. The fact of *Gertrud*'s existence is Dreyer's own reply to Erland's Pateresque cultivation of sensibility as an end in itself. Dreyer's refutation of Erland's cult of expressive withdrawal is represented by the film we are watching.

hers who maintains his relationship with her to the end. Near the conclusion of the film, he makes it possible for Gertrud to flee from the fragments of all of these broken relationships and to live out the remainder of her life alone, as a recluse and scholar. In the final scene he visits her one last time to talk about the past.

The important point is that each of these men has in one way or another abandoned (or never embraced in the first place) the narrative project of all of Dreyer's work: the attempt to put ideals into relation with forms of worldly realizations. (Even Axel, the perennial bachelor, in his state of permanent chastity has apparently given up on the realization of his feelings in the practical forms of an actual sexual relationship. Moreover, although it is only sketchily presented, the fact that he is a professor of psychology may also be intended to tell us that he has made a fundamental compromise, replacing feeling with analysis.) Gertrud alone refuses to resign herself to that separation of ideals and practical expressions. She wants to live her feelings and dreams, and to live them unrepressed by society's, or even language's, mediations and compromises.

She refuses to cut her ideals to fit the world's expressive systems even as she – at least initially – attempts to live them in an actual relationship. Gertrud refuses to speak any other language than the language of love – not the language of business, statecraft, politics, or even poetry. It is not for nothing that she is made a singer. It is as if the only expression she trusts is the pure

emotional expressiveness of song – although it is significant that in her one opportunity actually to sing in the
film (not counting one flashback scene) Gertrud faints
away from even that opportunity of expression. Silence
is the only expression for an idealism so pure.

Yet Gertrud is no Emma Bovary. She is neither fool
nor sentimentalist, and Dreyer is not interested in easy
satire. (The only Flaubertian archness or irony about
Gertrud's idealism in the film is confined to the con-
temptible Erland, which should indicate how Dreyer
would have regarded a Flaubertian reading of his film.)
When her relationship with Erland doesn't live up to her
expectations, Gertrud is absolutely dry-eyed and clearheaded about her position, and about the inhospitality of
the world to her ideals. By the end of *Gertrud,* she sees
as clearly as the most perceptive viewer how imperiled,
how untenable, how fraught with pain and inevitable
frustration her effort of translation is, even as she refuses to compromise her position in order to mitigate
her doom.

The central (and longest) scene of the film epitomizes
the complexity of Dreyer's presentation of the relation
between what we can imagine or feel and what we can
actually speak or live in the world. The occasion is a
gathering of friends and dignitaries to celebrate the poet
Gabriel Lidman's fiftieth birthday. (We are to understand that Lidman has a national following and that the
ceremony is intended as a grand public homage to a man
who is a kind of unofficial poet laureate.) Gertrud and

Gustav (the latter in his capacity as a minister of state and the former as the wife of the minister) are seated as official guests at the dais.

It is not accidental that *Gertrud* uses such an emphatically public ceremony, complete with elaborate formal presentations and a series of ceremonial speeches, as the dramatic device to bring Gertrud and her former lover together.[12] There can be no retreat into insulated subjectivity for Gertrud and the man who still intensely loves her and will remind her of it again on this night. There can be no photographic or visual privacy. *Gertrud* gives us a world in which virtually everything must be said and done out in public, in public forms, ceremonies, and language.

In this scene and in one more emotional scene that follows between Gertrud and Gabriel the next day, Dreyer forces Gabriel and Gertrud to negotiate every expressive hurdle possible. Their few moments of intimacy in the film are snatched from between interminable, polite encounters with others. All of the intimate moments in *Gertrud* are interrupted by the press of unexpected and unwanted social obligations and duties.

12 The scene has more than superficial similarities with the comparable ceremony in Frank Capra's *Mr. Smith Goes to Washington,* in which Jefferson Smith is publicly feted following his senatorial appointment. There is not sufficient space to go into the parallels here, but it seems clear to me that Dreyer was influenced by Capra – of all directors, the filmmaker who might seem, on a superficial acquaintance, to have the least to say to him.

Gertrud's and Gabriel's poignant scene at the birth-day party has to be grabbed during the few minutes that Gustav is away attending to some pointless public func-tion and from which he is due to return at any second. Similarly, the final, moving scene between Gertrud and Gabriel the next day is forced to take place in the few minutes that Gustav is called away to the phone.[13] Even Gustav's and Gertrud's own initial scene together (in which Gertrud announces her intention to divorce him) is interrupted by the sudden intrusion of Gustav's mother.

In two of the supreme examples of misery under glass in all of Dreyer's work, at the moment that she is under-going the greatest emotional distress of her life, Gertrud is enlisted to sing in public to please a government min-ister during the birthday ceremony; and, in the subse-quent final farewell between Gabriel and Gertrud the following day, Dreyer arranges the scene so that the parting of the two former lovers has to be conducted directly under the eyes of Gustav, who is, with true ministerial heartiness (and irrelevance), offering a toast to the future at the moment they are excruciatingly say-ing goodbye to each other forever.

But the resistance to the expression of pure feeling in the film is not merely the consequence of Gustav's (or his mother's) unexpected intrusions into otherwise inti-

13 One of the running jokes of the film – though it is really too sad to call it a joke – is that Gustav is repeatedly being called away from Gertrud's side by one ministerial duty or another.

mate scenes. Even when Gertrud and Gabriel (or Gertrud and Erland) are alone together, Dreyer reminds us of all of the obstacles that social discourse itself puts in the way of our expressions of ourselves. If adequate expression depends on language to a large extent, language itself nevertheless gets in the way of our deepest expressions. The cosmic distances between souls and the difficulty of building bridges from one heart to another with the forms of social and verbal intercourse have seldom been more powerfully documented in film. Everything in *Gertrud* must be enacted socially, played out almost as publicly as if it were on a stage, in the forms of social and verbal interaction between characters who – even if they are lovers or former lovers or husband and wife – are also in other respects at the same time almost complete strangers to each other.

The endless talk, talk, talk of the film – so much objected to by its initial audience – reminds us of the endless repressions, evasions, and subterfuges that all social intercourse repeatedly forces upon us. There can be no unmediated, pure expressions in the film. Everything is filtered, censored, controlled by the very nature of discourse and the human personality. That is why the only even partially adequate expression in the film takes place between the lines, in the pauses and silences, it seems. Dreyer's middle–distance photography emphasizes characters' social embeddedness. There can be no swoony Hollywood merging of souls. No melting of one character into another in the forms of glamour close–

296

ups. No blending of eyes into eyes (of characters' eyes into each other or of viewers' eyes into the characters') in point–of–view shots.

But, after these general observations about the nature of expression in *Gertrud*, let me return to the scene of Lidman's birthday festivities. To underline the formality and publicity of the expressive moment, Dreyer begins the scene with a procession of the young admirers of Gabriel's poetry marching toward his table to make a formal speech of homage. In a tracking movement whose elaborateness and stateliness emphasize the ceremoniousness of the event, Dreyer's camera follows the progress of the procession from a balcony at one end of the grand dining room, down a flight of stairs, and up to the table of honor at which sit Gabriel Lidman and the other dignitaries present for the festivities.

As the group marches toward the speaker's table, they sing a song of praise to Lidman. It is a moment roughly comparable to the singing of the "Marseilles" by the assembled company in Renoir's *Grande Illusion* – a diverse group of individuals are momentarily imaginatively united in a public ceremony and express their comity by singing together. What is most interesting, however, is how different Dreyer's understanding of such a moment is from Renoir's. To be joined together in such a community of song and shared feeling in the Renoir film is one of the supreme moments. It represents, for Renoir, an entirely desirable merging of the individual into the group, a satisfying expression of his personal energies in terms of group purposes and activities. But for Dreyer the relation between individual imagination and public expression is problematic in a way that it almost never is in Renoir. In the interactions that immediately follow this Renoirian moment of harmony, Dreyer opens to view accesses of private and socially inexpressible feeling that are designed to make us question not only the adequacy of this ceremony, but the adequacy of all public expressions of feeling.

It is not accidental that the music of the public sing-along is replaced by a very different music during a subsequent meeting between Gertrud and Gabriel in a private sitting room off the main banquet hall. The harmonized resonance of male and female voices singing in unison is superseded by the hesitations and silences of pained confidences. Those plangent, anguished tones and a violin and cello duet on the sound track usher us into an entirely different acoustic realm – a realm of intense feelings that will never be expressed in a community of shared experience. They represent everything that will never be converted into Renoirian expressive ceremonies.

But I am getting ahead of the scene. Let me return to the moment following the communal song and the traveling shot of the procession marching toward the speaker's dais. A young man steps forward from the group to make an elegant speech about the purity and truth of Gabriel's love poetry. He delivers an impassioned hymn in praise of perfect love as the basis for a union between

two individuals (and as an alternative to what he scorn-
fully describes as the older generation's acceptance of
"the convention" of marriage as an economic and social
institution). In his adolescent faith in absolute love as the
bond that unites two souls, the boy seems to be a young-
er, male version of Gertrud, but, as subsequent scenes
make clear, he is inserted into the film to establish an
important contrast. The boy represents a state of expressive naiveté or inexperience. In his paean to pure
love, the young man completely fails to acknowledge any
of the expressive requirements (and problems) that
Gertrud (and her creator) recognize. Even as she embraces an ideal of perfect love, Gertrud recognizes the
painful distance between the ideal and the reality. Even
in her earliest scenes with Erland, Dreyer shows that
Gertrud recognizes the expressive *labor* it takes to make
the translation from the ideal to the reality. (*Gertrud* and
its title character are quite clearheaded about practical
sexual and social realities of love affairs from the very
beginning of the film.) For the boy, on the other hand,
there is no need for an act of translation at all, which is
why the boy's belief in an *easy* relation of ideals and
realities is inadequate, and entirely different from Gertrud's more tough-minded beliefs.

I commented previously on Dreyer's general avoidance of shot/reverse shot techniques of intercutting between speaker and listener, and his avoidance of close–
ups, but this scene stands as one of a small number of
important exceptions in his late work to his general pref-

Controlling social and linguistic contexts that everywhere limit expression –
Gabriel Lidman at the birthday ceremony, and off in private with Gertrud

erence for middle-distance camera setups in which two or more interacting figures are visible at the same time. As the boy speaks, Dreyer intercuts shots of Gabriel's reactions, and uses them to make it clear that even if his poetry has been the inspiration for the boy's impassioned rhetoric, Gabriel is not taken in by it. Gabriel is not buying what he has been selling. As the young man effuses, Dreyer's judicious cuts show Lidman holding himself aloof from, and even seeming slightly pained by the boy's uncritical celebration of the rapturous merging of two souls in love.

It is not surprising that when he rises to speak in response, Gabriel, in effect, changes the subject. Even as he seems to be replying to the boy's speech and expressing his gratitude for it, he tactfully switches the topic from

300

love and passion, to a statement about the importance of intellectual strength and emotional control for the true artist. After all of the overheated rhetoric, Gabriel coolly speaks in praise of cool-headedness. He displays the tough-mindedness and dispassionate judiciousness that the boy lacks, a coolness and toughness of intellect that Dreyer himself as an artist so brilliantly demonstrates with this bracing shift of tone.

The third speaker at the festivities is Gertrud's husband, Gustav. With his speech the tone and subject matter shift once again.[14] Gustav's talk shows us the extent to which the preceding drama of the relationship of the heart and the mind has been completely lost on him. Dreyer emphasizes his ignorance by having Gustav deliver a disquisition on style as the unproblematic expression of thought and feeling. It would be almost comic if it weren't so pathetic. The conflict between imaginative ideals and the repressiveness of available forms of expression is something that has never occurred to Gustav.

Gustav's appreciation of Gabriel's poetry is confined to a neoclassical dissertation on its decorum and the purity of its style. The same poetry that authorized the

14 It is not too much to argue that these tonal shifts and corrections of vision are, in effect, the meaning of *Gertrud* – a film that takes as its subject the trajectory of exalted impulses braving hostile expressive environments.

They are also evidence that Dreyer is completely unsentimental and undeluded about Gertrud's predicament. He sees the expressive difficulty of her position as clearly as she herself does.

young man's lyrical effusion has, in Gustav's appreciation of it, become an example of "moderation," "reasonableness," propriety, and charm (in the most deadening sense of the words).

Dreyer is doing more than indicating the limitations of Gustav's statesmanlike devotion to neoclassical conceptions of expression. The tones of Gustav's ruminations serve as a foil to Gabriel's. They tell us how profoundly different Gabriel's passionate appreciation of the necessity of intellectual rigor is from the superficially similar emotional detachment and intellectual control of a connoisseur of stylistic effects like Gustav. While Gabriel's performance as a speaker (and Ebbe Rode's as an actor) communicates a state of intense passion carefully reigned in and difficultly modulated into an acceptable form of public expression, the tonal performance of Gustav (played by Bendt Rothe) communicates his belief in control and arrangement as ends in themselves.[15]

To expand this a bit, one might argue that Gustav is the equivalent of the formalist critic who has managed to turn all human expressions into value-neutral "texts" disconnected from messy "contexts," and all reading (or viewing) into passionless connoisseurship. Gustav sees nothing in Gabriel's poetry but words and "style." The stylistic container is emptied of content. His bloodless

---

15 The only moment that Gustav loses his masterful control of his emotions in the entire film is the explosion of grief and anger near the end in which he tears up and burns Gertrud's photograph, after her telling him that she has never really loved him.

understanding of expression is really not very different from that of recent formalist interpreters of Dreyer's own work, who see nothing in his films but the "play" of "empty" signifiers, evacuated styles, and self-referential allusions. In short, like the critics he reminds one of, Gustav represents a position on expression that could not be further from Dreyer's own, which is why he is such a distinctively limited character.

In contrast to Gustav's expressive poise and coolness (and praise of poise and coolness), Gabriel and Gertrud offer expressive disturbance and dismay – however carefully controlled and forcibly suppressed. They interest Dreyer much more than Gustav does, and are obviously much closer to his heart. They are deeply agitated and upset precisely because – unlike Gustav and unlike the boy speech maker – they recognize the real difficulty of the translation of their energies into practical social and verbal expressions. Gabriel's gestures, walk, tones, and posture speak powerfully throughout the film about his extreme emotional disturbance. Gustav and Erland are entirely more relaxed expressively, which is just their problem.

It is typical of the density and rapidity of *Gertrud* that in a few minutes, in these three speakers, in what is usually dismissed as a static, talky, transitional scene, Dreyer has succinctly "placed" each of them, and provided three different visions of expression. But *Gertrud* is nothing if not a study of multiple perspectives on expression, and while these speeches are being delivered, Dreyer adds a fourth perspective, which is different from each of the other three, by tracking down the length of the speaker's table to reveal that Gertrud is sitting there either ill or in anguish during the ceremony – whether in disillusionment at the fatuity of the sentiments expressed, in pain at the failure of life to live up to the ideals being talked about, or in weariness at the unreality of all such ceremonies and the inevitable falsifications of the public expressions it gives rise to. With the assistance of her dinner partner, she retires into a private room off to one side of the banquet hall while her husband is still slogging away praising purity of style.

In a film whose subject is the chasm between feelings and practical forms of expression, it is appropriate that after having rendered a public ceremony in some detail, Dreyer should now, in the following scene, invite the viewer, as it were, to step off to one side of the Renoirian world of shared public expressions.[16] As Gertrud moves into a sitting room to rest, Dreyer moves his film into a more private expressive realm, where more important events may take place.

One can only speculate about what a different direction the scene might have moved in if this were a Renoir film. That birthday celebration could have become an opportunity for the unfurling of a panorama of fascinating social interactions. Renoir could have turned it into a

16 Though, as I've already suggested, the ceremony has already pointed more to failures of expression and gaps of understanding than to Renoirian harmonies.

grand, seriocomic interplay of winks, nods, gestures, overtures, approaches, refusals, and flirtations. In his work it is almost never necessary for characters to leave a group completely behind in order to begin to speak together. The densely woven social fabric of his films always demonstrates how tightly knitted together the characters are, no matter what superficial differences or rivalries may appear to exist between them. Because they all speak an identical social language, Renoir's characters are always more cemented together than they are separated by any individual squabbles. Underpinning their minor, and ultimately trivial, disagreements is a profound and pervasive agreement to a universally intelligible language of gestures, actions, and words that is available to everyone and within which everyone can express himself or herself.

For Dreyer the real events are always inward. It is within the assertively private space and occasion of an encounter between Gabriel and Gertrud in a room off to one side of this public assembly that one of the most moving and painful scenes in all of his work, indeed in all of film, will take place. One must leave behind the public ceremony for the real events to start.

Gabriel excuses himself from the celebration and joins Gertrud. They are former lovers who were separated long ago, but Gabriel is still deeply in love with her. Though it is difficult to capture the spirit of his words in a bald summary of them, Gabriel proceeds to tell Gertrud that the man with whom she is now in love –

the composer Erland Jansson – doesn't love her and has, in fact, been dragging her name in the gutter by bragging to strangers about his sexual conquest of her. It is as excruciatingly painful for Gabriel to have to tell Gertrud this as it is for her to hear it, and he breaks down in tears as he speaks. For her it is a stunningly disillusioning discovery. As we (and probably Gabriel also) realize, in leaving her husband and attempting to begin a new life with Erland, she has burned all of her bridges. However, the impact of the scene resides less in the shock value of the tale Gabriel tells than in what the scene as a whole tells us about expression.

We have come a long way from the birthday ceremony. Under the pressure of the emotions the characters attempt to contain, language fails and breaks down. The former lovers are silent for much of the scene. The eloquence and volubility of the other room is superseded by stuttering, hesitant, near muteness. For long moments in the scene, Gabriel's feelings are displaced into stunned, blank iterations of Gertrud's name, and Gertrud herself is largely speechless through most of it.[17]

Gabriel is a poet. He has devoted his life to language. We have just seen how eloquent he can be when he is speaking in a public forum. Yet here he is virtually speechless. His stammering iterations announce the

---

17 In his pity, grief, and despair, Gabriel simply repeats Gertrud's name over and over again, as in the following moment: "Oh, Gertrud. . . . Gertrud. . . . Gertrud. . . . Why don't things turn out the way we imagine them?"

state of expressive crisis that *Gertrud* takes as its subject. Feelings can be spoken neither in the Renoirian ceremony nor (more than haltingly and despairingly) in his repetition of Gertrud's name.

As I noted about *Ordet*, one of the hazards of subtitles is that they encourage a viewer to become a reader of, rather than a listener to, the text. No greater disservice could be done to a scene like this one than to fail to listen to it. That is because the meaning of this scene is precisely that meaning itself has retreated from the semantic meaning of the words and moved into the subtext of tonal resonances underpinning them. One has to sit back and listen to Gabriel's and Gertrud's tones as they speak, as if the tones themselves were a musical sound track laid down almost independently of the words that they say. That schism is the point of the scene.

The tonal text of inflections, emotions, and imaginations is the text that matters throughout *Gertrud*. Even at their most desperate moments, Hamlet and Lear could fall back on the language of the Shakespearean soliloquy. *Gertrud* denies itself and its characters the possibility not only of soliloquies but also of almost all of the expressive resources of denotative language itself.[18] The reason the "text" of *Gertrud* can seem so tedious or pointless to an

18 As I will argue below, the flashback scenes and some of the stylizations in the drawing room scenes offer a kind of visual language that functions independently of spoken language and is more expressive than spoken language. Those scenes are the cinematic equivalent of the Shakespearean soliloquy.

audience prepared for Renoirian expressiveness is that virtually everything that matters in the film is expressed in an emotional "subtext." Dreyer never went further in the direction of indicating the fundamental limits of expression. The very operating premise of *Gertrud,* and of all of the main characters in it (excepting perhaps the statesman, Gustav), is that language cannot be trusted. Words only hide or conceal our feelings. No one in *Gertrud* can say what he or she means. The characters' gestures and words declare themselves acts of misdirection. Characters exist in an essentially oblique relation to everything they say or do.[19]

The whole emotional and imaginative text of the film is hidden somewhere underneath the visible and audible text of social expressions in it. That expressive gap is the fundamental fact that characters and viewers must come to grips with. It is that subtext that we and they must learn to hear and see. That should help to account for the blankness of the faces and the absence of eye contact between characters (which particular scenes in *Gertrud*

19 In this sense, Erland only differs from the other characters in that his expressive infidelities are manipulative while theirs are not. Although Erland cruelly attempts to profit from his insincerities, he is not in a *fundamentally* different relation to expression than any of the other characters in the film. Language betrays everyone here. It hides or represses true feeling as much for Gabriel the poet as it does for Erland the cynic. It is not too much to say that the central subject of *Gertrud* is the unbridgeable gap between personal impulse and all public expression. Erland is more blatant and extreme, but not fundamentally different from the others in this respect.

share with scenes in *Ordet*). It is what *won't* be publicly expressed – what won't be expressed even in facial expressions or shared glances – that Dreyer communicates in this negative way. Gabriel's gestures, walk, and posture as he sits or stands communicate intensities of feeling that even his poignant lines of dialogue cannot. What the passionate silences, the emotionally freighted inarticulatenesses, the overwrought (and semantically empty) iterations of the film express is the substitution of a fullness of feeling for an emptiness of actual social and linguistic expression. Imaginative richnesses of consciousness and emotional richnesses of feeling are asked to substitute for impoverishments of practical experience and failures of social expression.

In miniature, the scene between Gertrud and Gabriel in the drawing room enacts the fundamental substitutional process of *Gertrud* as a whole. Emotional presences and imaginative connections are called on to fill the void of social and physical absences and separations. *Gertrud* makes that process of imaginative and emotional substitution its subject, exploring the difficulty (perhaps the impossibility) of translating private states of consciousness into forms of expression that manifest themselves in worldy time and space.

The expressive crisis defined by *Gertrud* is as much Dreyer's as his characters'. The real poignancy of the expressive problem explored by all of Dreyer's films is its radical sincerity: It is not merely assigned to particular characters in a dramatic situation. It figures Dreyer's own problem as a transcendental filmmaker working in realistic narrative forms. Not only Gertrud and Gabriel, but *Gertrud* itself, in this scene and others, despairs of the meaningfulness of social forms of representation. As much as his actors are, Dreyer is forced to communicate his meanings obliquely. They do it in the pauses between the spoken lines, in catches of the voice, and in gestures. He does it in special acoustic, visual, and stylistic effects.

But, however glancingly and fugitively, meaning is just barely communicated. That is why, although a tone-deaf and visually centered viewer may see or hear little going on in a scene like this one, or may regard it as "empty" or "boring," anyone responsive to the characters' tones of voice and the emotional depths of feeling underneath the most prosaic and repetitive verbal expressions will find this scene among the most moving in all of Dreyer's work. The verbal and positional repetitions in this scene and others, the insistent parallels and echoes between one scene or shot and another that Dreyer builds into the film, which many critics have cited as evidence of *Gertrud*'s tedium or Dreyer's creative exhaustion, actually make the repeated words and paralleled situations *more* emotionally resonant – as a chant or a litany can become emotionally more powerful the more its words are emptied of literal significance. Connotative richness of feeling opens up as denotative meanings are drained away by the repetitions. In the largest sense, these verbal stalls and circlings are an extension of most of the other abstracting and simplifying aspects of the film.

It is *Gertrud*'s (and Dreyer's) excessive shift away from what is socially speakable that I want to consider in the conclusion of this chapter. How does a work, above all a dramatic work, communicate when it abandons faith in social forms and expressions? How does an artist express secret, private, almost inexpressible states of feeling and imagination?

As we have already seen in previous films, at a point of expressive crisis like this, Dreyer depends upon artistic style to "speak" in ways that the characters or their social interactions cannot. One of Dreyer's chief stylistic ways of speaking for and through the characters in *Gertrud*, when their own powers of speech are muted or stopped, is to use expressive musical orchestrations to communicate meanings. In this scene, for example, the music of a violin and cello on the sound track "speaks" for Gabriel and Gertrud when their voices are choked by shame and grief, throttled by emotion. Following so shortly on the birthday ceremony, we feel all the more how different in function this music is from the public song fest. It is not a way of uniting a group of characters in a community of shared feeling but of revealing private feelings that words don't express.

It is important that the music is on the sound track of the film – a stylistic device of the film itself – and not in the room with the characters. Insofar as the music does not exist in the actual world Gertrud and Gustav occupy, it is Dreyer's attempt to supplement his own text – to deflect attention from the manifest social and verbal text of his own film and toward a stylistic subtext underpinning it. The music is his attempt stylistically to "fill" the "emptiness" of the social and verbal text. It is an attempt to register the presence of emotional and imaginative energies that won't be converted into lines of dialogue or social interactions between the characters.[20]

Dreyer employs similar nonsource sound musical scoring in all of his sound films to pick up the expressive burden that characters' social interactions will not bear. The music in *Gertrud* functions exactly the same way that the music and the lighting effects functioned in *Day of Wrath:* to communicate meanings that Dreyer (or his characters) can't express in the structures of dramatic interaction. Just as the crucial fact about the shadows in *Day of Wrath* is that they are *not* traceable to naturalistic sources within the film, the crucial fact about the music in *Gertrud* is that it is not realistically explainable. They are stylistic effects of the film – purely imaginative effects that offer their meanings *in place of* social expressions.

Now, obviously, other films use tonal richnesses of expression, special lighting effects, and nonsource sound musical orchestrations also, but there is a difference between Dreyer's use of such expressive devices and the

20 Compare my discussions of comparable musical substitutions or deflections of attention in other films in my *American Dreaming* (Berkeley: University of California Press, 1985), 222–225, and *American Vision* (New York: Cambridge University Press, 1986), 258–260.

routine Hollywood stoking up of dramatic interest and emotion. These special effects are not used by Dreyer merely to emphasize the importance of an event or social interaction or emotionally to heighten its effect, but in an almost opposite way: to suggest the presence of imaginative energies that are otherwise invisible or inexpressible. The musical or lighting or tonal effect does not expand upon or editorialize about the social text; it deflects our attention from it, it attempts to *substitute* its emotional meanings for absent social significances. The shadows and light on Anne's face, the music on the sound track between Gabriel's and Gertrud's lines, the tones of Gabriel's voice "speak" in ways that the characters' practical words and actions cannot. Imaginative events, as rendered through such stylistic heightenings of the text, are offered not as enhancements of but as *alternatives* to social ones.

Gertrud takes its place along with *Day of Wrath* as one of Dreyer's two most heavily orchestrated and evocatively photographed films precisely because in both films the orchestration and the lighting are called upon to communicate what cannot be said in the forms of dialogue and social interaction within them: energies of eroticism and imagination that won't be incorporated into the repressive ideologies of family, church, and state in the earlier film, energies of idealism and emotion that won't be expressed in the forms of social interaction in this one.

In an essay he completed shortly after finishing *Day of*

313

Wrath, Dreyer approvingly quotes Heinrich Heine's familiar maxim that "where the words come out short, the music begins."[21] But he significantly goes on to argue a more radical position than Heine's, one that might be reformulated as "where there can be no words, there must be music."

Insofar as *Gertrud* makes a viewer supremely attentive to the ways words conceal rather than reveal, the ways social interactions betray characters rather than serve them, the ways language represses rather than expresses intensities of feeling, its stylizations are a crucial way of supplementing its text, of moving it out of the realm of inadequate social expression and into a realm of more adequate imaginative expression. Yet Dreyer's point is ultimately a tragic one – that our finest ideals and desires will not be "realized" in the structures of social and linguistic interaction. The effects are merely stylistic. They are not available outside of film. Musical soundtracks and special lighting effects are not available to us in life.

In this respect, like both *Day of Wrath* and *Ordet,* *Gertrud* pits realism against itself. Dreyer locates his film at the mysterious interface where the real and the unreal come together. Even if its characters did not talk as much as they do about their wishes, dreams, and desires, many of *Gertrud*'s scenes would seem designed to en-

---

21 "A Little on Film Style," reprinted in Skoller (ed.), *Dreyer in Double Reflection,* 141.

courage us to treat it as a dream film. The result is that even as Dreyer and his characters scrupulously honor the forms of realistic dramatic interaction, the events and interactions in the film are simultaneously pulled in the opposite direction: so that we will not willingly suspend our disbelief, but that we should never quite forget the stylized, dreamlike artificiality of the film. I want to hold off considering *Gertrud*'s dreamlike coda for the time being, but there are many aspects of the main narrative that one might cite as examples of Dreyer's deliberate dreamlike stylization of events:

There is the voice-over narration that Dreyer uses to tell the story of Gustav's visit to the opera house to look for Gertrud one night (and within which Gustav talks about how "we dream our lives away"). There is the beginning of Gertrud's meeting in the park with Erland in which the lighting is so unnaturally diffused and Gertrud's costume and appearance are so strangely girlish (and stagy, as if she had cast herself in a theatrical production) that the scene looks as if it were being presented not as it really happened, but as Gertrud imagined it. There are the dozens of art objects Dreyer places around the characters in different scenes (pieces of sculpture in the park, works of art on the walls of rooms, and the music played and songs sung in different scenes) that make the sets look as if they were less realistic locations than psychodramatic projections of Gertrud's fantasies (or, again, as if they were stage sets designed to *remind* us that they are stage sets). The

315

proscenium effect of the settings, blockings, and photography seems intended not to draw a viewer in, but rather to grant him or her a slight, but crucial imaginative *distance* from events. Dreyer induces a moderate degree of abstraction that parallels the states of abstraction he dramatizes in his characters. He cultivates our meditativeness.

Beyond those things, there are the insistently symbolic uses of more mundane props (like Gertrud's mirror, the tapestry she comments on, and her photograph). Dreyer's photography of Gertrud's image in the mirror in her home is particularly strange and evocative: three times that we see her image in the mirror, he deliberately places his camera in a position from which Gertrud seems to have an existence only as a virtual image – her actual body is invisible, she floats above the ground, her mirror image is all.[22] Then there is the use of music and other sound effects (principally the sounds of clocks ticking and chiming), which are repeatedly used as formal effects to mark the beginning or end of scenes and to encourage a viewer to compare or contrast one scene with another, all of which keep nudging us away from treating the film as a series of realistic depictions, and

22 There are two other uses of mirrors in the film: another time in her home when Gertrud symbolically indicates the end of her relationship with Gabriel by blowing out the candles on the mirror (which he gave her), and a briefer glimpse of Gertrud's image in a mirror in a room at Lidman's party.

toward considering events and objects abstractly, allegorically, symbolically.[23]

Moreover, in addition to employing a "flash-ahead" coda at its conclusion (a coda that itself contains further verbal flashbacks and "flash-aheads" embedded within it), *Gertrud* is the one Dreyer film to employ extended flashback sequences during the course of its narrative: in the first of which, near the start of the film, we see Gertrud's initial visit to Erland Jansson, which occurred several months before the events of the film begin; in another of which, near the end of the movie, Dreyer flashes back to the day on which Gertrud decided to break off from Gabriel Lidman, many years earlier.

In the flashback scenes, *Gertrud* becomes an outright dream film. Reality, in any ordinary waking sense of it, is simply left behind. The flashbacks are deliberately stylized in their presentation (in their voice-over effects, their lighting and photography, their pantomimic acting, and their use of costumes and theatrical gestures and inflections) to remind us that as we watch them we are seeing not reality as it might be said to exist indepen-

---

23 The pervasive metaphorization of shots, events, and objects is, in effect, only an instance of the general derealizing tendency in the film. As I explained in the *Day of Wrath* chapter, the metaphoricity of Dreyer's shots and scenes is a way of moving the viewer beyond being a mere realistic consumer of facts, events, and objects in the film, and encouraging him or her to participate imaginatively (along with Dreyer and the characters he cares most about) in the transforming, substituting, and enriching acts of consciousness that *Gertrud* takes as its real subject.

317

dently of a particular human awareness, but the transformations of consciousness enacted by a character.
They are lighted, acted, and photographed to communicate that they represent not actual, but imagined ver-
sions of experience. Each uses an extremely simplified
or ritualized form of pantomimic acting, largely avoids
dialogue or the depiction of realistic social interactions
between the characters, and is photographed with gauze
over the lens (or the use of a diffusion filter) to call
attention to its nonrealistic quality.[24]

Dreyer is not, of course, suggesting that any of *Gertrud*
is actually dreamed, but that much of it *might* have been
dreamed: some whole scenes, and many fleeting moments within others. That is to say, such stylistic effects
register events and movements of consciousness that do

24 The connections with what Dreyer did in *Vampyr* are important. Notwithstanding all of the differences between the two films, *Vampyr* comes
the closest to *Gertrud* in its interest in how consciousness (which is
expressed in both films through stylized effects of photography, frame
composition, lighting, and camera movement) transforms events in ways
that have no correlative or form of expression in so-called reality. The
subject of *Vampyr* is, in effect, the transforming power of imagination –
which is why virtually every important shot within the film is assignable to
a special point of view (sometimes that of the protagonist, David Gray,
but at other times that of the camera itself as a distinguishable consciousness, as in *Ordet*). The distinctiveness of the camera's movements
and perspectives is meant to remind us of the distinctiveness – that is to
say, the nonobjectivity, nonneutrality – of events of consciousness.
Events of consciousness – not words, actions, or practical events – are
the true subject of films otherwise as apparently different from one
another as *Gertrud, Day of Wrath,* and *Vampyr*.

not (or cannot) correspond to actual worldly events and movements. Dreyer deliberately alternates between these flashback/memory/dream sequence scenes and moments and the drawing room conversation scenes and moments. The first are photographically enhanced in various ways (with diffusion filters and the selective use of overexposure and light spilling into the camera); the second are generally flatly fill-lighted. The first avoid conversational interchange and border on being played as pantomime at moments; the second are pained, awkward, frustrating attempts at talk between two characters. The first are visionary; the second, social in their presentation.

The alternation of the two sorts of scenes or moments is the point. The question asked in all but words is how does one bring the energies of the one into the expressive structures of the other? How does one speak the energies of imagination and desire that are documented in the one, in the language of society and dramatic interaction of the other?

Gertrud (like *Vampyr*) makes us aware of all of the ways consciousness transforms reality under the pressure of our desires, even as it equally reminds us of how reality may fail to live up to our imagination of it and may fail to allow us to express the transformations of desire in the forms of our lives. The transformations stay metaphors, effects of style, tonal plangencies, dreamlike enhancements. The works of art scattered throughout the film (paintings on walls, sculptural figures, a tapestry, pieces of music, even a score framed and hung on the wall of Erland's room that looks just a little like a still from the credits sequence of *Day of Wrath*) and the examples of writing in the film (Gabriel's writing about love or Gertrud's love poem about herself) celebrate expressions of consciousness that have no practical equivalents or social corollaries. This great work of art celebrates acts of consciousness recorded in works of art and acts of writing that are able to generate meanings and connections that don't exist in any more worldly form.[25]

What I am describing as the dream-film quality of *Gertrud* is part of a larger project of what I previously called the partial narrative derealization of reality in Dreyer's work. Events and objects hover half-way between being symbolic and being realistic. For example, in the scene I've described in the drawing room during the birthday celebration, just before Gabriel Lidman comes in, Gertrud points to a tapestry on the wall immediately behind her of a naked woman hounded by dogs

25 The way many of the film's effects actually seem designed to remind us that we are witnessing a *work of art* (and not merely eavesdropping on reality) seems, in the largest sense, a celebration of the power of artistic transformation in general. It is as if Dreyer is giving thanks for all the ways that art itself is different from life – all the ways art alone can express energies of consciousness that life inevitably represses. Although he couldn't have known that this would be his last film, it is fitting that this celebration of the powers of art should occur in his final film.

For a somewhat fuller discussion of the expressive function of deliberately stylized or dreamlike moments in film see my article "Love's Dreams," in *Persistence of Vision*, no. 6 (Summer 1988), 57–59.

and tells Axel Nygren (who has stopped by to comfort and attend her) that she dreamed that dream the night before. She says that she was the naked woman surrounded by baying hounds. The effect is suddenly to render the tapestry and the interchange itself strangely unreal in at least two ways: once for the viewer of the film and once for the characters in it.

In the first place, in terms of our experience of the movie, what was previously merely an incidental prop on the set suddenly becomes not only important, but symbolic. In the second, in terms of Gertrud's experience, what was previously merely an object in her surroundings is suddenly transformed into a spectral emanation of her consciousness. The tapestry, which we thought to be mere, dead, inanimate reality a few seconds earlier in the scene, is suddenly derealized and animated metaphorically – turned into the stuff of human consciousness or made an extension of it.[26]

I have already alluded to another similar partial derealizing effect involving not an object, but Gertrud herself. Dreyer photographs Gertrud so that, while her ac-

26 In all of this I am assuming that Gertrud's "explanation" of the tapestry is insufficient to "justify" its presence in the film naturalistically. In fact her explanation of the tapestry in terms of her dream only makes it more strange and its presence in this scene less understandable. There is no adequate explanation of why this particular tapestry should appear in her dream. The connection between the two remains artificial and uncanny, and the presence of the tapestry within the film remains inexplicable, which is to say, we remain aware of it as an artistic effect, an expression of consciousness in excess of narrative logic.

tual body is not visible on camera, her reflection is visible on screen in a mirror (a mirror that we are told was a present from Gabriel, her former lover). As she stands in front of it, it is as if she had not a physical body, but a body imagined into existence in memory and desire, conjured into visionary presence through the gift from Gabriel. (A comparable effect is achieved in the scene in which Erland and Gertrud sleep together for the first time. While he plays a nocturne on the piano, she undresses in another room. Dreyer contrives it so that we see only her shadow on the wall behind him, as if her body were not the reality, but her image were.)

As such effects illustrate, Gertrud is, in the most profound sense, never more than a virtual presence even in her own film. She is as fugitive and intangible as the ideals she embraces. This is not merely a technical observation. It is the most artistically daring aspect of the film, and potentially the most baffling to a viewer unprepared for its radicalism.

Gertrud is not merely a realistic character (as one might encounter one in another sort of film) with exalted ideals about love. She is something much more daring. She is Dreyer's most sustained attempt to dramatize the consequences of an existence that won't be pinned down to realistic forms of expression or categories of understanding. She is larger and more elusive than any actual, practical representation of herself can ever, anywhere, in any way embody.

The various representations of Gertrud in the film –

in the disembodied mirror images, in the tapestry, in the poem she composes for her epitaph in the coda scene, in the photograph of her that Gustav tears up (paralleling the scene of her tearing up another photograph of herself in Gabriel's apartment), in the sketch Gabriel makes of her – don't bring her into focus for us but do the opposite. Before our very eyes, they distribute Gertrud outward, away from any fixed representation. They tell us how incompletely she is represented by any realistic representation. Her self is dispersed among various representations, each equally inadequate and partial.

Like her shifting descriptions of herself as a mouth, sky, clouds, a lover, her identity is entirely fluxional, and will only be represented by a series of moving substitutions – a sequence of endlessly replaced figures. She is representationally elusive and mercurial. She is a figure of imagination and desire unable to be pinned down to any form, and in fact fleeing from all stable or fixed forms. She is energy in motion.[27]

At one point, Erland says to Gertrud, "I don't know who you are," and the problem that his observation summarizes is that Gertrud is precisely what won't be

27 Joan and Anne are earlier manifestations of this same phenomenon. All three defy the realistic representational structures of the world (and of their films) to comprehend or define them – with equally tragic results. Yet insofar as the figure of Gertrud is closer to our conception of our ordinary experiences than either earlier figure, and is at the same time just as uncompromising in her transcendentalism as the earlier figures, *Gertrud* seems to go further than the two earlier films to represent the problems of bringing the transcendental inpulse into everyday life.

Images of Gertrud proliferated away from any center of physical presence –
Self-dispersing representations and imaginative displacements

"known" that way. Each of the men around Gertrud attempts to repressively "know" her, to limit her to a restrictive identity, and each fails precisely because she won't be limited in his way.

That should help us to understand one of the additional significances of the many repetitions of Gertrud's name in the film, which I have already called attention to. Gertrud is repeatedly named in the course of the film – by Dreyer in the first instance in giving her name to its title, but, more importantly, by each of the men around her. But the effect each time is not of reaching her, but of failing, falling short. Gertrud is exactly what will never be addressed, never be reached or identified, never be brought into focus with a fixed identity.

Her name is the film. Her name is invoked dozens of times by everyone around her. But the point is that she is what can't be named. She won't be grasped by such acts. She is desire. She is need. She is hunger. She is a principle of imaginative movement, of unappeasability, of insatiability. She is the imagination of possibility, a dream of freedom and self-definition that will never be confined to an actual social identity.

She is the character all of Dreyer's cinema has been pointing toward. Even more purely than *Day of Wrath*'s Anne, Gertrud is a principle of imaginative energy that won't be limited to a social identity, expression, or function. That is her doom and her audacity. Gertrud is a figure beyond the efforts of figuration of the men around her, a figure almost beyond the effort of figuration that is Dreyer's narrative itself. If she moves beyond worldly self-representation and understanding by the characters in her movie, Gertrud even more radically almost moves beyond artistic representation in the film in which she stars, and beyond understanding by its audiences, insofar as they want to pin her down to a social identity.

No scene demonstrates this better than the coda. It is a scene that Dreyer added to his stage play source, which concludes merely with Gertrud – in a Hedda Gabler–like moment – leaving her husband and home at the final curtain. Dreyer's final scene jumps ahead thirty years to show Gertrud living alone in monastic simplicity somewhere outside of Paris. Now an old woman, she receives a visit from her old friend Axel Nygren. It was with his help that she fled her marriage so many years before. Axel is now an old man, and not having seen her in the intervening years, he uses the excuse of presenting her with a book on Racine he has just published to pay her what they both obviously feel is a final visit. She holds a brief conversation with him in which she speaks of her refusal to forsake her ideal of love or to compromise it. Walling herself off in her austere study, Gertrud has, like Coriolanus, given up the whole universe in order to hold on to her imagination of a "world elsewhere."

How are we to feel about this scene? Some viewers would argue that it demonstrates the ultimate sterility of Gertrud's life (or of Dreyer's vision). She lives and will obviously die alone in a Spartan setting. Dreyer avoids glamorizing her existence in any way. None of the austerities of her life are elided or avoided. In a daring touch, at one point in the scene, Dreyer positions the camera to reveal a view of the hard, narrow bed at one end of the room in which she lives. The obvious implication is that the woman with the most exalted conception of sexual relations in all of film now sleeps alone, and will continue to sleep alone until the day she dies in that same bed.

In the course of her conversation with Axel, Gertrud

briefly attempts to offer a practical justification for her decision, and to defend the fullness of her life in terms of her opportunities for reading and pursuing her intellectual interests, but it is crucial to our understanding of the scene that the meaning of the scene and the meaning of Gertrud's life (to her and to us) are *not* reducible to the practical conditions of her existence, or to the practical justification of it that she expresses to Axel.

The meaning of the scene is understandable only abstractly or metaphorically, in terms of its formal allusions to other scenes and aspects of the film, in relation to the cinematic styles and meanings that preceded it. Dreyer is telling us that it is only in the achievements and accumulations of consciousness in time (Gertrud's consciousness, Axel's consciousness, and – comprehending both even as they go beyond either – the consciousness of their creator and the consciousness of a viewer of the film) that ultimate significances are made. The justification of Gertrud's life does not reside in any practical activity or expression of herself in that room or out of it. In effect, Gertrud's mistake earlier in the film, with each of her lovers, was to attempt to live her consciousness. What this scene tells us (and what she realizes by this point) is that her consciousness must be its own reward. Insofar as the coda works formally by means of metaphoric references and internal resonances with other aspects of the film – and not pragmatically to suggest that Gertrud's achievement involves practical or social arrangements – Dreyer is telling us that it is acts of consciousness that make meaning, not worldly actions or words.

All of Dreyer's work has been leading toward this recognition. Joan is not important to Dreyer for her worldly heroism, but for her private convictions and passion. Anne and Herlofs Marte must give up their places in the world to hold onto their visions of themselves. Even Inger must finally stop her efforts at match-making and soothing hurt souls, must die to the world, and lie still and silent in order to become empowered as the center of a spiritual family, as the creator of a visionary community.

Like a reincarnation of the earlier imaginative absolutist, Joan of Arc, plunged into Victorian society, Gertrud finally represents a quality that can't be measured in the world and that has no practical way of expressing itself in it. (Even the callow Erland – in his twisted and cynical way – realizes something close to this when he calls Gertrud "proud," but adds that hers is a pride of "soul" and not what "society" would call pride.)

I want to conclude by teasing out some of the formal resonances in the final scene. In the first place, the coda is designed to refer us back to the first scene of *Gertrud*. It is the only other scene in which Dreyer presents an older woman, and his intention in the coda is obviously to encourage us to think back the whole length of his film in order to compare it with that opening moment. In the earlier scene, Gustav's mother drops in on Gertrud and Gustav and gives us an image of old age that Dreyer contrasts in every way to the one Gertrud presents. It is an image of old age as consisting of endless tippling, gossip mongering, chitchat, and social trifling. Gustav's mother is a silly old fool who has mortgaged her soul – if she can even be said to have such a thing – to social climbing. She is a slave to the opinions of "the court," "society," and the "best sellers" she devours (but whose authors or titles she can't even remember). Her conception of life is as governed by conventional judgments as Gustav's conception of poetic expression. She rambles on about how Gertrud has been "a good wife" who has conducted herself "irreproachably," as if there were nothing problematic about social values, as if they were an even passably adequate basis for ultimate judgments. It is exactly those sorts of values to which Gertrud's life and Dreyer's whole film offers an imaginative alternative.

The genius of Dreyer's aging of Gertrud in this coda is that in turning her hair white, in heavily making up her face with powder and giving her an ashen complexion, in washing out the expressive contrasts and avoiding modeling her features by using diffused lighting, and in hushing her voice with the whispery tones of old age, Dreyer finds a means physically to desubstantiate or derealize Gertrud's appearance in a way that repeats the imaginative or metaphoric derealizations of the earlier film.

Gertrud's physical paleness (her hair and face are

The derealizations of art, spiritual possession substitutes for dispossession –
Gertrud in the coda losing herself in memories, wishes, dreams

virtually flat white) repeats the visual effect of the whitened, diffused lighting that we saw previously in the flashback scenes of the film, as if she were actually blending into the world of her memories, bleeding out of life and out of view as she becomes more purely a spiritual being. What is most interesting about this derealizing tendency, however, is that as Gertrud becomes less physically present and socially active (or, in terms of the film, less visibly modeled and dramatically assertive, as she is paled and faded by the hair dye and pancake makeup and fill lighting and as her voice is quieted), she actually becomes more spiritually compelling and powerful in Dreyer's text. Physical, social, and verbal absence intensifies imaginative and spiritual presence.

Compare the way in earlier scenes, as I have already noted, Gertrud is represented by virtual, rather than actual, images: reflections in mirrors, shadows on walls, symbolic representations in works of art. The substitu-

330

tion of spiritual presence for physical unavailability that has been going on throughout the film is, in a sense, completed and literalized in the final scene. As an old woman, Gertrud more or less ceases to have an actual sexual, bodily, or social identity, a real presence at all. She has become as desubstantialized as her wishes, desires, dreams, memories.[28]

She actually lives the renunciations, the spiritualizations, the withdrawals, the simplifications that the style of the whole preceding film has endorsed. In this sense, she realizes the most stringent and abstract qualities of Dreyer's style. She realizes the states of intense emotionality and spirituality that the style of his film has cultivated all along.

Furthermore, in a sense, this scene derealizes itself by dispersing itself into an alternating series of flashbacks and flash-aheads. There really is no present in it: only a

28 In the final scene Gertrud's dephysicalization occurs most vividly at the moment that she reads to Axel a poem she wrote at the age of sixteen about love. Not only does she assert in the text of the poem that she has no actual existence, but only an emotional one; but while she reads the poem (asking that we "look at her"), Dreyer cuts away from her image to show a shot of the written text of the poem itself. Written texts are important throughout Dreyer's work insofar as they represent purely imaginative presences that leave the limitations of bodies and socially mediated forms of expression behind. But this text – in asking us to look at "Gertrud," while Dreyer denies us a look at her and inserts a look at the text itself – more than any of the other uses of texts in his work gestures towards the ultimate disembodiment of the figure reading it. It is as if Dreyer is showing us that Gertrud has *only* an imaginative presence at this moment.

series of memories of the past and predictions of the future (at one point, Gertrud tells Axel of already having selected her grave site and her epitaph and asks him to pick a flower in memory of her after her death). In the most uncanny moment of all, Gertrud actually turns the present moment into a memory of the past enacted at some point in the future. As Axel is leaving, she tells him that she looks ahead to the future day in which she will look back on the present and "your visit will be a memory."

Gertrud is Dreyer's most rigorously extended experiment in cinematic abstraction in an effort to induce an answering state of abstraction in the viewer. Significant actions of an external sort are almost eliminated. Settings are simplified and props reduced to a minimum. Events and scenes are paralleled and formally compared until they seem as ritualistic as Kabuki. The pace and rhythm of the actions and interactions are retarded to the point that they take on an almost incantatory quality. The names of the characters are repeated so often that they cease to be names at all, and instead become almost pure sound, marking time and reverberating in the air like the sounds of the clocks that tick and the chimes that ring in the background of many scenes.

Though they are probably the most criticized aspects of *Gertrud,* the repetitiveness of the film's events and language contributes powerfully to Dreyer's narrative project. The repetitions of a few simplified settings, of characters' blockings, and even of their words (as when

Gertrud and Gabriel repeat each others' names) empty the items of realistic, denotative meaning (as repetition always does), the better to substitute a connotative richness of emotional significance to the positions, settings, and names (as ritualized chanting or ceremonial litany does).[29]

In this sense *Gertrud* is the supreme example of the impulse that has been driving all of Dreyer's work. The physical simplification of settings, the austerity of appearances, the slowing of the pacing, the minimalization of superficial forms of expression and eventfulness, and the paring away of superfluous props and costumes – all of these worldly impoverishments – are in the service of a supreme imaginative enrichment. *Gertrud* renounces external eventfulness in order to cultivate internal eventfulness. It stops one sort of action so that another sort can begin. It immobilizes the characters the better to

29 Dreyer's interest in the expressive effects of litany or chant also throws light on the expressive function of the ceremony of ritualized singing, marching, and speech making at Gabriel's birthday party, and on why Dreyer would choose to put this scene at the center of the work. The expressive premises of the ceremonies staged in that scene are, in effect, the expressive premises of *Gertrud* as a whole. The emptying out of practical meaning in that scene figures the possible enrichment of imaginative meaning that Dreyer seeks in his whole film. In the reduction of a scene to the depiction of a stylized ceremony in which virtually everything said and done is merely the expression of a formula, Dreyer attains the state of perfect scenic abstraction that he courts in other ways throughout his work. The birthday party ceremony represents a condition of imaginative plentitude attained in the absence of all truly personal expression of it.

represent in them, and to sponsor in a viewer, the possibility of meditative movement. Sitting still in silence (for Gertrud or a viewer) becomes the occasion for emotional movements and flights of imagination. The film and its title character renounce possibilities of expression in the world in order to entertain possibilities of expression that the world won't sustain. Moments of characters' silence (for example: the silence of the characters in the powerful concluding shot of the film) mark the point at which the text begins to speak most imaginatively.

The most daring aspect of *Gertrud* is that Dreyer attempts to represent a figure who *lives* the state of imaginative exaltation and worldly abstraction that his style evokes. Each viewer will have to decide for himself or herself if he succeeds or fails, and to decide if Gertrud herself is a success or a failure. Each viewer will have to decide if she finds a way to humanize Dreyer's stylistic effects, or if, on the contrary, she gives up her humanity in the process.

In the coda, Gertrud comes emotionally closer to Axel and allows herself to speak more intimately and personally with him than she allowed herself to do in any of the earlier encounters with the men in her life (except for the brief and doomed affair with Erland). This is not to argue for her frigidity earlier. Thirty years before, she was so vulnerable to emotion, so able to be wounded, so passionately involved with her practical decisions that she couldn't attain this serenity of vision, which comes only with the disinterestedness of visionary disengagement. Dreyer is clearly arguing in favor of this state of imagination as a substitute for the turmoil of actual worldly engagements. In our contemplation of it, we have life more intensely and importantly than we do in the heat of words and actions. In renouncing social expressions and the practical realization of our dreams in the forms of ordinary experience, we attain the possibility of attaining them in our imaginations.

It is a tragic recognition, and is Dreyer's final word on the relation of imagination and realistic representation. The enriched consciousness is finally alone, cut off from expressing itself in verbal and social forms. That is why this film itself, and never more so than in this final scene, has to renounce verbal forms of expression and social forms of interaction between characters. We are in the realm of reverie and dream and metaphor.

One might call attention to one false note in the coda that reveals almost as much about Dreyer's complexity of feeling about his heroine as the truths of the scene do. Dreyer goes to some lengths to point out that Gertrud subscribes to a daily newspaper, listens to the radio, and supervises the work of a hired man, as an obvious attempt to argue that to some degree she is *not* cut off from the practical world of men and affairs. But it is a false step. The references to the newspaper and the radio, and the brief conversation with her handyman are completely unconvincing to a viewer, in a film that tells us differently, if we trust the tale and not the intentions

335

of the teller. All of the rest of the coda, and indeed all of *Gertrud,* tells us that it is only in leaving the world behind that one can hold onto a soul. Even though Dreyer may want to tell us otherwise, Gertrud is finally "free" (the word she uses to describe herself) only when she leaves the compromises of society and social expression behind. Only in dying to the world can one be born spiritually. Only in worldly renunciation can there be imaginative gain.

But having said this, one should recognize that the waffling on Dreyer's part is not artistically trivial, but extremely revealing, because it takes us to the heart of an ambivalence that energizes all of his work. It represents an uncertainty that we have encountered in the earlier films, that is equally present in this final film. Even as his film tells us otherwise, Dreyer unconvincingly attempts to suggest that Gertrud's imagination doesn't ultimately estrange her from the world. He apparently could never quite resign himself to that. Inger is only his most vigorous attempt to argue that imaginative energy is directly translatable into practical, familial expression. Directly, in *Ordet,* and indirectly in the other films, Dreyer, in effect, fought to deny the insight about the aloneness of the imaginative individual that his own work (and career) repeatedly forced upon him.

That is only to say that, in the deepest view of the matter, Dreyer himself *is* Inger or Gertrud. His works are energized by the same quixotic and doomed attempt to live ideals, to translate spirit into practical expressions as his heroines are within the works. He is spiritually in league with his heroines, conspiring with them, urging them on, half believing that their translations from one realm to another can be made, even as his films tell us and him, almost against his will and despite their aspirations, that their efforts must fail. His heroines' states of uncertainty and need and hope – in the absence of practical achievement – are their creator's as well.

A small gesture and sound effect at the very end of the coda epitomize the complexity of feeling that Dreyer creates about the worldly renunciations and imaginative substitutions in *Gertrud*. In the final seconds of the movie, after Gertrud concludes her conversation with Axel, as he departs, she waves goodbye to him from her study. Dreyer photographs the gesture so as to remind us of an earlier farewell wave that occurred at the end of one of the most passionate and touching previous scenes – the scene, thirty years before, in which Erland Jansson and Gertrud first slept together, and specifically the moment at the end of the scene, in which Erland waved goodbye to Gertrud as she left his apartment. Dreyer dramatizes their parting from one another on the morning after they have spent the night together by showing Gertrud sharing a cigarette with Erland and then expressing her love for him with the most complex, evocative, and tender series of interwoven glances and dramatic gestures in the entire film.

In evoking that touching earlier moment in its final seconds, *Gertrud* suspends us between a consciousness of the present and the past. We remember both Gertrud's earlier hope and her ultimate disappointment. We remember the earlier scene as the single evanescent moment in the previous film in which Gertrud and her creator were beautifully able to express her dream of love in the forms of a practical human relationship, in the dramatic structures of nuanced verbal and social interaction between two characters. Dreyer's delicate choreography of the exchange of the cigarette and the interchanged glances between Gertrud and Erland in that earlier scene represented a possibility of the actual, practical, shared expression of two persons' feelings that was not present in any other scene in the entire film.

Gertrud's farewell to Axel at the end of the coda thus suspends a viewer between a feeling of infinite resignation and renunciation, on the one hand, and a memory of Gertrud's grand, daring, joyous attempt actually to live her dream of love in the form of a practical human relationship, on the other. Dreyer wants us to respect and cherish both the sublime hope and the final tragic renunciation.

Simultaneous with the wave, in those final seconds of the film, Dreyer inserts the sound of a bell tolling on the sound track. One might understand it literally as marking a specific time or event, or symbolically as tolling the passing of youth, life, and pleasure (or even as tolling Gertrud's beckoning death). But like most of the other effects in the coda, Dreyer invites us to understand this sound neither literally nor symbolically, but rather *formally* in terms of its vibratory resonance with the effects of the whole preceding movie. In short, Dreyer does not want us to leave the film and import practical facts about bells from outside of it in order to understand the chimes. Nor does he want us to interpret the ringing sounds in terms of a set of stock metaphoric meanings (for example, to allude to Gertrud's death or aging). Rather his goal is the opposite: to hold us *in* his film, to keep all of its stylistic resonances reverberating in the echo chamber of our consciousnesses.

Bells have tolled previously to mark crucial moments in *Gertrud,* and this final knell brings all of those earlier sounds of bells and chimes and clocks back to resonate in a viewer's consciousness (which is clearly larger than even Gertrud's consciousness at this moment). One recalls the ticking of the clock in the initial scene of the film; one recalls the sounds of the clock on the night Gustav went to the opera to look for Gertrud, the night she slept with Erland; one recalls the chiming of the clock on the final evening of Gertrud's flight from her home.

The point is that with this final set of sounds all of these earlier sounds of bells and chimes and ticking sounds come back to enrich our consciousness in non-realistic ways. They exist not to remind us of real clocks and clock sounds, but of all of the clocks and sounds that have come before them in the film. They function stylis-

339

tically to evoke states of feeling that exist in works of art outside of literal significances and realistic meanings, and beyond all practical forms of expression.

In relying on these sounds and this gesture to communicate meanings in this way, Dreyer himself is turning away from practical forms and structures of expression as surely as Gertrud is. The sound of that bell echoes in a viewer's consciousness as the film ends, and for a long time afterwards. But it is, after all, only an artistic effect. It refers to nothing in the world. The sound is good for nothing; it makes nothing happen. It represents an enrichment of consciousness that is an end in itself. For Dreyer as for Gertrud, such enrichments of consciousness may have no practical form of expression, and no worldly consequences or correlatives.

I would suspect that the disastrous history of his own vexed expressive career as a filmmaker may have led Carl Dreyer to feel closer to Gertrud than we can guess. He was not that far from being as much of an expressive failure as she – nor that far from being as much of an imaginative success. We should not allow ourselves to forget that he was, as an artist at the end of his life, almost as neglected and alone, and living in a world of his own, as she. She has nothing to show for all of her efforts but her poetry and memories; he has nothing to show for his but his films – almost nothing according to the standards of worldly value.

Gertrud suggests that for Dreyer as for Gertrud, the final brave recognition is that there may be no possible

340

realization of our vaulting ideals of love, freedom, and transcendence in the world. Like the wave and the bell, the only consequence of the dream of love may be an enrichment of our consciousnesses, like the enrichment that this whole film figures. But, for Dreyer and for Gertrud, however tragic that conclusion, it is no reason to abandon love's dreams.

Epilogue:
A world elsewhere

They are lonely; the spirit of their writing and conversation is lonely; they repel influences; they shun general society; they incline to shut themselves in their chamber in the house, to live in the country rather than in the town, and to find their tasks and amusements in solitude. . . . Meantime, this retirement does not proceed from any whim on the part of these separators; but if any one will take pains to talk with them, he will find that this part is chosen both from temperament and from principle; with some unwillingness, too, and as a choice of the less of two evils; for these persons are not by nature melancholy, sour, and unsocial, – they are not stockish or brute, – but joyous; susceptible, affectionate; they have even more than others a great wish to be loved. Like the young Mozart, they are rather ready to cry ten times a day, "But are you sure you love me?" . . .

And yet, it seems as if this loneliness, and not this love, would prevail in their circumstances, because of the extravagant demand they make on human nature. . . . Talk with a seaman of the hazards of life in his profession, and he will ask you, "Where are the old sailors? do you not see that all are young men?" And we, on this sea of human thought, in like manner inquire, Where are the old idealists? where are they who represented to the last generation that extravagant hope, which a few happy aspirants suggest to ours? In looking at the class of counsel, and power, and wealth, and at the matronage of the land, amidst all the prudence and all the triviality, one asks, Where are they who represented genius, virtue, the invisible and heavenly world, to these? Are they dead, – taken in early ripeness to the gods, – as ancient wisdom foretold their fate? Or did the high idea die out of them, and leave their unperfumed body as its tomb and tablet, announcing to all that the celestial inhabitant, who once gave them beauty, had departed?

Ralph Waldo Emerson, "The Transcendentalist"

343

Gertrud is, in Emerson's phrase, an "old idealist." Dreyer understood, as deeply as Emerson did, the tragedy of that predicament. Gertrud's loneliness is profound. As Emerson argues in "The Transcendentalist," the paradox is that the loneliness results not from melancholy or misanthropy, but from love. The exorbitance of the need for social relationship, the "extravagant demand [made] on human nature" is the source of the individual's ultimate tragic estrangement.

Gertrud repeats the overall narrative progress of *Day of Wrath* and *Ordet*. A character reaches outward at the beginning of the film, moving beyond social walls and imaginative boundaries, in a daring attempt at social connectedness and emotional relationship. Yet the effort is doomed. The possibilities of realizing one's ideals in the form of actual social relationships which are evoked early in the narratives are abandoned by their ends. The second halves of all three films reverse the direction of the narratives' and the characters' initial movements outward. Anne, Inger, and Gertrud are forced to withdraw from the actual societies of relationship they attempted to bring into existence. Spiritual or imaginative communities take the place of actual, worldly relationships.

The most common visual metaphor that Dreyer uses to communicate this double movement is one involving the opening or closing of doors. Early in their narratives, in important scenes, Anne, Inger, and Gertrud each

344

open doors and move outward through them as a sign of their ability to connect up with other characters. Anne and Gertrud actually leave their homes in several scenes, and move outdoors beyond their films' confining interiors. Inger leaves the farmhouse in which the rest of *Ordet* is set and goes out into the barn to comfort Morten. But then, in the second halves of the films, the metaphor is reversed. In the counter-movement that concludes each work, each character is forced to withdraw back behind a closed door. Anne, Inger, and Gertrud are immobilized within confined spaces (of which Inger's coffin is only the most extreme example).

As my previous chapters have suggested, Dreyer's visual style photographically parallels this two-fold process. The stylistic correlatives to the spatial and social movements of Dreyer's central characters outward, across boundaries or through doors early in their films are the searching, reaching movements of Dreyer's camera through the spaces of his sets and, specifically, his use of visual depth to communicate imaginative possibilities of movement. Similarly, in the final scenes of the same films, the flattening of the screen space or the use of a shallow depth of field in a shot parallels the central characters' acts of expressive withdrawal or physical stasis.[1]

---

1 In a still subtler version of this process, photographic movements into or out of the plane of the screen (for example: the movements of the camera in the first half of *Ordet*), or representations of spatial depths within a particular shot which entice the viewer to look "through" or "past" the

None of Dreyer's films uses the opening of doors and the movements of its central character through them early in the work more expressively than *Gertrud*, although, in line with all I have said, the film ultimately reverses its direction, to close doors around Gertrud, finally to shut her up behind one in its final scene. After all of the openings of her heart toward Erland, after all of her brave movements away from her home and marriage, after all of her doomed attempts to reach out, Gertrud finally is forced to retreat – both literally and metaphorically – back behind a closed door, to withdraw back into a room physically even smaller and more confining than any of those from which she fled. After dramatizing the opening of doors, *Gertrud* is finally about their closing around her. It is a film about the necessary renunciation of worldly ties, movements, and expressions.

Since this renunciatory impulse is probably the most difficult aspect of Dreyer's work for the average viewer to come to grips with, I want to conclude with a consid-

two-dimensionality of the screen on which the film is projected (for example: the shot of Gertrud undressing in Erland's bedroom, which Dreyer composes to emphasize the sheer depth of the space into which we are looking) are used to suggest opportunities of movement and possibilities of relationship. In contrast, in the final scenes of the same films, the stasis of the camera positions and the reliance on lateral (side to side) movements of the camera and right-left blockings of characters' movements communicate the need to "look beyond" physical and spatial forms of movement and connectedness, to entertain purely imaginative relationships between figures.

eration of it. One way to get some perspective on Dreyer's practice is to consider the example of another artist
in another medium, an artist who is nevertheless quite
similar to Dreyer. Emily Dickinson frequently relied on
the same metaphors that Dreyer uses involving the closing of social doors and the opening of spiritual ones. Her
work can, perhaps, help us to understand the complexity
of Dreyer's and Gertrud's final stance. In the lines that
follow the one that I quoted as the epigraph to the second section of this book, Dickinson writes explicitly
about windows and doors and rooms, and about the
relation of the visionary to such worldly confinements:

I dwell in possibility
A fairer house than prose
More numerous of windows
Superior of doors
Of chambers as the cedars
Impregnable of eye.[2]

There are at least two ways to read the third and fourth
lines. Since they employ parallel syntactic constructions
("numerous of windows . . . superior of doors"), and
roughly equivalent physical objects (and equivalent dictional choices to describe them) namely, "doors" and
"windows," probably the most common reading is to take

2 I should note that I quote the manuscript reading of the text. In his
standard edition, Thomas Johnson changes the second "of" to "for,"
although this change (like his weird placement of em-dashes in many
lines) lacks manuscript authority.

their meaning to be parallel. Read thus, to "dwell in possibility" is to be able to move though more "windows and doors" on experience than are available when one lives merely "prosaically." To "dwell in possibility" is to be able to substitute imaginative movements in place of the immobilities that the actual world imposes.

What the shutting of doors in *Gertrud* encourages us to realize, however, is that the third and fourth lines may also be read in the opposite way: not only as being parallel and equivalent, but as presenting contrasting alternatives. In this entirely less bland interpretation, Dickinson's lines tell us that withdrawals into privacy and secrecy and loneliness are necessary in order to empower the imagination. In the metaphors of the two lines, they tell us that shutting worldly doors is necessary in order to be able to open imaginative windows.

The soul indeed reaches outward in other than worldly ways; but it does so by withdrawing inward in solitude. The lines tell us that the erection of barriers – the walls, the doors, the secrecy – is as essential to an understanding of what it means to "dwell in possibility" as grand, visionary movements beyond barriers is. Dickinson tells us that the doors make the windows possible. The contraction, the shutting-up, the withdrawal is necessary for the expansion, the opening, the movement. The social dispossession or worldly relinquishment is the price of the spiritual enfranchisement and enrichment.

That double recognition is what *Gertrud*'s coda also expresses. Dreyer tells us that, as painful as it undeniably is, we must close certain worldly doors in order to open spiritual windows. It is an undeniably painful recognition, one that even Gertrud has to have forced upon her. She (and perhaps her creator too) accepts it only reluctantly and at the end of her film, but it is an absolutely essential recognition nonetheless, if we would understand the deepest springs of Dreyer's work.

At the end of each of Dreyer's three final masterpieces, social, verbal, worldly expressions of the self ultimately fail and are abandoned. The central characters are left immobilized and silent. However, if Dreyer's derealizations have succeeded, if his redirection of a viewer's attention away from realms of social value and practical interaction to realms of spiritual value and emotional transaction have been successful, the final state of practical and verbal relinquishment within his text is converted from a condition of social loss to one of imaginative gain. The viewer who has been educated by Dreyer's style understands that final immobilization as a form of imaginative movement. When the final door shuts in front of Gertrud – even as it forcibly insists on the social renunciations and romantic failures of her life – Dreyer intends that we experience an imaginative opening more powerful than any worldly closing.

Dickinson's lines can help us to understand some of these things insofar as her metaphors about doors and windows and rooms are quite similar to Dreyer's. But, perhaps even more importantly, Dickinson's poetic style can throw light on Dreyer's cinematic style. That is be-

349

cause Dickinson's style, like Dreyer's, shows us how style itself can create new ways of knowing. Her poetic style, like his cinematic style, has radical designs on our minds. It forcibly works to redirect our attention and to alter our states of awareness in ways that are strikingly similar to what Dreyer does in his films.

In the first place, note how Dickinson's lines are built around a bizarre "derealizing" process similar to the one in Dreyer's films. Common-sense diction is dislocated into representing entirely uncommon-sense conceptions. Concretions are transformed into abstractions. The reader is forced to translate qualities or objects across realms in the same way that the viewer of Dreyer's work is. If we begin reading Dickinson's verse thinking that the meaning will be physical, practical, conventional, the very first line – with its deliberately paradoxical reference to "dwelling in possibility" – wrenches us in the opposite direction.

But if reality is "derealized" by Dickinson's forceful shifts of reference, just as happens in Dreyer's work, unreality is also "realized." Dickinson tells us in her first line that she doesn't dwell in a normal "prosaic" house, but then uses thoroughly domestic metaphors about doors and windows and chambers to describe where she does dwell. The consequence is that the same sort of cognitive dissonance is induced that Dreyer creates in his films. We have to shift into a special way of understanding in which prosaic references to ordinary things represented by the most mundane dictional choices (the mean-

350

ing of: "dwelling," "fairness," "houses," "numerousness," "doors," "superiority," "windows," and
"chambers," in these six lines) are transformed into gestures *away from* obvious, easily understood, worldly
things, yet without completely leaving such practicalities
and common-sense understandings behind either. We
can't stabilize a reading either in the purely physical or the
purely metaphysical direction.

It is crucial that accepting the spiritual meanings in
Dickinson's work typically does not involve jettisoning
the physical or realistic meanings. Rather the reader is
suspended somewhere between the two, in exactly the
same way that Dreyer's work suspends a viewer *between*
practical and spiritual understandings of events and objects. Dickinson works to dislocate our perceptions so
that they end up being just slightly at an angle to both
realms. And just as in Dreyer's work, this complex abstracting process moves us into a complex state of abstraction. We are propelled to a certain imaginative distance from realistic objects and meanings, even while
not quite losing contact with realistic objects, events,
and significances. In sorting all of this out, the reader is
thrown into a meditative state of mind, quite similar to
the state that Dreyer's films induce in a viewer.

In short, Dickinson works stylistically first to disori-
ent, and then to reorient and complicate our understanding. Like Dreyer's, Dickinson's style is a style of
intentional, forceful redirection of attention. She wants
to bewilder us, to mystify us, at least momentarily. She

wants to mess up and to slow down our reading process, precisely so that we can be shaken out of fixed positions and common-sense assumptions. Her goal is to open up new, less stable, less assured possibilities of understanding – new ways of seeing and feeling as alternatives to our common sense, ordinary, practical understandings. In being confused, messed-up, slowed down in this way, we enter into a different, less practical, more meditative and abstract relation to words and things in her work.

Thus Dickinson's use of paradoxes, oppositions, misdirections, and juxtapositions of the prosaic and the abstract are not merely eccentric "touches" in her technique, but are the fundamental means by which she dislocates our perceptions (by dislocating language) and induces special states of a meditativeness or abstraction in us. The fifth and six lines of the excerpt above are the most vivid demonstration of her use of paradoxical language as a deliberate means of changing the way we understand her writing.

Dickinson disorients us logically and perceptually in order to reorient us imaginatively. Her writing yanks us around, in this instance, deliberately switching its terms of comparison in order to enlarge our view. Line five suggests that the relation of "chambers" and "cedars" is based on the numerousness of either term, but line six shifts the comparison to one involving their mutual concealment and obscurity. The basis of the comparison in effect reverses itself, shifting from "countability" to "uncountability," from accountable presence to unaccountable absence, from eminent visibility to egregious invisibility. Furthermore, while the assonance of "chambers" and "cedars" pulls the two words together, and the use of "as" suggests a parallelism, the visual imagery presents a deliberate paradox insofar as the two terms could not be more opposite: chambers are interior spaces defined by exterior boundaries; and cedars are exterior spaces defined by internal boundaries. As Wallace Stevens (himself a poet in the Dickinsian vein) might have put it, reality is made a more than a little "hard to see." The juxtaposition of the two images literally makes things hard to see – which is, of course, the point of the sixth line. In repelling physical sight, we are forced into a relationship to the lines that is defined by the substitution of insight for sight that all of Dickinson's (and Dreyer's) style urges on us.

I want to conclude with one final connection between Dreyer's style and Dickinson's. Her style can teach us a lesson about "hardness" that Dreyer's style also teaches. The sheer muscularity of Dickinson's style, the violence of its dislocations of meaning, the difficulty of our comprehension of it, the labor of understanding it asks of us, tells us how hard it is to lever oneself away from practical, worldly realms of value. The difficulty, the continuous labor of meaning-making embodied by Dreyer's style (and embodied in the difficult, laborious performances of his greatest characters, and by the performances of viewers attempting to rise to the challenge his style presents) teaches us the deepest lesson of all: the lesson that spiritual values have to be labored into existence at the greatest expense, at a nearly exorbitant cost. They cannot be merely reclined into or inherited. That is why Dreyer will probably never be a filmmaker for the masses (or even for critics and reviewers) who want their truths less arduous and less complex.

As *Gertrud* above all demonstrates, for Dreyer the making of spiritual meanings will always be a difficult task, a labor of love with no rewards in the world. The spiritual meaning maker labors alone and in the dark. The values brought into existence by the active soul are fragile. Its creations are vulnerable. They are continuously in danger of loss, decay, or misunderstanding. They are brought into existence in local acts of creation that have meaning within particular circumstances. They are not excerptable from the specific contexts and conditions that stimulate them. That is why it is hard to generalize about them. Such performative virtuosity does not make itself available to our abstract appropriations. Such strenuous acts of genius do not lend themselves to mass consumption. They can never become part of popular culture.

For all of these reasons, both Dickinson and Dreyer were probably resigned to the neglect and misunderstanding their work suffered during their lifetimes. In the words of another verse by Dickinson, their careers and their works ultimately demonstrate that

The soul selects her own society
Then shuts the door.

Filmography

Mikkel	Emil Hass Christensen
Johannes	Preben Lerdorff Rye
Anders	Cay Kristiansen
Peter Petersen, a tailor	Ejner Federspiel
Anne, his daughter	Gerda Nielsen
The minister	Ove Rud
The doctor	Henry Skjaer
Peter's wife	Sylvia Eckhausen

GERTRUD

Script	Carl Dreyer, based on the play of the same name by Hjalmar Söderberg
Photography	Henning Bendtsen
Editing	Edith Schlüssel
Music	Jørgen Jersild
Songs	Grethe Risbjerg Thomsen
Released by	Palladium Film, December 1964
Running time	116 minutes

Cast:

Gertrud Kanning	Nina Pens Rode
Gustav Kanning	Bendt Rothe
Gabriel Lidman	Ebbe Rode
Erland Jansson	Baard Owe
Axel Nygren	Axel Strøbye
Gustav's mother	Anna Malberg

VIDEO AVAILABILITY OF DREYER'S FILMS

The Passion of Joan of Arc (1928) is available from Facets Multimedia, Video Yesteryear, Tamarelle's French Film House, Western Film and Video

Vampyr (1932) is available from Facets Multimedia, Video Yesteryear, Hollywood Home Theater, Tamarelle's French Film House

Day of Wrath (1943) is available from Facets Multimedia, Western Film and Video, Tamarelle's French Film House
Ordet (1955) is available from Facets Multimedia, Western Film and Video, Tamarelle's French Film House
Gertrud (1964) is available from Facets Multimedia, Tamarelle's French Film House

SUGGESTIONS FOR FURTHER READING

The screenplays to *The Passion of Joan of Arc, Vampyr, Day of Wrath,* and *Ordet* are printed in Carl Theodor Dreyer, *Four Screenplays* (Bloomington: Indiana University Press, 1970).
- The screenplay to the unproduced *Jesus* is printed in Carl Theodor Dreyer, *Jesus* (New York: Dell, 1972).
- The screenplay to the unproduced *Medea* is printed in Jytte Jensen (ed.), *Carl Th. Dreyer* (New York: Museum of Modern Art, 1989).
- An excellent anthology of Dreyer's interviews, essays, and lectures is available in Donald Skoller (ed.), *Dreyer in Double Reflection* (New York: E.P. Dutton, 1973).

357

Index

359

About the author: Raymond Carney is one of a new generation of interdisciplinary studies scholars engaged in studying film in the context of other arts and other post-Romantic forms of expression. He has published essays on painting, dance, drama, film, literature, and criticism in *The New Republic, Partisan Review, Raritan, The Georgia Review,* and many other journals. His previous books include *American Dreaming* and *American Vision,* and editions of works by Henry James, Henry Adams, and Rudyard Kipling. Professor Carney has served as an artistic advisor to the Whitney Museum of American Art and has been a Fellow of both the National Endowment for the Humanities and the Stanford Humanities Center. He currently is a Professor in the College of Communication at Boston University and is the General Editor of the forthcoming *Cambridge Film Classics* series.